FROM APE MAN TO HOMER
The Story of the Beginnings of Western Civilization

FROM APE MAN TO HOMER

The Story of the Beginnings
of Western Civilization

H. E. L. MELLERSH

Illustrations by
SALLY MELLERSH

LONDON
ROBERT HALE LIMITED
63 Old Brompton Road, S.W.7

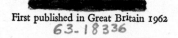
First published in Great Britain 1962

63-18336

PRINTED IN GREAT BRITAIN
BY EBENEZER BAYLIS AND SON, LIMITED
THE TRINITY PRESS, WORCESTER, AND LONDON

CONTENTS

70131

ACKNOWLEDGEMENTS

I gratefully acknowledge permission, granted by the publishers, and by the authors, editors and translators, or their representatives, to quote from the following books:

The *Aegean Civilization* (Gustave Glotz; Routledge & Kegan Paul)
Ancient Near Eastern Texts relating to the Old Testament (J. Pritchard; Princeton University Press)
Ancient Records of Assyria and Babylonia (D. D. Luckenbill; University of Chicago Press)
The Ancient Worlds of Asia (Ernst Diez; Macdonald & Co.)
Egypt of the Pharaohs (Sir Alan Gardiner; Oxford University Press)
The Epic of Gilgamesh (R. Campbell Thompson: Luzac & Co.)
The Hittites (O. R. Gurney; Penguin Books)
The Iliad (R. V. Rieu; Penguin Books)
The Legacy of the Ancient World (W. G. de Burgh: Macdonald & Evans)
The Literature of the Ancient Egyptians (Adolf Erman; Methuen & Co.)
The Odyssey (E. V. Rieu; Penguin Books)
The Sumerians (Sir Leonard Woolley; Oxford University Press)
The Tell El-Amarna Tablets (S. A. B. Mercer; Macmillan & Co., of Gt. Britain and of Canada)
Ur, the First Phase (Sir Leonard Woolley; Penguin Books)

H.E.L.M.

LINE DRAWINGS

CHAPTER I

The Nature and Heritage of Man

MANKIND was both lucky and unlucky in the timing of its arrival upon the world scene.

Our genus, the culmination of the mammalian pattern of life, found the rest of the mammals there in such a rich profusion as had probably never existed before and certainly would never exist again. In this, man was lucky. But he also happened to come to existence when the earth's surface was suffering or about to suffer one of its infrequent bouts of chill, a sort of undulating fever in reverse, when over half a million years or so the ice pulsated backwards and forwards from the poles no less than four times and at its greatest spread reached to where now stand London and New York.

This book, however, is one of history not biology and the reader does not need to condition himself to thinking in terms of millions of years, more particularly so since the date of the early hominid's entry is in dispute and varies in estimation from half a million years to nearly two. Our true concern is *Homo sapiens*; and only as the evolutionary creator of his character and physique are we interested in his near-human and half-human progenitors. The age of the men of our own species is also in dispute; they do not for certain turn up in the palaeontological records until a mere few thousand years ago, say thirty or forty. They can therefore have suffered for certain only the mischance of the last of the four ice ages. Indeed it may be that the harsh and rigorous conditions acted more as a challenge than a discouragement to men, a challenge that was accepted and overcome, and so much so that the final disappearance of the ice even seemed to them a catastrophe rather than a blessing. In which case the timing of their entry upon the world scene was lucky on both counts, they having possessed the courage to make it so.

Though there may be no need for the reader to think in terms of biological time-spans, something at least of the biologist's outlook he may usefully borrow, the concept that is to say of man as a natural

9

phenomenon and the successful culmination of the evolutionary process. For this book is an attempt to relate as a consecutive story the earlier parts of mankind's history. It will seek not only to connect the happenings in Egypt with those in Sumeria, with those in the land of the Hittites, with the spread of the Aryan-speakers and so on, but also to show a real and logical connection between these later peoples of history, if ancient history, with those vague and distant persons to whom have been given such impersonal names as *Homo sapiens*, Palaeolithic Man, Aurignacians, Maglemosians, and the rest. The connection will be the more real and obvious if both reader and writer continually bear in mind that mankind is in truth a single biological species, and that in its history it is no more than continuing the planet's evolutionary process—though continuing it very much in its own new and distinctive way, which is not so much to adapt itself to its environment as to seek to adapt environment to its own heartfelt needs and wilful desires.

Homo sapiens, then, facing his environment, brave new man facing a very old and refractory world, Adam and Eve expelled from a state of animal innocence because they have dared to think. Of course they cannot help but think; and to think hard and successfully with Nature's new instrument, the large and convoluted brain, is their only hope of survival. It will be well to consider shortly what were man's assets and equipment for the task in front of him. Biologists make much of the idea of "eye, hand and brain", a mutually co-operative and stimulating trio; it is by now perhaps a well-worn idea, but none the worse for that. By the time that the mammals arrived on the earth, Nature had long evolved a most successful ground plan for a living creature. This is the vertebrate pattern, wherein a head and brain, questingly in front, send back, through a protected nerve cord, messages from the impressions that they receive to a symmetrical double pairing of limbs, jointed and digited, which offer great potentialities of motion and response. To this the mammal added firstly warm-bloodedness, which saved it from freezing and so vastly extended its range upon the earth's surface, and secondly those *mammae* or breasts which have given it its name and also, more importantly, the ability, not to mention desire, to suckle, fondle and hence love and educate its young. The mammal spread over the earth, a supremely active creature, with good sight and superlative powers of smell; it proceeded, in a volcanic burst of evolutionary activity, to differentiate itself into a vast variety of types that took advantage of particular environments and specialized in exploiting in some particular way the potentialities of its splendid ground plan. The grazer grazed efficiently, the browser browsed, the cat tribe became a killing mechanism to which their instincts as well as their teeth and claws were bent, the seals turned their arms into flippers, and the bats their hands into wings. And so on. One line, however, the theory goes, eschewed all such specialization. Instead it went up into the trees—unless it had already gone there for safety—and there, as it was forced to do for survival, it developed sight at the expense of smell and its digited appendages into grasping hands and feet. From tree shrew through creatures like unto the modern tarsier, lemur, monkey, ape, it reduced its snout, bulged its eyes, grew its fingers—and enlarged its brain. It enlarged its brain because its improved stereoscopic vision enabled it to examine things that its improved hands could pick up, and both processes stimulated the brain's activity.

Finally came a descent again from the trees. Mankind's ancestors were not the only kind to do this, but they, it seems, were the only kind to do something else, assume an erect posture for which a life in the trees had partly but not wholly prepared their limbs. Opportunity was given for further and more thorough handling of things, for further fruitful co-operation of brain, hand and eye. The rest of the story is familiar. Increasingly these creatures *thought* about what they picked up and examined. They began to use what they had picked up, the stick with which to poke and slash and beat, the broken flint with which to gouge and scrape and cut and tear. They did not throw away these handy extensions of their own limbs but kept them, envisaging their use at another time; they took the flint and purposely knocked it into better shape, and whittled the stick and scraped the bone with the sharp flint. *Homo faber*, man the smith, the toolmaker, had arrived.

He had arrived as a testimony of what could be done if brain-power were stimulated and improved. Man, of course, had other assets. He had most excellent supple limbs. He had not the strength of the bear or the speed of the horse or the swimming power of the porpoise; but he was a good second-best to all three of them. He had by far the best vocal cords of the lot—and he had those hands, with the long fingers and the opposable thumb. But all these are as nothing compared with the brain. The human brain makes of man a quite different animal from all the rest, evolved but unique. He alone develops *conceptual thinking*, beyond, that is to say, the merest rudiments of it which is the best that even the other primates can display. He alone is self-conscious, introspective, able to conjure up in the mind's eye the remembered past or the imagined future. He alone can think, "Today I threw that stone and missed; tomorrow I will wait and get nearer!" or "Today I saw her; tomorrow I will kiss her!"

That last is not a pointless and tasteless example; or, at least, it is written for a purpose. For if we are to consider man's assets in terms of his animal inheritance then we must consider whether there do not exist disabilities as well. Man does indeed inherit animal instincts and partake of the nature of the beast; and even when such instincts are refined they may be over-powerful. Human beings, for instance, unlike most of the rest of the animal kingdom, find the sexual impulses almost always with them and not a matter of strictly seasonal urge. This is in the nature of a sublimation but yet a difficult one. Sex ceases to be a blind compulsion at certain times; but it does remain a compulsion difficult to control. And it is not only difficult because it is ever-present, but also because of that human power of conceptual thinking, because of the imagination. The same could be said of many other urges. It would almost be true, and relevant, to say that man had acquired not a better brain but quite simply, "an imagination". Anyone, I believe, in looking at the manners and customs and activities of early men must at times obtain the impression almost of their possessing minds and imaginations that do no more than plague them: the brain is too big for its owner, uncontrollable, over-active, fantastically imaginative. The owner therefore tortures himself, as no animal ever tortures himself, in the effort to control his baser instincts and evolve a satisfactory way of life in company with his neighbours.

Whether that is true or not, it will be readily agreed that man had a difficult task before him. He had an animal inheritance—of all, that is, except the physical tools of mastery or adaptability, the wolf's fangs, the tiger's claws, the mole's spade-like forepaw, the zebra's protective camouflage. To compensate for this loss he had only his reasoning brain, tempered or bedevilled by his imagination. As we see man's early history unfold, whether we are considering a tribal tabu or a law of Hammurabi, the quiet skill of a cave painter or the ferocious ethics of an Achilles, we shall do well to bear these abilities and disabilities in mind. From the time of the entry of our own true species into the world, to Homer's time when the stage was at least set for the real and rapid creation of our Western civilization, man does not change his unique but difficult nature.

From an evolutionary point of view, indeed from any point of view, man's early history is a success story. But it might have been more successful, certainly more quickly and consistently successful; and there are times when it looks as if it were not going to be successful at all: it is an old and bitter joke that our species is only very questionably "Man, the wise". Civilization was a slow-growing and tender plant, and it was perhaps a miracle that it grew.

But grow it did.

CHAPTER II

Prelude: The Old Stone Age

THE story of Palaeolithic Man is in the nature of a curtain-raiser to true history; almost, since so little happens, one might compare it to a tableau or transformation scene, where change is so small and so slow that, as it were, only a small amount of impersonal and rudimentary machinery is needed to convey the desired effect to the audience. None the less, the palaeolithic is an interesting time, and even an admirable time, when men rarely show themselves at their worst and often at their best. It, of course, has its significance; for if change was slow time was long and a way of life that lasts for thousands upon thousands of years must leave its mark on character and memory and what we call inherited instincts.

Men's embryonic years need not have been called a Stone Age. The name, one might contend, was due to an accident, that it was their flint tools that led to the discovery of earliest man. But to think this would be wrong. Great skills there may have been with withy and wood and bone. But flint was the master tool, the tool that fashioned all other tools, the sharp thing, the weapon. We are right then to think of early men's lives as bounded by flint and the technique of making flint tools. The skill was a great skill and a mystery, handed down, no doubt, along the male line. The time spent, the inordinate time spent, was never wasted. The poor tool was discarded. The perfect tool became an heirloom, a tool to talk about and around which to weave tales of prowess and magic.

Even more significantly perhaps, early man's life is bounded by hunting. He is, essentially, the Mighty Hunter, only excelled in courage and skill, if at all, by the Red Indian of the last century who had learnt to ride the horse conveniently brought to him by the Conquistadores. Palaeolithic Man ate animal, lived animal, thought animal; as we know, he finally drew animal.

His history is governed by changes in climate.

It is a history already more than nine-tenths passed when *Homo sapiens* comes upon the scene. Beginning in the sub-tropics of Asia and

Africa—as half-man or ape man, Austrolopithecus and then Pithecan-
thropus—the human race, having established itself, must have, as it
were, pulsed inwards and outwards over the world's main land mass,
the Euro-Asian continent, as the ice ages pulsed outwards and inwards
from the poles. Its happiest hunting-grounds must always have been
the park lands and great grass steppe lands, where the colossal herds of
browsers and grazers roamed. But there were animals that preferred the
tundra country, between the ice and the steppes, mammoth and
reindeer in particular; and as these followed their food men followed
them. The masses of water locked up in the ice caps, by lowering the
sea-level, would help man to wander by creating land bridges where no
land bridges exist today. It looks as if the greatest and most adventurous
wanderer was the species we have called Neanderthal Man. Perhaps
he wandered even too boldly and too near to the ice.

Whether or not we possess any genes from Neanderthal Man in our
blood is still a matter of controversy, but the major opinion is against
it. William Golding's novel, *The Inheritors*, gives a more likely picture:
the two species side by side in the times of the last Ice Age, *Homo
sapiens* inexorably inheriting the earth, *Homo neanderthalis* being dis-
possessed of it. The Neanderthalers in this book become for the reader
a pathetic, pitiable group, and perhaps they really were: cursed with a
sturdier but less nimble frame, a large but not a well-fronted brain;
envying and almost willing to worship the master race who, however,
treat them with loathing tempered at best by whims of amused
tolerance, as we might regard a tamed bear. It has been pointed out
that if the discovered remains of Neanderthal Man, of which there are
many, are arranged in time sequence, their primitiveness, the clumsi-
ness of their bones and the thickness of their skull, increases rather than,
as might be expected, decreases. The Neanderthaler was perhaps
evolving in the wrong direction, adapting himself too thoroughly to
the rigours of the ice. *Homo sapiens*, however, Man the Wise—an
unconscious wisdom—gained from the ice's rigours a hard schooling,
the benefit of a challenge accepted, but took the more difficult way of
not altering his physical make-up and was rewarded with the luck of
the ice's final retreat. He might well have said, catching a glimpse of
some envious and miserable remaining Neanderthaler skulking round
the outskirts of his hutments and his fire and awaiting inevitable
extinction: "But for the grace of God, there go I!" There are those who
say that in our race-memory of the Neanderthalers lies the germ of the
stories of ogres. It is not impossible, though perhaps not likely. What

is certain is that the two species did live concurrently; and the co-existence must have had some considerable effect on the survivor, rather as if the Abominable Snowman had been seen lately on Hampstead Heath or looking up bewilderedly at the Statue of Liberty. One of the first finds of *Homo sapiens* was in the cave of Cro-Magnon in the Perigord; and there there was brought to light the evidence of murder: three men, a woman and a child obviously done to death with violence. It is at least possible that here was shown one incident in a ruthless war of extermination, a round that contrary to the usual went to the weaker side. It is clear that one culture, the Neanderthaler's *Mousterian*, gave place with dramatic suddenness and completeness to another, the Cro-Magnon people's *Aurignacian*.

We have no need to review all the "cultures" of the Palaeolithic Age, which are based on the kinds of tools they used. For thousands, perhaps hundreds of thousands of years, the half-men forerunners of true men used the great fist-tool, the *coup de poing* or hand-axe, made from a core of flint; they continued to use it with a conservatism that is almost incredible. Neanderthal Man learned to make use of the flakes that were knocked off the core, somewhat more handy and delicate tools. What *Homo sapiens* did was fundamentally to use flint so skilfully that not only could he produce a variety of tools but also tools that were capable of producing further tools out of other and more recalcitrant materials. He learnt to produce flakes of an even thickness from a more or less cylindrical core: he produced the knife blade. He then went further and produced from this blade an engraving tool, the *burin* or chisel, broader on one side than the other and strong enough not only to etch his drawings on bone and ivory and antler at the workman's whim but, what was of more practical importance, fashion without breaking these tough materials into picks and shovels and cleavers and harpoons and awls and needles. The blade and burin are as far advanced from the hand-axe as the modern machine tool is an advance on the Iron Age lathe.

In fact, though we have called the palaeolithic era a curtain-raiser to history we must not underrate its achievements. By the time that these first certainly known men of our species, the Aurignacians, appear in Europe they are already thriving and established. They have come, it is now thought probable, from South-West Asia, Palestine and Syria way. They clothe themselves, adorn themselves; they are savages, but they have many skills. They will continue their way of life for something in the neighbourhood of another dozen thousand years, a

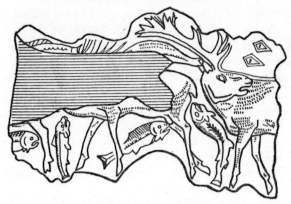

The stag that looked back. A beautiful etching on bone
by a palaeolithic (Magdalenian) artist

span six times the length of our distance from the birth of Christ. By
our standards, therefore, whatever progress they made was very slow
progress. But do not let us make the mistake of imagining that progress
was non-existent, that in describing a "cave man" we have done justice
to all Old Stone Age men of all times and in all places. It is not even
very sensible nor very complimentary to call him a cave man; true that
his remains have most often been found in a cave, but there they were
safe to remain, and if a gorilla can make a windbrake we must credit
the earliest true men with the ability to make a hut or at least a shanty.

The truth is that the cave must have become no more than a winter
shelter and that men, restless and nomadic and hardly possessing a word
for home, were for the rest of the year hunting and following the
animals. Great progress must have been made in the very art of hunting
itself, growing no doubt into an ever more organized, more efficient
and more communal exercise. There is evidence of this.

The discoveries towards the end of the last century at Predmost in
what is now Czechoslovakia surprised the archaeologists of those days
and can surprise us still: a stratum up to thirty inches thick of the ashes
of countless fires seeded with the bones of innumerable beasts. The
bones of all the animals usually hunted were there, great and small:
bison, auroch, horse, reindeer, elk, musk-ox, wolf, fox. The bones of
one creature in particular were there, the great hairy mammoth. At
Predmost was a strategic position where the herds seasonally passed
through a gap in the mountains between the plain of Hungary and the
larger plain that extends across from the Atlantic to the Urals. Men

2

took advantage of this position and managed to leave behind the bones and tusks of nearly a thousand mammoth. Yet among their weapons of flint and bone and ivory was nothing that could have inflicted a mortal wound on the great tough-hided beast. How then did they kill them—drive them over precipices, into pits, into deep snow? In any case there would have had to be given the *coup de grâce*. These men must have been brave, tough, resourceful; well-organized hunters. Their dwellings, judging by finds of similar mammoth hunters near Kiev and in the Ukraine, would have been huts half-submerged in the ground for warmth and covered with skins. Skins and furs of the foxes and wolves they killed they no doubt used to cover themselves. Awls and needles, and sinew for thread, they possessed.

At Solutré in the Loire valley there is evidence of even more successful hunting and mass slaughter, this time of the horse. The Solutreans made perhaps the most beautiful, razor-sharp flint spear-heads of all time.

More than in their tools, it is in their art, their less utilitarian art, and in the evidence of thoughts on life and death which they have left behind, that the palaeolithic people interest us and show us that they were not only the ancestors of the men of later history but their equals and their closest counterparts.

Speech and the control of fire appear to have been two of man's earliest achievements. They say that many birds are fascinated by and love literally to play with fire; perhaps it was early inquisitiveness, inherited from his monkey-like forebears, or from even farther back, that made man first conquer his instinctive fear of the leaping and consuming flame. As for speech, the very ability to think conceptually demands and creates the need of speech—which fact, though making the invention inevitable, does not make it any the less outstanding. We must not, however, credit the palaeolithic hunter with a very great vocabulary nor a very flexible instrument. With virtually only one occupation and one interest, the first men would have had no need for many words: different words no doubt for a male bison, a young bison, a mother bison, a virgin bison, for bison steak off the rump or off the loin; but abstract words, such as, shall we say, *position, movement, speed, intention, doubt,* must have been much harder come by, however great the need for them, as must have been also the more subtle moods and tenses of verbs to express not only past and future but the wished for and the provisional. Primitive languages creak and are cumbersome in expressing such refinements, though they may in the latter end achieve subtleties of which we nowadays feel no need. To begin with, the expression of anything but the immediate here-and-now must have been difficult. William Golding makes his Neanderthalers suffer mental agonies in their efforts to express what they imagine, as opposed to what is actually before them. "I see a picture," they say, frowning, which is a good touch: very possibly it was in this very ability to express themselves that the race *sapiens* excelled beyond its rivals. The later elaborations of hunting, the need to work together in it, to give and understand words of command, must have developed speech, at least in its practical if not its poetical aspects.

How far men needed speech, either poetical or abstract or material, in order to be able to think is hard to say, but *impressive* words, either harshly so or melodiously so, must have helped him, words to cogitate upon and to roll around the tongue and around the brain. *Death* in their languages might be a harsh word, and *love* a beautiful, or an insistent one.

A horse may fear the smell of the blood of its companions, many a beast and bird may pine at the absence of its mate or master; but these facts do not necessarily indicate any true awareness of death on the part of any animal. To man, with his powers of conceptual thinking, the concept of death must have been one of the most powerful, not to say shocking. Was the dead body still alive somehow, at least until its decay; was there a spirit, that remained alive in a dreamlike way and as in dreams? Those were inevitable questions. And "Is there anything that can be done about it?" is surely man's next question, since he is a worrying and wilful sort of creature who does not easily acquiesce in facts that he deems unpleasant. It is significant that even the Neanderthalers sometimes buried their dead with care and respect and that from very early times our own race not only laid possessions with the departed but bequeathed to them such symbolic aids to a renewal of life as the dusting of their body or bones with the bloodlike red of ochre.

With this we are brought to consider the very idea of magic, which is so important a concept in the lives of early men—one that will hardly even begin to fade before we approach the end of the period that is covered by this book. The idea of magic is closely bound with the word just used, *symbolic*. There must be something slightly tortuous and indirect, or more than slightly impractical and sentimental, in the mind of man, both man ancient and man modern, in that he is so affected by the symbol, the word or thing that reminds him of something else, that stands, *significantly*, for something else. The regiment's banner is more poignant than the regiment itself, more personal, more touching; the word *cross* and the word *crescent* pile high in the mind of Christian and Moslem associations and concepts for which he is willing to give his life. To the primitive mind the symbol is equally affecting and even much more real and significant: the shift is only a matter of degree, only a single step. The symbol is for him not a substitute, it is a reality—indeed a super-reality—by its associations more significant than the true reality behind. Red ochre is not merely symbolic and reminiscent of life-giving blood; *it will give life as blood gives life*. It will do so because man believes so; and man believes so because he most wilfully wishes to believe so. Magic is man's effort to control his recalcitrant environment; it has been called, rightly, his first ignorant substitute for science.

And in spite of the mistakenness of its fundamental premise, which is that "like effects like", magic did often work most successfully. In sympathetically considering magic we must never fall into the error of ourselves accepting it, for it is indeed a terrible flaw in man's way of thinking that will hold him back for millennia. But we must not on the other hand, which is perhaps more likely an event, despise it or dismiss it or belittle its power. Magic worked for two reasons. One was that men sought to make happen by magic what would inevitably happen in any case. Afraid that the beneficent sun would not rise the next morning, men did not fail to ensure its return by symbolically enacting that return. If they had been told that their magic was ridiculous they would have simply pointed to facts: *it had worked*. The other reason for magic's power is the sensitivity of man's mind to suggestion, something very deep and not wholly explicable even to ourselves. Let a primitive man of any era be told by his medicine man, his *shaman*, that he is going to die, and he will die. Tell the most sophisticated modern man that the latest drug will do him good, and give him without his knowledge water instead, and good undoubtedly will be derived by him. The two examples are parallel if not identical.

So we may turn to the most spectacular example of palaeolithic man's resort to magic, his paintings and etchings on the walls and ceilings of dark and inaccessible caves.

It is, of course, an assumption and no more that the cave paintings were executed for magic purposes; and we may like to think that the artist's stature is lowered if he has to be credited with only a utilitarian motive. But we should be wrong to feel so. The artist can experience aesthetic satisfaction even though he does work for reward, and indeed satisfaction is increased by reward. To receive, therefore, the awed plaudits of all his tribe, either while he worked or afterwards or both—which if we may draw analogies from present-day aborigine Australians he certainly did—such was surely the reward most likely of all to soothe his savage and untutored breast, balm greater than the highest fee. And that there was magic interest behind the paintings is a highly reasonable assumption from many signs. There is first the fact that the paintings are almost always in the deepest recesses of a cave system, difficult of access for both artist and audience, yet creating an awe-inspiring effect when, dimly lit by the flickering torches, they do finally impinge on what we may call the pilgrims' vision. The great cave of Lascaux has often been likened to a cathedral. Secondly, the beasts are often shown pregnant or wounded, with spear and darts thrust into their sides; at Pindal in the Spanish Asturias a mammoth has the position of its heart carefully depicted. Negative evidence is the fact that human beings are very seldom shown, and then in unrealistic, stylized ways: if to draw naturalistically is to give power over the creature drawn, then to draw humans would be an anti-social rather than a social act. The most striking evidence of magic is in one of the few human figures shown, the so-called Sorcerer from the cave of Les Trois Frères. This fellow is doing what the witch doctor has done until recently—he may still do it—and must have done from the beginning, which is to crown himself with the horns or antlers of the beast, in this case antlers, to dress up in its skin, and to prance about in what to us looks ridiculous but to his fellows no doubt a delightfully symbolic imitation. To super-impose as it were one magic on another, that of imitation by drawing upon that of imitation by dancing, may seem a little complicated and inexplicable; but we are in any case deceiving ourselves if we imagine that we shall ever do more than gain a dim understanding of the workings of the palaeolithic mind. The idea of *like producing like* does seem established: the symbolic imitation, whether by drawing or dance or both, that will produce both fecundity in the beasts that supply men's living and mortality before the enhanced skill of those men in the hunt on the morrow. To say that men's skill was not enhanced by the inspiration and confidence given by such magic practices would be ridiculous.

As is well known, the first of the painted caves to be discovered was at Altamira, and the Spanish landowner who (with the help of the quick eyes of his little daughter) effected the discovery had great difficulty in making an incredulous and sceptical world believe that the paintings were not either a few mere hundred years old or fakes. Nowadays we err in the opposite direction by ceasing, through familiarity, to wonder at all. Perhaps the best way to end this chapter is to quote from an appreciation of Cro-Magnon Man, the first men of our own kind that we know of with any familiarity. This is by Geoffrey Bibby, whose book *The Testimony of the Spade* certainly shows no dulling of the powers of appreciation by familiarity. Taller, stronger, more handsome than ourselves, Mr. Bibby says, Cro-Magnon Man wandered into Europe when the Ice Age was at its height,

"The Sorcerer"

and succeeded in carving out a living for himself in the face not only of inimical nature but of an inimical rival race, over which he had no obvious material advantage:

> "The only point in which he was already head and shoulders above his Neanderthal adversary was in artistic sensibility—and it is not impossible that it was this sensibility, with the greater imagination and breadth of conception which it must have induced, that decided the issue between them."

We already know which way that decision went.

CHAPTER III

Fertility and Invention

THE end of Palaeolithic Man, that is to say of his way of living, was miserable. He did not go out spectacularly, rather he retired grumbling. There is little sign that he wanted to change, that he had any inner urge to do so; if environment and climate had not altered he would in all likelihood have been content to remain a savage and a hunter until the end of time. But the environment and the climate did change, as it must do sooner or later; and the incentive came from without.

By the time that the change came the men of the great hunting era had spread themselves over most though by no means all of the habitable globe. They could not go where the ice caps remained, though from probably 20,000 years ago a slow and no doubt fluctuating final retreat of the ice had started. They could not yet reach any island more than a few miles from a shore. However, they were still helped by the locking up of water in the ice, and either land bridges or nearly complete land bridges enabled them to reach first America and then Australia. Exactly when the Americas became populated is still a matter of dispute and only this much can be said for certain: the original immigration came from Asia, via Siberia and Alaska, and it was not *later* than 8000 B.C.

But though man had spread more universally than any other animal had ever spread he had as yet done so very sparsely. He was capable, with the rest of life, of proliferating in alarming geometrical progression; but as with the rest of life he was so far kept inexorably by nature from doing so. His command was not yet great enough.

8000 B.C., that is to say, in round figures, ten thousand years ago, seems to be a crucial date in human history. By then the ice's retreat, for long a disconcerting acceleration, was reaching its end and the after-effects were becoming apparent. In the higher latitudes the seas were rising, so that, for instance, the land between what we know as England and the Continent, after perhaps a couple of thousand years freed from ice and studded with meres and rivers, was shortly to succumb to the North

Sea. More universally, tundra and steppe were changing to forest. Nearer the equator, the climate was becoming drier and deserts were forming, or increasing.

The heyday of the free-roaming browsers and grazers was over. And so therefore was the heyday of the men who lived off them. The beasts could only seek for or follow their wonted climate and environment to where in remnant it continued. Man, the new successful animal, must now, if he could, show the stuff that he was made of and do better.

Mostly he did do better. A minority took the conservative way. They followed the beasts who followed the climate. Up northwards through Europe their traces have been discovered and their final story pieced together. The mammoth they finally exterminated, but the reindeer remained; making some concession to change, they turned their

Bow-and-arrow hunters. Spanish rock painting

attention at least partly to the big mammals of the sea. Stubbornly but heroically they pass out of history—leaving their skill and way of life, perhaps, too, in some degree their genes, to another stubborn gallant residue, the present-day Lapps and Esquimaux.

If all men had taken the conservative course there would have been no growth towards civilization but only a slow decline. Fortunately this was not so. The remainder of men, the large majority, took two courses, either hunting in new ways, or finding a substitute for hunting.

To hunt in new ways was the obvious solution, though no doubt it entailed some pretty agonized rethinking. Methods, and weapons, had to be thought out afresh. These people might well be called the bow-and-arrow hunters. Often, too, they can be called the shore-hunters, the beachcombers—or, to use an unfamiliar term that seems to have found favour with the archaeologists, strand-loopers. Surrounded by the ever-thickening forest, the old hunters seem often to have made for the water's edge and to have settled there. Such a move was perhaps the result of a sort of claustrophobia, or to put it more positively, and more complimentarily, a sort of inherited agoraphilia. Perhaps it was mere common sense, the making of the most of two sources of food, the seas and lakes and rivers, and the land of trees; perhaps the shore formed a kind of bridgehead against the wild-beast dangers of the forest. Their way of life is usually known as the *mesolithic* or middle stone age. It is a term of doubtful benefit; having invented it the archaeologist becomes involved in argument as to whether such and such a culture should be called mesolithic or not, or in explanation that there were many parts of the world where the mesolithic stage was never passed through at all: he does better seldom to think in terms of it.

Maglemosians, Capsians and Azilians most warrant attention. They all had something to offer posterity, or at the least something to be remembered by.

Maglemose is Danish for *big bog* and it is in Denmark that remains of this type of culture were first found, in fenland, on islands, at lakesides. The Maglemosians existed, living remarkably the same sort of lives, right across the lowland belt of Europe, from England to Russia. Sometimes they are called the Kitchen Midden people because their village site is typically a colossal mound of discarded oyster and cockle-shells; they lived literally on their own refuse heap, and one would imagine a pretty smelly one at that. Their way of life strikes us as likely to have been squalid and unheroic, a sad deterioration from the open hunting life of the palaeolithic peoples. But that is something of a superficial reaction, and we must be fair to them. Times may well have been hard, and if often the only way to keep alive was to hunt for shell-fish, then at least keep alive they did. And the remains that they have left behind show that they also hunted larger and more active game, the red deer, still even the auroch, and the dangerous forest boar. They were great fowlers too. Perhaps to retrieve for them, certainly to help and befriend them, they tamed the dog: here is a foretaste of what is to come. As Kipling once explained to children, it may have been the woman who had the patience and intelligence to make the moral conquest; but it was the man in his hunting who benefited the most. A second womanly conquest is suggested by another find in one of the Danish kitchen midden sites, a comb. Not the first comb of history surely, since women can hardly have delayed long to discover the advantage, and the attraction, of sleek hair; but at least it is something to set against the stinking fish-pile. It may be added that this way of life was to persist in pockets long after the surrounding Europeans had progressed to what we at least would regard as a better way of life; it must have been far from unbearable therefore.

Capsian is North African, with an offshoot into Eastern Spain. These people indulged in a most lively form of rock painting. There is no mysterious hiding of these paintings in deep caves, and no shying away from the representation of the human form. Sometimes men are still queer and stylized; but more often everything is gay and uninhibited and natural: the girl climbing up a rock-face to rob the wild bees of their honey, matrons in long gowns, men with imposing feather head-dresses, and hunters prancing about with abandon and doing tremendous skilled execution with great bows. If the art of the palaeolithic

Capsian *joie-de-vivre*

Aurignacians and Magdalenians was largely magic, then the art of these later Capsians was *joie de vivre*: the concept of these so-called mesolithic times as poor ones of difficulty and transition does not always seem to hold good.

The Azilians take their name from a cave on the French side of the Pyrenees, though their like are found as far north as Bavaria. Their contribution is an art, so-called, that seems to us at first little more than ridiculous: round smooth pebbles painted with stripes and dots and circles. Two patient palaeontologists, Breuil and Obermaier, have, however, put some sense into them, by comparing with other scratchings or drawings or paintings going back in time and so extracting a number of series each beginning with the human form and progressing step by step to something more conventionalized and less recognizable until there is reached the Azilian pebbles. Without doubt, then, some at least of the pebbles are showing the human figure, though so highly

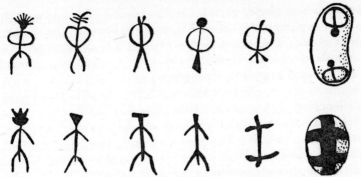

Azilian pebbles and the human form

stylized and so badly copied as to have become quite unrecognizable. This says much for the piety of the Azilians but little for their intelligence. In his book *Ancient Hunters*, W. J. Sollas has told of a meeting with an Australian aborigine who possessed very similar painted stones. She made it pretty clear they were to do with ancestor worship.

One thing all these peoples show, and that is a continued and developing skill in the making of tools and implements of flint and bone. The typical flint is now a *microlith*, no more than an inch or so in length, usually crescent-shaped and delicately worked to give one straight or curved razor edge. These were fitted into wood or bone, often in rows, to produce spears and harpoons and arrows. Later, similar pieces were to be fitted into the first sickles.

Now, the use of the sickle is to cut grass or cornstalks. We are introduced to the great "revolution" which took place within the Stone Age, to the twin invention that was going to transform man's way of life and set him free from being a mere food-seeker, hunter, preyer upon Nature. It is an event that in archaeological language divides the Old and Middle Stone Ages from the New, that ushers in the ways of using flint that are known as Neolithic. A change vastly greater than that, however, is involved.

To fail to recognize the significant connection between seedtime and harvest does not necessarily show a lack of intelligence; rather it suggests a carefree nature, regardful of the truth of "sufficient unto the day" and regardless of the passage of time: some primitive peoples are said not to have recognized a connection between the sexual act and the birth of a child. However, the connection, and the way to exploit it, will sooner or later occur to some receptive mind, particularly if hunting is beginning to grow less easily rewarding. It would be likely to occur in places where hot sunshine and sufficient rain made the wild corn's growth a spectacularly quick affair. The ensuing steps are inevitable: to sow the grain with conscious intent, carefully to tend and weed it during its growth, triumphantly to harvest it—cut it, dry it, winnow it, store it, grind it, cook it, eat it. This could and did happen in hill-and-meadow countries of the Near East and East, and in the warmer climates of America. The result was the growing of wheat and barley, of rice, of maize. Rice-growing, coming later, was probably a matter of imitation, but maize-growing must almost certainly have been an independent discovery; it does seem very likely, however, that all the peoples of Europe learnt to become farmers from one single source, the Middle East.

If to control crops is a possibility then so also is to control herds. This other of the new techniques may have arrived more gradually, a scarcely noticed progression from mere efforts to guide the wild herd, through odd occasions of midwifery of the cow in difficult labour or the feeding of the orphaned lamb. Husbandry seems to have become established, however, at much the same time as the raising of crops. The grain and the straw would be both a temptation to the beast to approach and a bait wherewith to catch it and reconcile it to captivity.

What should be realized is that if the growing of crops entailed one sort of patience, the purely passive patience of waiting for ripeness, then the domestication of animals involved men and women in another and even more difficult kind of patience, the active kind that goes with regard and love. It is superficial to think that those who live on animals and kill them cannot love them. All primitive hunters have had a regard for their animals, a regard that has concerned and often worried them deeply. But the husbandman has a greater regard; a mutual trust has to be formed. In fact man, in becoming farmer and husbandman, was instituting a change of more than the world about him; he was instituting a change within himself: besides modifying his way of life he was modifying his character—it would not be altogether wide of the mark to say that in beginning to tame nature he went at least some way in taming himself.

From the middle or beginning of the Seventh Millennium B.C. and in the course of three thousand years or so—a long span by modern standards, a short one by palaeolithic—men learned to grow many crops and tame many animals. Of the grains there was, besides barley, wheat and rice, millet in the Far East and sorghum in Africa; those, with oats and rye later in northern Europe, were to give man his staple food, his energy-producer. He soon learnt to parch or "pop" the ground grain in ovens and to make gruel and biscuits. Gruel left to itself will often ferment, and a sort of beer may be nearly as old as agriculture itself. The use of yeast to make leavened bread and better beer probably did not come until the beginnings of the Bronze Age. To supplement the protein of his reduced meat supply, the leguminous plants or pulses were soon cultivated: peas and beans are spectacularly large in size and easy to store. Egyptians first grew the lentil. Another lack, of animal fat, was made good by cultivating the olive, sesame, rape and flax. Flax was to give not only linseed oil but also from its fibres a thread more easy to spin and weave than the somewhat hairy, wiry wool of the early domesticated sheep. The date and the vine were being grown in the Middle East by the Fourth Millennium; and by the time that the Neolithic Revolution had penetrated to the lakesides of Switzerland orchards of a better apple than the crab had appeared. Of the taming of animals the order in time was probably: goat, sheep, cattle, pig. The draught and pack animals came later, the ass and onager at about 3000 B.C. These must have been times of great experimenting, often exciting, no doubt sometimes disastrous. The tale of poisonings we shall never know; we do know that the early Egyptians tried to tame, without much success, antelopes and gazelles, monkeys, and hyenas. . . .

It is often said that the Neolithic Revolution released the tide of progress towards civilization because men were able for the first time to create a surplus of food beyond bare necessity and, less tied to a hand-to-mouth existence, had time in which to think. But the hunter must have had leisure on occasion. Perhaps it was only the leisure of the cat tribe, carnivore repletion which results largely in sleep. The hunter too must sometimes have possessed a surplus of food, indeed he probably suffered chronically from a perpetual swing between too much and too little. The point is that with the best will in the world— and the most developed taste for high meat—he could not make great use of his surplus. To the word surplus, then, we must add the qualification, *storable*.

Some of the season's harvest had to be put aside for next season's sowing. The rest, if men were sensible, was carefully stored and doled out as a ration, either a voluntary or an enforced ration. As intimation of this, early settlements on the fringes of the Nile have left traces of straw-lined pits for storage.

Three important developments are going to arrive from all this. The agriculturist is going to cease to be a universal and perpetual roamer. Secondly, the need will arise, and will be met, for leaders, for big men who will take responsibility and tell all the little men what to do. Thirdly, with the village forming, with the head man willing and eager to control, a larger community will spring into being. There must, of course, in palaeolithic days, have been those who took command of the hunt; the little family group, wandering in its sparsely populated world, must have had its Old Man or its Old Woman, or both, who exercised some authority and restraint. But these are minor figures compared with the sanction-wielding, awesome, hierarchical figures, wearing the symbols of power, hedged round with dignity and the support of only lesser great men, that were by slow but certain steps now arising. Man's first chains and his first exploiters were being shaped. That is one way of looking at the new situation. Man's first substantial opportunities, as a being who can plan and abstain and control and co-operate, were being taken—that is the other way of looking at it.

The new inventions and techniques of neolithic times were considerable, fresh conquests leading to fresh needs.

There was the container, the vessel, the jar, the cooking pot, needed as never before. Men discovered that fired clay could change its nature and become reasonably fireproof, totally non-porous and wellnigh indestructible. The long story of pottery was begun, a story of art as well as utility, since shape was at the potter's command and surface invited decoration. As our first motor-car was a

Reminiscent of a leather bag. A neolithic pot

horseless carriage so the first pots resembled the gourd or the clay-smeared basket or the leather bag with its string-tied mouth that they had replaced. The potter's wheel was a good long time in coming.

The axled wheel for transport was even slower in arriving. Perhaps only a road creates a demand for a wheel, and it is the wheel that largely creates the demand for a road. Mesolithic people dragged sledges about. But the early Sumerians of about the Fourth Millennium are the first people that we know had wagons on wheels, because they left behind models of them: the real thing, of course, may have come earlier.

With the boat the Neolithic Age made much greater progress. The desire to fish more effectively, the frustration caused by the unfordable river, must have long ago forced men to dare sit astride the fallen log and sew up and blow up an animal skin and hang on to it. Now the smooth strong neolithic axe is going to make possible the dug-out canoe, in Egypt papyrus rafts are going to evolve into prowed boats, and people are going to venture out into the Pacific, not always so pacific, in catamarans. For the first time the *isolated* islands of the world, those out of sight of any other land, will begin to receive their quota of brave and adventurous men.

Sewing with the string of leather or with gut was practised by the hunting men; but spinning and weaving are neolithic inventions. The *idea* of weaving may be no more than an elaboration of plaiting the withy, which half-man may have done when he made his windbrake, but the loom soon becomes an elaborate mechanism—as soon, that is to say, as a thread exists to encourage its development. At rudimentary spinning anyone can try his hand, with combed-out wool from the hedgerows, a skewer for a spindle and a small potato for a whorl or weight at the spindle's end. He will need patience, however, as well as a wetted thumb and forefinger, to start the miraculous process going. The neolithic woman who could tame a wild auroch or a timid sheep certainly possessed patience enough. A piece of woven linen has been preserved for us from one of the earliest Egyptian cultures, at the lakeside of Fayum, some fifty miles south of Cairo. The find dates at about 4500 B.C.*

Another new invention in these centuries prolific in advance is the permanent human habitation. *The home* arrives. Near to Jericho, which lies at the northern end of the route from Egypt to the land that flowed

---

*Most people nowadays have heard of the "carbon-14" method of dating that has brought a so much greater accuracy to our estimation of the age of things past. The method depends on the fact that all living things, animal or vegetable, absorb from the atmosphere and throughout their lifetime a modicum of the radio-active isotope of carbon called carbon-14. After death this carbon is slowly lost, at a steady and calculable rate. Beyond an age of 70,000 years the residue of carbon-14 is too weak to be measured by present instruments; the method is most reliable over a range from 5000 B.C. to the beginning of the Christian era.

with milk and honey, there is and has been for thousands of years a perennial spring of fresh water; and here excavations have lately uncovered traces of building of earlier and earlier date until amazingly one is in the Seventh Millennium B.C. And the houses from the start must have been very pleasant. One small discovery in particular shook the complacency of the diggers: the supposedly most modern hygienic invention of rounding the join of floor and wall to prevent the harbouring of dust was known to the housebuilders of ancient Jericho.

The house of stone remains in the ground for the archaeologist to discover, but not, of course, the log cabin. But that too was possible for the neolithic agriculturist, and there is no reason to suppose that he failed to do so. For he had the tool for the job.

The stone tool that has been ground and polished constitutes the badge and name-plate of the New Stone Age men, as did the microlith of the mesolithic hunters, the blade and the burin of the later palaeolithic and the flake tool of the Neanderthal men. Both the hoe and the hafted axe, now invented, would in use *acquire* a polish, and it was soon found that such smoothness gave an advantage that was worth imparting from the beginning. So it was done—and harder, igneous rocks were for the first time also used in the process.

In fact, the polished axe is the great and significant tool of the Neolithic Age: it will be made finally with such perfection that metal axes will later copy exactly its lines; it power will so impress people that it will become and remain a portentous symbol until beyond Roman times. Its significant power was first not that it could fell humans but that it could fell trees. Not always but very frequently, with greater frequency as the agricultural

The polished and hafted stone axe

way of life spreads northwards, the first job for the farmer was not to till his land but to clear it of scrub or forest so that he might begin to till it. Modern experiments have been made by Danish enthusiasts with genuine neolithic axe-heads that had existed, and had not been sharpened for 4,000 years. Two lessons were first learnt: that the axe must not be socketed too tightly but must have room to vibrate slightly in the haft; that swinging from the elbow was more effective than the normal swing from the shoulder of the man armed with an axe of iron. When those lessons had been learned, 600 square yards of silver birch forest were cleared by three men in four hours. . . .

Finally, however, the Neolithic Age men must not be credited with too great an efficiency, nor must it be thought that with the end of hunting as their main livelihood men had ceased to become trekkers and wanderers and had settled down to a permanently ordered way of existence.

To some extent inefficiency in agriculture and a renewed propensity

Rock painting: the hunter with his dog?

to migrate across the face of the earth were no more than cause and effect. True, the home had come into existence, true that the lucky men who had found a very fertile spot would not be likely to move from it. But the ordinary run of slash-and-grab farmer, who, with no scientific knowledge, would soon exhaust the fertility of the site he had cleared with his axe, would in a few years' time have to find another. The herdsman, too, would move, not only seasonally but sometimes more permanently and drastically when climate or weather was against him. Even the neolithic people's very success would make for movement. Man, like any animal, tends to proliferate up to the possible limits, and increased food was creating increased population. The village would, as it were, spawn further villages; when pressure grew, even if the original settler did not move his son and his family might have to do so. "And there was strife between the herdsmen of Abraham's cattle and the herdsmen of Lot's cattle. And Abraham said unto Lot: 'Is not the whole land before thee? Separate thyself, I pray thee, from me.' "

Greater trouble would arise when the good lands were so filling up that Abraham's simple solution was not possible. Or when chiefs and petty kings were less amenable and more self-important than the biblical patriarch.

CHAPTER IV

Interlude: Ways of Thinking

THE story has now reached the point of leaving the featureless plains of history, the generalities of the palaeolithic and earlier neolithic ages, where peoples are undifferentiated. It arrives at the point where peoples become distinct, soon even individual persons will be distinct, or if not distinct at least discernible. First, however—calling in anthropological knowledge to supplement archaeological—we must take a last look at the old, indistinguishable people, to take some note of their spiritual as opposed to their material achievements. What they thought and believed influenced not only their behaviour but the behaviour for a long time of those who followed after.

It is not easy to enter into the thoughts of early man. Fundamentally perhaps he was as materialistic in his outlook as ourselves, since his primary aim was undoubtedly his own welfare in this life on earth.

But his ways of trying to achieve his object were not nearly so materialistic, nor so individualistic: he was aware that external nature was largely inimical, and man's nature not easily controllable; and if he could get by with some feeling of security from the vagaries of either he would be happy to forgo a good deal of what we should regard as the inalienable freedoms. External nature and the laws that governed her he did not understand in the least. But he was not confounded by his ignorance: he was not aware that he did not know. . . .

Man is, to use a phrase of Gerald Heard's, "sensitively aware", out-standingly so compared with the rest of the animal kingdom.

Man is aware of his body, his own and other people's, not only because he can see and feel it better, at least than any quadruped, but also because he can visualize it, contain it in his conceptual thoughts. He will decorate it, therefore, and significantly so. Clothes will be for warmth, and even so paint too, mixed as it will be with earth and oils and fats. But from the beginning both will have a symbolical significance, a meaning for the onlooker: man, as he continues to do, will "dress for the occasion".*

Even more, man will be aware of his fellow-man's countenance. Of all creatures he has the most expressive face, and his eyes mirror the subtle and complicated thoughts behind them. Men soon became rightly aware that in the head and behind the eyes lay the seat of intelligence, which discovery may indeed have led to the unhappy habit of cannibalism, a practice indulged in to assuage spiritual and not gastronomic yearnings and that typically selected the brain for eating, so that its virtue might pass to the participant.

Of all mutual awareness that between sex and sex must have been the most deep and troublesome to man. Most creatures during the time that they live in flock or herd are virtually neuters; then when their gonads come to life again and the seasonal urge is upon them they drift off to perform a ritual and to form pairs or a male-mastered harem. Man had also the instinct to herd, or more probably the intelligence and reason to see the advantages of co-operation; but he had also his ever-present sexual urges and the paramount need to regulate and sublimate them. The result has been the invariable presence in all primitive societies of the strictest and widest taboos against incest. With it has gone some form of exogamy: the outlet was without and not within the family circle. And the rules and customs have often been so strict and so complicated and so fierce as to seem almost hysterical, the actions of a society fighting off by any means a deadly danger. The very concepts of sexual love and of brother-sister relationship must never connect: Malinowski tells of how amongst the Trobrianders of the South-west Pacific, should a brother by chance witness his sister's love-making, and there be no way of hiding the fact, then in shame and guilt all three would commit suicide. Incest in fact—brother and sister, son and mother, often in much less close relationships—was the deadly sin, more deadly, more guarded against, than murder.

And no doubt rightly so. Murder destroys the individual, but incest if left unchecked could make family life unbearable, unthinkable, would in the end destroy it. Murder may be held in check, if expensively, by the blood feud, as is reflected in the laws of Hammurabi, even in those of our own recent Saxon forefathers. But incest is another matter. Here is something wide and deep and spiritually dangerous—incidentally,

---

*A seaman, sole survivor of a nineteenth-century missionary expedition to Tierra del Fuego, told afterwards how he had been stripped, depilated, and painted. This, one imagines, was not primarily a torture but a discipline: he was improperly dressed.

much over-simplified by us if interpreted solely as one colossal Oedipus complex—that must be controlled. It is the health of the clan, its spiritual health, that matters.

That is the point, and why this example of incest taboo has been considered at some length.* Men are aware of their spirituality and disturbingly aware. They are also aware that they belong to a community, and that they must if necessary be ruthless in maintaining the healthful existence of that community.

And as time went on the size of men's communities increased: from family or clan of two or three or four generations to tribe or collection, either more or less closely knit, of clans; from village to town, to group of towns, to nation. The practices devised to maintain the spiritual health of the larger community were manifold but ran to a pattern. Foremost was the idea that such health depended upon the *virtue* of all members in accord with the well-known workings of the influence of magic. Not only would the imitative dance or the slaughter depicted on the cave wall help towards the hunt's success but the hunter's sexual continence before the event would strengthen him, whilst the incontinence of his wife in his absence would weaken him—as would indeed the lack of fortitude of his children, the eating on any of their parts of an acknowledgedly weak or timid creature, or even the presence on their hands of fat or grease that would convey its property to the hunter and make of him as we would say a butter-fingers. So we may fairly imagine—judging by similar habits of still surviving primitive hunters —did the ideas of what have been called sympathetic and contagious magic, dual aspects of the fundamental idea that like influences like, elaborate themselves. And those elaborations had all, no doubt, to be remembered, and who to remember them better than those knowledgeable ones, the older men of the tribe? Great responsibility devolved upon the older men.

So much was this so that the entry into man's estate was a time of great importance, to be impressed upon the youngster by means of ceremonies of memorable, indeed often of shocking, import. The girl at puberty in all primitive societies had her initiation ceremonies too, but they were usually milder, inculcating the more patient and passive virtues. The male was finally told secrets, of the methods of ensuring the safety of the tribe. But this was only after he had proved his manhood and at the same time received some irrevocable badge of this manhood and of belonging to the tribe: circumcision, the knocking out

*The interested reader should turn to *Nature into History* by Leslie Paul (Faber, 1957).

of a tooth, the lopping off of a finger. Amongst the palaeolithic cave paintings there appear quite often—for instance at Gargas in the Pyrenees—the silhouettes of hands with lopped-off fingers.

Great responsibility, too, devolves upon the dead ancestor. It has already been seen how early in man's history arose a care for the dead. This grows in elaboration. It does not always seem a matter of sentiment; sometimes it has more the appearance of self-protection, certainly of self-interest. Man must have had an ambivalent feeling towards his dead, and, perhaps rather naturally, a respect and fear. He entertained little doubt as to their influence upon the living; and sometimes he wanted to be free of that influence, sometimes to benefit by it and turn it to his advantage. He seems often to have thought that the influence remained only whilst the flesh remained; so that on the one hand he mummified, and on the other, as is shown in some of our own Long Barrows, he bundled aside with complete lack of ceremony the bones of the previous central figure to make room for the next august and influential occupant of a family mausoleum. Skulls, the containers of the seat of the intellect, were much considered. Amongst both modern and ancient primitives—the Maoris, the neolithic people of Jericho— skulls have been decorated, made more lifelike with clay modelling and cowrie shells for eyes, and set up in the house, as more sophisticated ages would set up a picture of the deceased or his favourite weapon, though in this instance with a more practical purpose. Here, in the skull of the great one whose greatness cannot of a surety have wholly disappeared with death, existed essentially the great *influencers* of human affairs; and one would seek naturally to influence the influencer. Man's early life, the life of both the hunter and the inexpert agriculturist, must have been one long struggle for luck, one long wilful effort to turn one's luck to good, to discover it in advance by omens and to do all in one's power to make those omens satisfactory. Men therefore supplicated, importuned, made offerings to, propitiated the set-up skull, where resided the spirit of his ancestors.

Therein lies one way in which was demonstrated the birth of religious feeling—giving to the phrase the widest definition possible, such as "the belief in spiritual beings superior to man". Another path that led to religious belief and custom began undoubtedly in animism, the feeling that all the aspects of nature around one—the stream that sparkles, the stone that trips, the animal that evades or succumbs—have behind them a spirit. And once again, and inevitably, comes the idea of influence, the idea that the spirits of these physical phenomena can be influenced by greater spirits with mightier magic power—in fact, by gods.

To bring in the word *God* unfortunately tends to cloud the issue for us. For we find it impossible to regard the conception as primitive man must have regarded it. To him a god was no more, or less, than a super-power of the spiritual and magic world—a world indivisible from the material world—that he could importune, coerce, bribe, placate, thank or worship. It was his own very particular spiritual power, particular to his tribe—in fact, the spirit of the tribe. It might take animal form if it wished, or at least have an animal as its familiar or its symbol. It not only might take human form but probably had once been human, could become human again, and even in some cases had as yet been nothing but human. Yet it was, none the less and indisputably, a god.

With the Neolithic Revolution men's ideas concerning magical influence took a new turn, and a turn towards darkness rather than light. Certain discoveries, certain "facts of life", things that we either take for granted or from which we turn an embarrassed eye, affected early man

profoundly. One, that was to come a little later, would be the unnatural but pleasant practice of drinking the milk of the cow, the idea of the symbolic motherliness of the cow; another and earlier would be the spectacular virility of the bull. The queerness and potency of women had always struck them, indeed awed them: their menstruation, their powers of procreation. The fertility of women was something both to delight men and to frighten them. The fertility of Nature—without which the fertility of women was a menace— was a miracle to be fostered and multiplied by all the influences within man's power. And now the newly observed miracle, that the dead seed could be brought to life, seemed perhaps the most impressive of all. Since a farming community is likely to be more devastatingly

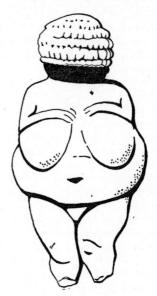

Fertility personified: the "Venus of Willendorf"

affected by a harvest failure or a murrain among its beasts than the hunters who in scarcity can at least hunt elsewhere, it was also a

miracle imperative to perpetuate with success. The idea seems to have
grown up universally that the dying and rebirth of the corn, reflected
as it was by the seasonal dying and rebirth of all nature, had to be and
indeed only could be kept going by the magic influence of the dying
and rebirth of men. In particular by the blood of men. In a gruesome
and practical way the idea was sound: the blood of men, as of beasts,
does nourish the crops by a purely chemical process. But the idea was a
mystical one; and men believed that the normal processes of nature
were not merely helped by blood sacrifice but would fail without
them. Men fell back on an already ancient idea, that the virtue and
conduct of man influenced the beneficence of nature. They added to
this, inevitably, the idea that the more important the man the greater
his influence. They considered their chiefs and kings who, with the
elaboration of society, were coming into existence; and they evolved a
theory that the king must die in his prime and be renewed by another
and younger and more virile king if the benign influence, and hence the
crops, were not to fail.

Do not let us suppose that such a practice was universal. But the belief
in the active influence of the great ones does seem universal—there was
a plague at Thebes, it may be remembered, solely because of Oedipus's
undiscovered sin—and, though the stark logic may soon have been
toned down in practice, human sacrifice as a spectacular way of
influencing and pleasing the god does become a common occurrence
in neolithic barbarism.

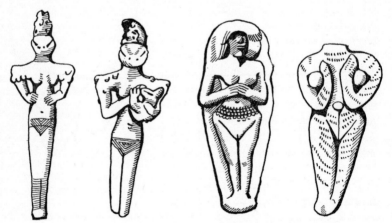

More fertility figurines, from Sumeria and Palestine

By way of summary this much may be said. Man, unblessed with the easy, mechanical nature of the insect, is seeking to become a social creature. His imagination and his wilfulness, his ignorance and his wrong-headedness, do not make this task easy, and he himself realizes that he has to take drastic steps to achieve his aim. He realizes that for his own spiritual health there must be a spiritual health of his community. He realizes too, more practically, that for his community to continue to exist it must gain and retain sufficient powers over the fertility of Nature. To achieve both aims he will if necessary be quite ruthless to the individual, and the individual will realize and accept the situation.

Man will equally be ruthless if necessary in his dealings with other communities. He knows that the path of progress towards a fuller life, though not necessarily easy of discernment, is sure to be beset by difficulties and that he must struggle to overcome them.

CHAPTER V

River and Flood

ALMOST the "Neolithic Revolution" seems to hang fire. The change is fundamental, but it is very slow. For many hundreds of years men must have been not so much agriculturists as hunters supplementing their diet, no more full-time farmers than the present-day city commuter who grows his own vegetables and keeps a few hens and perhaps a pig. For many more hundreds of years the new secondary inventions —weaving, pottery, the making of clay bricks—helped to make life easier and towards the forming of village communities. Jericho stands out as a near-town, a precocious child as it were. But no further startling advances are made; there is smoke but no fire, the real glow of civilization, pulsing and bursting outwards, is not yet to be seen. The face of the world is preparing itself and men are awaiting their opportunity. Certain great rivers, growing less fierce and turbulent, ever dropping their silt from the higher reaches, are about to present themselves for harnessing by men.

Those rivers are, in particular and as is well known, the Nile on the one hand and the parallel pair, Tigris and Euphrates, on the other.

There are also the Indus and the Hwang Ho or Yellow River. A suspicion will always arise that the Westerner, in describing the beginnings of his own civilization, will tend to play down beyond all reason the East and the East's contribution. But even had the early civilizations in the Indus valley been discovered before those of the Nile or Mesopotamia—which is in itself unlikely, for there was so much less to discover—there is no doubt that the balance would have later righted itself and the sites in the Middle East have soon taken precedence in archaeologists' estimation. Harappa and Mohenjo-Daro are not to be ignored. But their day is later, in the middle of the Third Millennium, and they are in no great way originators. China's civilization, though it is so old and more continuous than Europe's, can similarly make no claim to be the earliest.

Another cause of much friction and little light is the debate as to which of the two civilizations, Egyptian or Mesopotamian, made the greater contribution to progress and which came first. As both took something like a thousand years to "come" and developed by such small and multiple stages that to choose a particular point as that of arrival is impossible, any dispute as to priority in time is practically meaningless. As to priority in greatness or contributions to progress, any decision there is no more than a matter of opinion and predilection. The surprising fact is how closely parallel in time the two separate developments run; the important fact is that each has an enormous contribution to make. I think that, if anything, we should let favour fall more upon the Egyptians, and, for this reason only, that, most of Mesopotamian discovery being so much more recent than Egyptian, we need to make some compensation to restore a true balance. Since for the best part of a couple of millennia neither centre indulged in any serious rivalry with the other, we shall do well to follow that example and think of the two as complementary and not competing. Though they may in general follow the same sort of pattern, in detail their histories are different. Their geography is different; and, as Sir Leonard Woolley, who excavated in both places, has said, "Man must adapt himself to his surroundings even while he masters them, so that geography does affect history." One difference is that, whereas Egyptians remain Egyptians, the peoples of the Two Rivers present to us a confusing kaleidoscope of names: Sumerians, Akkadians, Babylonians, Assyrians, Chaldeans.

Sumerians in their sheepskin skirts

A dumpy little man, with an enormous nose and very often a benign not to say self-deprecatory expression, wearing a heavy flounced sheepskin skirt below a bare torso: that is the self-portrait that the Sumerian has given to us of himself. Half a century or so ago he was a more or less mythical figure, mentioned in the Bible as inhabiting the plain of Shinar, leaving behind some cuneiform writing in an unknown tongue, and passed over by the historians under some such title, now seen to be misleading, as "the Early Babylonians". Excavations have in the interval completely changed the picture and the growing certainty with which their script is being transliterated and translated will clarify it still more. The Sumerians are the people who opened up the land at the head of the Persian Gulf; they have a history of well over a thousand years.

Their believed beginnings tend to be pushed back farther and farther by the archaeologists, and the process may not yet have stopped. Dates are vague: let it suffice that we begin before the Fifth Millennium B.C. is over and stop—so far as this chapter is concerned—when a Dynastic record of kings becomes reliable, just about at the round figure, 3000 B.C. First, in very bare outline the story is something as follows. (The names of peoples or cultures, called after the sites where their characteristic belongings and pottery were first discovered, may appear confusing; but they are universally used and to omit them would make the reader's reference to any more detailed history of the Sumerians less helpful.)

Once the Persian Gulf must have extended to at least where Baghdad now stands. But from each side a river, the Karim from Persia and from Arabia the nameless river that once filled the Wadi al-Batin, perpetually poured in their silt so that, some 300 miles south of the gulf's head, there formed a bar across the entrance. This in turn helped to pile up the silt from the Tigris and the Euphrates. Gradually this great inland sea changed its aspect: in the words of the Creation story of Genesis, the waters were gathered into one place and dry land appeared, islands that grew and extended and joined. This land was amazingly fertile. And men were not over-slow in discovering the fact.

First probably arrived a people of already well-organized neolithic life and of considerable artistic skill in pottery; they came down from the hill-country of what is now north Syria and south Turkey, the Tell Halaf people. Next came a migration from the north-east, from the highlands of Iran, the biblical Elam, where soon Susa was to be

founded.* These Al Ubaid people, equally advanced in their barbaric
culture, fond of painting gay and spirited birds and beasts on their
pottery, peacefully and slowly took over from the Halafians and also
extended farther south as the water receded. These in turn were
absorbed by fresh arrivals from the north-west, the Uruk or Erech
people, followed by a last wave, this time again from Iran, the people
of Jemdet Nasr. By this time the polyglot population is calling itself
Sumerian and there will begin the "Dynastic" period, of what we may
call documented history. By this time also two outstanding inventions
have made their appearance: the use of copper, and the use of writing.
Somewhere between one of these changes of culture, Sir Leonard
Woolley believes between Al Ubaid and Uruk, came a disastrous
flood—the flood, no doubt, of the biblical Noah and of his Sumerian
counterpart, Uta-Nipishtim, of whom more later.

What is remarkable about all these changes is that there is no good
evidence that any were achieved with violence; they seem to have been
infiltrations rather than conquests—the one that occurred after the
Flood may well have been more a matter of repopulating an empty
land. There was continuity, even though the only material signs of
culture that we have to build upon, paramountly the types and
fashions of pottery, do show these definite breaks: all the peoples of
these four cultures were living in the same land of flat fertility and, as
has been observed, environment does shape a man's life even while he
is shaping his environment. What is going to happen to these people,
what must happen to them if they are to survive, is that they will find
themselves *organized* by a higher authority. However fertile this
newly appeared land might be it could not under the burning sun
produce its crops without irrigation; and a multiplicity of irrigation
systems particular to each private individual would be an absurdity.
Men had to learn to co-operate, to understand that "I may do what I
like with my own" was a disastrous belief, that disputes over land and
water must be settled by a higher authority that none would question.
Their solution was, in fact, something of an extreme one: the land
belonged to the God; and there was a King who described himself as
"tenant-farmer of the God"; and everyone obeyed him and lived
under his protection. The king, an instrument of divinity and quite
possibly himself to assume divinity at death, developed a pomp and
majesty and an increasingly complex household of priests and civil

*Difficulties arise from the continual change of the names of countries throughout
history. We will stick to what seems the most familiar name.

servants—the one, surprisingly enough, scarcely distinguishable from the other. As a consequence there rapidly developed in Sumeria a large collection of god-dominated, king-led city-states.

With the ancient Egyptian's generic type we no doubt feel more familiar. But our idea is likely to be influenced by those ubiquitous statues of a later, more military and more self-advertising age, proud kings with stern yet sensual lips. Sensual per-haps the Egyptian was in that he loved and appreciated the good things of life on earth; but I think he was a much merrier person than the statues would give us to believe. He seems to have been a rather taller and much more slender person than the Sumerian. Because of a convention of drawing it is difficult to imagine the ancient Egyptian other than long and almond-eyed, a full-eyed effect even in profile. Since from the earliest times both sexes had used powdered malachite on their eyelids as a protection from the glare, and since most cosmetics and ornamentation in the early days fulfilled more than one if not all three of the purposes practical, symbolic and beautifying, probably Egyptian eyes would have seemed to us striking. In contrast to the almost over-powering beardedness of the Semite, even to the occasional beardedness of the Sumerian, the early Egyptian either disliked hairiness as much as the Fuegians of Darwin's time or else was naturally free from it: since beardedness in all eyes seems to go with venerable kingli-ness, the Pharaoh of later times wore a ceremonial wooden one: perhaps we may throw a general glance of pity at the burden-someness of the regalia and ritual of early kings, by thinking what an encumbrance a wooden beard must have been.

The benign Sum-erian: a statuette from Ur

Herodotus called Egypt most aptly "the gift of the Nile": in that sun-soaked, rainless climate any habitation without the blessed river would have been impossible. When the rains come and on the moun-tains of the Nile's source the winter snows melt, the ensuing torrent will grind the boulders in the river's bed and carry the fine silt for thousands of miles to spread at length over the lower reaches, a flood that is the reverse of a catastrophe, a yearly beneficence whose occurrence, though not extent, can be confidently predicted. Egypt is a narrow strip of a country, seldom more than seven miles wide until it spreads out at the river's delta, in some parts enclosed by cliffs and over all its length edged in impressive contrast by the desert.

The earliest people who had the courage to change their way of life and accept this gift of a river that virtually did their ploughing and watering and manuring for them are known as the Tasians, arriving probably from the shrinking oasis of the Fayum. Here, as with the Sumerians, we have a sequence of cultures based on pottery finds, one worked out by the great Egyptologist and founder of modern systematic archaeology, Sir Flinders Petrie. It runs: Tasian, Badarian, Amratian, Gerzian. The first two peoples are neolithic but good pottery-makers and linen weavers; the same or similar people, even more adventurous, were to arrive finally at Windmill Hill in England. With the Amratians comes copper in quantity. Yet this is still the chalcolithic, the "copperstone" age, for many tools and weapons continue to be made of flint. There are stone knives of this culture that archaeologists regard almost with awe, so beautifully are they made; the suggestion is that they were, in fact, awesome objects, tools of some ritual such as circumcision. The Egyptians, even from the beginning, are efficient craftsmen, masters of their material. With the Amratians arrive the first brick-built houses, together with something very different, evidence in all probability again of ritual rather than mere sophistication or coquetry: ladies' wigs.

As in the Sumerian changes of culture, there are signs more of peaceful infiltration than of military conquest. The change to the Gerzian culture does, however, seem an exception. These people produce a formidable weapon, a hafted and pear-shaped mace. Later times were to relegate the mace to a lower category, permissible to fighting Christian bishops for instance, but the Gerzians seem to have found it sufficient to their purpose. Their most interesting relics are vases painted with pictures of boats, many-oared, twin-cabined and carrying their fetish or flag, while as background is shown what is believed to be their country of origin, a country of pointed hills. Whatever may be the exactly correct interpretation of these pictures, and whether these most early of ships were Egyptian or foreign— Cretan perhaps—one thing is certain: trade is growing. To settle down in a land of fertile mud flats may be an obvious thing to do, but it was not necessarily an easy thing, and there were certainly balancing disadvantages that had to be overcome—the greatest and most obvious of which was that the land provided little else but mud. In neither Egypt nor Sumeria could all men sit at home. Some had to seek abroad, near or far, for many of life's necessities: timber, flint and other stone, even the right kind of clay for pots. The prospector, the sailor, the trader, were in fact arriving.

The Nile is a more easily navigable river than the Tigris or Euphrates and the Egyptian must have become a river boatman before he became a sailor. The raft of papyrus-bundles soon became a prowed boat of the same material. But the presence of this great river, so mild after the last of its cataracts, had a much profounder effect upon the people who lived on its margins than merely to convert them into boatmen. It was a highway, a connecting road, and it is not by chance that Egypt's early history differs from Sumeria's in that it not only reaches a "Dynastic" period earlier but that there is only one line of dynasty instead of many and that a genuine unification of the whole country comes about.

It is not an easily won unity nevertheless. The Pharaohs are throughout known as lords of the Two Kingdoms, Upper and Lower Egypt, the lands of the river-strip and of the delta respectively, and it was only by conquest that the famous first Pharaoh of the First Dynasty known as Menes, but also as Narmer, managed to unify the country. It is a unity that in times of weak rule disintegrates; but is one that always returns, and for 2,000 years it will be a unity under native rulers. For two millennia Egypt, suffering a couple of lapses into misery and chaos but otherwise remaining with remarkable conservatism her true and unchanging self, continues as an important, influential and independent country.

And such constancy required more than the innate conservatism and bidableness of Egypt's people; it needed efficient and elaborate central control. From exactly the same causes as in Sumeria—irrigation being as necessary if full advantage of the Nile's yearly flooding was to be taken—Egyptians were forced to co-operate and to submit to being organized. And if the Sumerians' response to the solution was of necessity drastic, in that they made themselves wholly subservient to a series of priest-supported king-gods, the Egyptians', while not very dissimilar, can claim to have been immediately spectacular. King Menes, on the authority of Herodotus, successfully accomplished such a major engineering feat as that of diverting the course of the Nile, for the purpose of the more safely and imposingly building his great capital city of Memphis. In fact, in the last centuries of the Fourth Millennium there existed in Egypt no longer a people of neolithic barbarism, but a people of many arts and some science, possessing the beginnings of a reasonably flexible form of writing, and about to enter upon what was all over the world to prove a long and successful era, the ages first of copper and then of bronze.

Sumeria, too, developed early her own form of writing—of which, and of the Egyptian, more in the next chapter. In one aspect Sumeria does appear in advance and, in its turn, spectacularly so—unless perhaps we prefer to call it being in retard. Before the Fourth Millennium was out, Sumeria was staging a manifestation of religious fervour, and of the sort of communal ruthlessness in the pursuit of mystical benefits that we considered in the preceding chapter, as can hardly have been exceeded in any age and as has certainly never been exceeded in the startling effect produced by its discovery upon the modern age of archaeologists. A description of it will serve well to end this chapter that covers the advances towards complexity that were being made while men still lived in a world where tools were mostly or wholly made of stone. The discovery was that made by Sir Leonard Woolley of the burials outside the ancient city of Ur of many royal personages and their attendants.

For these burials a great square shaft was dug, straight and deep into the soil and approached by a downward-sloping ramp. In this pit was then built a domed tomb, and here was laid the royal body upon a bier, surrounded by objects testifying to its former wealth and likely to serve the soul's pleasure in the world to come. Then, as Sir Leonard Woolley describes the scene in the book, *Ur, the First Phase:**

There came down the ramp into the pit, whose earth sides were masked by reed matting, the whole company of those who were to accompany their royal master to the other world; ministers of the household, musicians, dancing women, male slaves and soldiers of the guard, even the chariot drawn by oxen or by asses, with the drivers, the grooms and the animals, assembled in ordered ranks at the bottom of the pit. Presumably some kind of service was held (in Queen Shub-ad's grave the fingers of the girl harpist were still

*(King Penguin, 1946).

4

touching the strings of the lyre), and at its end each took a little cup, filled it might be from a great bronze vessel set in the pit's centre, and drank a draught of a narcotic and lay down in his place and slept. And, from above, the mourners threw in the earth of the pit's making and buried the sleepers and the tomb chamber, and stamped the earth down and made of it a level floor for the next stage of the ceremony.

Queen Shub-ad's was one of the most spectacular of the burials unearthed, though not with the largest immolation, the greatest

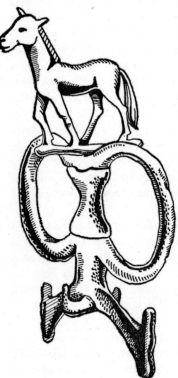

Rein-ring from Queen Shub-ad's chariot

number being seventy-four bodies in one pit. All her regalia, as many will remember, was found and in sufficiently good condition to be re-arranged or reconstructed. All the maids-in-waiting wore great wigs and elaborate head-dresses, and the queen herself had even a spare wig beside her. There were enormous lunar ear-rings and multiple necklaces of blue and gold. The lyres were of beautiful workmanship. The little mascot ass above the rein-rings of the chariot was exquisite.

But the wonder that these dis-coveries leaves in the mind is something deeper than at the beautiful workman-ship of the grave goods or the fact that so early had men learnt to build the arch and the dome. The exact signifi-cance of the burials is unascertainable. Queen Shub-ad is shown in no list of reigning sovereigns, and it has been argued, therefore, that here is a ritual burial of a surrogate, a substitute for the crop-controlling king or queen who must symbolically die so that there may be Nature's resurrection. Others, Woolley included, dismiss such an idea. What we must see, and all we really can see, is some intense religious conviction, and a ruthless-minded society that is willing to put that conviction into force. There was found nowhere sign of struggle or of rebellion against the edict of death, and there must surely therefore have been an unshakeable belief on the part of all the victims in a happy reawakening in the service of the buried great one who was in some way being translated to the kingdom of the gods. Or if not that then a resigned and unquestioning acceptance of the need of the sacrifice for the common good. There is that hand of the girl who plays her harp until the moment when her last sleep overtakes her. There is also another girl of whom Sir Leonard Woolley tells us, one in whose pocket was found unrolled and unused a silver hair ribbon with which she presumably had not had time to deck herself. What pitiable agitation, governed by an overriding compulsion, lies behind that find?

A following of these lines of thought and acquiescence much further could have landed the Sumerians into as bloody-minded and masochistic a wrong-headedness as in a different way was in action when Cortes and Pizarro conquered Mexico and Peru. Once again civilization is shown to be a tender growth beset by many risks.

The Ur "standard", showing feasting, husbandry and trade

DATES AND EVENTS, 3400 TO 1400 B.C.

B.C.	Europe and the Aegean	Asia Minor and Palestine	Egypt	Mesopotamia	The East	B.C.
3400		Jericho in existence	Pre-dynastic Period	Al Ubaid		3400
3300				Uruk or Erech		3300
3200				Flood (?)		3200
3100			First Dynasty: Menes	Jemdet Nasr		3100
3000	Palaeolithic	Neolithic			Neolithic	3000
2900				Queen Shub-ad First Dynasty of Ur	Elamites in Persia	2900
2800		"Troy I"			Yellow River civilization begins	2800
2700	Neolithic		Old Kingdom begins			2700
2600		Early Bronze Age	Cheops Chephren Pyramids	Ur-nina		2600
2500	Minoan civilization begins			Eannatum	Indus valley civilization begins	2500
2400		"Troy II"				2400
2300				Sargon		2300
2200	Windmill Hill People in Britain	"Troy III, IV, and V"	Pepy II First Intermediate Period	Naram Sin	Mythical Chinese emperors	2200
2100			Middle Kingdom begins			2100
2000	Entry of Aryan-speakers Mid Minoan culture	First entry of Aryans Assyrian traders		Third Dynasty of Ur	Aryans in Persia	2000
1900			Sinuhe			1900
1800	First Stonehenge The Megalith Builders	Abraham "Troy VI"	Sesostris III			1800
1700	Beaker People	First Hittite kings Hyksos in Palestine	Second Intermediate Period	Hammurabi	Aryans in India	1700
1600	Last Stonehenge	Mursilis I	Hyksos invasion	Hittites in Babylon	Indus valley civilization ends	1600
1500	Late Minoan culture Mycenae	Hittites conquer the Mitanni	New Kingdom	Kassites in Babylon	Shang Dynasty Chinese writing	1500

CHAPTER VI

Writing and Legend

THE really significant breaks in the human story are not between Stone Age, Bronze Age, Iron Age. It is truer to say that the two breaks lie between:

Old Stone Age
and
$\left\{ \begin{array}{c} \textit{Middle and New Stone Age} \\ \textit{Bronze Age} \end{array} \right\}$
and
Iron Age

—adding that we may consider ourselves as still in the Iron Age though entering perhaps either the Atomic Age or the Age of Astronauts or both.

Here are man-made divisions, for our convenience only. One archaeologist has said that the discovery of the use of copper and bronze merely "enriches and helps to amplify" the New Stone Age, which is a helpful phrase. We now approach the Bronze Age, rich, progressive, often peaceful though not ending so. We also enter the Third Millennium. This is something much less vague. The Sumerians of Queen Shub-ad, for instance, living round about 3200 B.C., were nevertheless already skilled workers in gold and familiar with copper, though as elsewhere their tools were almost wholly of stone; the archaeologists would say that they lived in a *chalcolithic*, a copper-stone age, another and a fairly recent effort at categorization which we have mentioned already.

The Third Millennium sees in the Middle East the full and extensive use of the written word. As mankind's major invention after speech, writing deserves our attention. Sumeria was probably ahead of Egypt in this. But since the Egyptian hieroglyphics are so much more spectacular and beautiful than any writing in cuneiform, and since, with a typically unshakeable conservatism on the part of their users, they continue to show in their established form more of the bones of their structure, it is on hieroglyphics that we will concentrate.

Writing begins with pictures—the sort of thing indulged in by repute by Red Indians and described so delightfully, and soundly, in Kipling's Just So Story, *How the First Letter Was Written*. But, even though the pictures became so stylized as to arrive at a sort of shorthand picture, the method is cumbersome and very inadequate. The next step is a widening process, a sort of shorthand of ideas. A pair of legs, for instance, does not mean merely a pair of legs but the abstract conception of walking, or standing, or running; to draw a scribe is certainly to convey "a scribe", but it can also convey the concept of "writing". There arrives, beyond the simple *phonogram*, the *ideogram*.

But the limitations are still severe. To take a simple difficulty, how does one convey a proper name? If the person owning the name is well known, then a portrait can be made. That does not get one very far. There is a famous Egyptian palette, the personal eye-palette (used, or meant to be used, for mixing his malachite eye-paint) of Menes or Narmer. This surmounts some of the difficulty and shows the trend. Narmer is seizing a kneeling and near-naked individual by the top-knot and seems about to destroy him. But who is he? To the right of his head is a little double sign, showing a sort of enclosure—a lake?—and a fish harpoon. The unfortunate man comes from and represents the people of the fishing lake (probably the Fayum); he is lord of the people of the fish-lake or, as we might say, Lord Fishlake.

But what if the name had not been so easily and directly representable? To turn to an English name, not to be childish but to make the exposition easier, how would the difficulty be overcome if the man had been Lord Southampton?

The answer is again well known. The solution is to use the pun, the child's game of the rebus. You split the word into syllables; and, ignoring the fact that strictly speaking you are being inaccurate if not downright ridiculous, you draw a weathervane showing S for South, a boiled ham, and a large barrel which the initiated in such matters know to be called a Tun. South-ham-tun.

You may have been ridiculous but in the process you have taken an enormous step forward, depicting not things but sounds; not pictograms, not ideograms, but phonograms.

In fact, from there the rest of the way, all the way, to a proper alphabet, is comparatively plain sailing. You have established an artificial convention and you can do what you like with it. You may take "open" syllables, those with only one consonant—as English examples, say, *be* and *hit* (aspirates, as well as vowels, will receive scant attention), shown by a picture of a bee and a boxing glove respectively, and you let these two pictures represent the sounds, the irreducible sounds, *b* and *t*. The meaning of the original pictures will be forgotten, the pictures themselves will become unrecognizably simplified—and an alphabet will have arrived.

Actually, for the Egyptians it was never plain sailing. It was rather as if they wilfully took on board a small but not wholly inefficient drag anchor and a large pair of bellows on which to blow on the sails from the opposite direction to that of the wind. This is interesting, for it shows something of the Egyptians' basic character, which was to help towards their long prosperity and unity and their final fall. The Egyptians—it is a universal trait of the times but they possessed it more noticeably—were much more conscious and traditional artists than they were practical scientists. They had built up their pictograms with great skill and patience into things of beauty and startling economy of line. They did not write them, they drew them, often painted them. Their object, therefore, was not to produce the most efficient and easily readable script possible but to produce the most beautiful and impressive script possible, both for their documents and their monuments, while at the same time doing their laborious best to ensure that their meaning was plain beyond any doubt. The result was a curious compromise, a sort of duplicated writing. On the one hand many ideograms and even simple pictograms were retained; and in order to make them as little ambiguous as possible (since the same pictures might also be used as phonograms, and since in Egyptian no vowels whatever were shown) these would be followed by a sign called by modern linguists a phonetic complement. This is rather as if after a picture of a pair of legs we put an R if running were intended and a W if walking were meant. Conversely, the Egyptians after their phonograms used pictures (which are now called *determinatives*) again to ensure that the reader knew exactly what was intended. This is as if we (writing phonetically) were to put down *wich* and then to add either a woman on a broomstick or else some sign or other—a useful determinative that the Egyptians actually used was a roll of papyrus— to show that the word belonged to the immaterial, unpicturable, abstract category. The total result was never something easy to read but always something elaborate and impressive and a work of art. As an example:

The three first signs read *ch-q-r* (vowel sounds, of course, unknown).*
They mean, literally, hunger. But the meaning required here is
"pauper". Next, therefore, we have one determinative, a man with
hand to mouth, which is used to denote hunger, or thirst, or speech,
and then *another* determinative, simply a man, who shows the human
connection, that is to say "hungry man" and not just "hunger".
Finally, two further facts to stress the Egyptian's preoccupation with
art rather than efficiency. The convention was to write the signs of a
word in a neat square, turning some of the signs sideways if necessary
to do so. In order to fit, in particular, the monument, the writing might
run either up and down, or from right to left, or from left to right—the
animal and human figures always facing inwards to the beginning of
the writing.

Cuneiform writing shows a surprisingly close parallel development.
It, too, has determinatives and like Egyptian can retain two or more
signs, fining down from different pictograms, for the same sound. It
does not come in the end, however, to possess such a wealth of signs,
which is understandable since from the start, being scratched on tiles
rather than painted on papyrus or carved on stone, it possessed little
beauty and, becoming a collection of wedge signs of only a small
variety of shapes, soon lost any that it may have had. Cuneiform,
however, easily wins over its Egyptian rival in adaptability: invented
by the Sumerians, it becomes the writing of, amongst others, the
Babylonians, the Assyrians, the Hittites and finally the Persians. It
even becomes for a while, in its Babylonian form, the instrument of a
lingua franca, an accepted diplomatic language such as was French in
the nineteenth century—a fortunate fact to which we owe, as will
be seen, a considerable addition to our knowledge of the Second
Millennium.

Cuneiform reached no nearer, perhaps not so near, to the true
alphabet. It showed vowels but would not show a sound without them:

*This omission of vowels explains at least partly the lack of consistency in our trans-
literation of Egyptian names. Other sources, e.g. the Greek version of the name, may give
a hint; but these hints tend to be valued differently by each Egyptologist.

all a matter of open syllables, where the vowels had to remain whether they were wanted or not.

Writing, in both centres of advance, grew in fact fairly rapidly into an adequate if rather portentous and clumsy instrument. Its power, the new power that it gave to its users, was considerable. That is a point that we must realize and that must have struck the first users—the first victims particularly—like a blow. It increased the mandate of the great one. He could write his message and deliver it by his messenger: the messenger would indeed read it to the recipient and not hand it across, but that awestruck recipient would soon learn to know that the potshard or the papyrus did indeed magically extend the word and the threat and the order of the ruler. With the seal of the great ones he was familiar, that signet ring or little cylinder carved in the reverse of relief that with its symbolic picture made plain and authentic the possessions and personality of the ruler. But here was something more, much more. A second use of writing was equally practical, and equally helpful to the ruler. Coupled with figuring—which is in its elements a simpler matter and must have come sooner—it enabled the ruler to keep accounts, in particular store accounts. If the king, who is tenant-farmer of the god, is to live with his increasingly elaborate household off the hard work of his peasants, and if there is as yet no money or other means of exchange, then he must indeed have a storeroom, and a tally of what at any time is in it. The very introduction of accounts and inventories, on a sort of prehistoric equivalent of Parkinson's Law, would increase the size and elaboration of the king's household.

Writing emancipated itself from the severely practical in two ways. Firstly, it got itself mixed up, inevitably, with magic. If to draw the likeness of somebody—the equivalent with modern primitives is to take his photograph—is to gain power over him, then not only to know his name but to write down his name was to gain even greater power. Similarly, if spells and incantations were potent things how much more potent and precious was a shard or a scroll or an amulet with the magic words thus made permanent and more than the mere breath of the mouth.

All that sort of thing could, however, be regarded, at least by the user, as no more than another very *practical* way of using writing. Literature comes later, though it comes at last. It comes in the form of the narrative of the exploits and good deeds of the great king, or of his officials and nobles, graven on their monuments or painted on the

walls of their tombs. Or it comes in the form of the poem or story, not
to be read by the generality but to be read and learnt by heart and
proclaimed by the professional storyteller. Here are the great sources of
information for later generations.

There is one epic story that we may examine here and at once, for it
concerns an early king of Sumeria and shows how Sumerians felt and
thought. It must be realized that the story was written down much
later than the actual events—such of them as were actual—or even
than the original stories as first handed down by word of mouth. But
in the same way the *Iliad* and *Odyssey* were probably not written down
until some time after Homer, and even Homer himself was telling of
events of four centuries or so before his own. Yet with intelligent
allowances we can learn a great deal of truth from Homer.

The Gilgamesh (or Gilgamish) Epic comes down to us originally
from the seventh century B.C. library of Ashur-bani-pal, who amongst
other things could be called a classicist and antiquarian, concerning
himself with his country's past rather as Charles II of England was
interested in Stonehenge. Later-found versions date something like a
thousand and fifteen hundred years earlier. Gilgamesh himself is shown
on the Sumerian king lists as fifth of the First Dynasty of Uruk or
Erech. This dates him at about 2850 B.C., that is if he was ever a real
person and not merely a mythical hero. But only eight farther down in
the lists we come to Mes-anni-padda, and Sir Leonard Woolley dug up
at Ur definite evidence of that ruler and of his son.

Here then is the oldest known poem in the world. It has been translated, by R. Campbell Thompson,[*] into blank verse of simple rhythm
and fittingly archaic diction, giving it perhaps a fortuitous resemblance
to *Hiawatha*. In such things as standard epithets—"broad-marketed
Erech" for instance—it has a real resemblance to Homer's poems, and
in its loving repetitions of descriptions and conversations a likeness to
any later epic or indeed fairy tale.

The story begins with the inhabitants of Erech beseeching the gods
to release them from the thrall of Gilgamesh, an episode put in to show
perhaps not so much his unpopularity as his power. He is described as
two-thirds divine, one-third human (a nice problem for the geneticist),

---

[*]*The Epic of Gilgamish, A New Translation* (Luzac, 1928). In the following quotations
the author's use of round and square brackets, to indicate any freeness of translation or
restoration to the often mutilated texts, are omitted. A prose translation, by N. K.
Sandars, has recently been published as a *Penguin Classic*. This gives a different weight to
the various sources and has a different ending.

and as wearing a crest that "towers like an aurochs".* Then, with reluctant admiration:

> *He is our shepherd . . . masterful, dominant, subtle. . . .*
> *Gilgamish leaveth no maid to her mother nor daughter to hero,*
> *Nay, nor a spouse to a husband.*

He has, in fact, the *droit du Seigneur* and uses it.

Gilgamesh owes at least some of his divinity to being son of the sky god Anu, and the rest of the gods rightly take the people's supplication thither. Anu is responsive, if showing no great paternal affection, and orders the appropriate goddess to mould from clay a hero who will fight and overthrow the tyrant. Enkidu is created. He is a Caliban figure, sprouting hair "like barley" and living with the deer and cattle.

A chance hunter meets Enkidu and rushes back in terror with his tale. He has met a man,

> *Like to a double of Anu's own self, his strength is enormous.*

But the father knows another whose "strength is enormous" and tells his son to report to Gilgamesh. The son does so.

Gilgamesh is interested. But how to get the great innocent beast-man to leave his friends the cattle and come to Erech? A ruse is thought of: if Enkidu can be made to lose his innocence, to know carnal delights, then his cattle will disown him and the experience will have humanized him. A decoy is sent in the shape of a temple prostitute. Decoy and hunter patiently wait for Enkidu's appearance by the drinking pool. At length the beast-man arrives:

> *So beheld him the courtesan-girl, the lusty great fellow,*
> *Oh but a monster all savage from out of the depth of the desert!*
> *" 'Tis he, O girl, O, discover thy beauty, thy comeliness show him,*
> *So that thy loveliness he may possess—O, in no wise be bashful.*
> *Ravish the soul of him!"*

The brave girl is in no wise bashful, and all goes according to plan. Enkidu, losing the friendship of the beasts, seeks human friendship, cleaves to the courtesan, and agrees to come and meet Gilgamesh:

Bos primigenius, wild bull.

"Up, then, O girl, to the Temple, the holy and sacred, invite me,
Me, to the dwelling of Anu and Ishtar, where, highest in power,
Gilgamesh is, and prevaileth o'er men like an aurochs—for I, too,
I, I will summon him, challenging boldly and crying through Erech,
'I, too, am mighty!'"

The courtesan promises Enkidu a triumphal entry, with dancing girls to welcome him and eunuch priests clashing their cymbals.

Meanwhile, Gilgamesh is having strange dreams, and asking his mother for interpretation. He is struggling with one as powerful as the god Anu, and then suddenly he finds himself embracing his adversary. His mother's interpretation is simple:

This is a stoutheart, a friend, one ready to stand by a comrade.

The dream and prophecy are in fact fulfilled. Gilgamesh, exerting his rights over Enkidu's girl, gives him plenty of cause for fight, and the ensuing combat is terrific. Enkidu, strengthened by human food, wine and "the bread-cakes of Erech", is almost more than a match for Gilgamesh:

Snorting like bulls, and the threshold they shattered, the very wall
quivered.

Then suddenly it is all over. The fury of Gilgamesh abates; Enkidu finds himself paying compliments to Gilgamesh. The hero apparently is as anxious to gain a true comrade as is the lately humanized beast—it is as if Hercules instead of wearing the lionskin had gone off to further adventures with the lion.

To Gilgamesh there does come at once the idea of a noble adventure with Enkidu. It is none other than to go to the great forest of cedars, to cut down some of these cedars, and to fight the terrible ogre Humbaba, who guards them.

Enkidu agrees. But it is rather a long time before they set out. First Enkidu, who knows a little more about the ogre—"flame in his jaw and his very breath Death"—on second thought tries to dissuade the hero. Gilgamesh replies in proper vein, that is with heroics: we are all mortal, he says, and if he should fall at least his name will be established for ever. He adds that he needs the cedar, anyway. Then the tools and weapons are cast, celts and swords and armour. Next, Gilgamesh consults the Elders. They advise against the risky expedition; in any case, let Enkidu go in front! Gilgamesh then asks his mother to intercede for him for the blessing of Shamash the Sun God. His mother, attiring herself appropriately, which is splendidly, does so. But, being a fond mother, she cannot refrain from reproaching the Sun God too:

> *Why didst thou give this restlessness of spirit*
> *With which didst dower Gilgamesh, my son?*
> *That now thou touchest him, and straight he starteth*
> *A journey far to where Humbaba dwelleth,*
> *To counter warfare which he knoweth not,*
> *Follow a path which he knoweth not? . . .*

Finally, Enkidu, warned by a dream, is prostrated for twelve days and wants to cry off the whole thing. Gilgamesh's reply is simple: "Shall we, O friend, play the coward? . . ."

They will not. They approach the forest of cedars:

> *Eke they beheld the Mount of the Cedar, the home of th' Immortals,*
> *Shrine of Irnini [Ishtar], the Cedar uplifting its pride 'gainst the mountain.*

Now it is the turn of Gilgamesh to have a dream, indeed no less than three dreams, from which he wakes in a fright; it is Enkidu's turn to enhearten his master. . . .

The account of the fight with the monster Humbaba is partly lost. But like so many fights in fairy stories it is something of an anticlimax, since the gods always seem to make it too easy for the hero. Shamash, the Sun God, is mindful of his promise to the hero's mother and to Gilgamesh's own supplication:

> *Wherefore against Humbaba he raised mighty winds: yea, a great wind,*
> *Wind from the North, aye, a wind from the South, yea a tempest and*
> *   storm wind,*
> *Chill wind and whirlwind, a wind of all evil: 'twas eight winds he raised,*
> *Seizing Humbaba before and behind.*

The result of the fight, one would think, was a foregone conclusion. In triumph "they cut off the head of Humbaba".

The sequel is by no means so happy. Towards Gilgamesh the hero, handsome and successful, the goddess Ishtar now casts her eye—with a look of invitation in it.

The rash Gilgamesh refuses to respond, pointing out to the goddess in most unequivocal terms that it is expensive for a mortal to have to support a goddess for a wife, and ending with an inspired vituperation of all importuning females, goddesses in particular:

Thou'rt but a palace which dasheth the heroes within it to pieces . . .
Thou'rt but pitch which defileth the man who doth carry it with him.
Thou'rt but a bottle which leaketh on him who doth carry it with him,
Thou'rt but limestone which letteth stone ramparts fall crumbling in ruin.

Ishtar, like any self-respecting goddess, Homeric or earlier, rushes to seek revenge from the great Lord of Heaven. Anu, hinting however that she perhaps has got no less than she deserves, fashions for Ishtar a great fire-breathing bull and sends it down to Earth.

A hundred men fight the bull, two hundred, three hundred. All are vanquished. Then along comes Enkidu, seizes him by the horns and by the thick of the tail, and vanquishes him. In triumph the two heroes, "the two brothers", offer up the bull's heart as sacrifice to the Sun God outside the gates of Erech. Ishtar in shrieking rage mounts on to the ramparts. And Enkidu, above himself, adds to his sin of *hubris* the sin of impiety, which is perhaps an over-mild term for his next act, which is to execute towards the goddess a gesture of monumental indecency.

The great pair are allowed their triumphal entry into Erech and the ensuing revels in their honour. But then Enkidu in a dream has a presentiment of the goddess's revenge, which is death. He is stricken by a fever, and first curses the courtesan girl as being the prime cause of all his troubles. Shamash tells him he is wrong and promises him the compensation of great fame after death. Reconciled and resigned, Enkidu tells his friend Gilgamesh of his approaching end, when, as in his dream, and with no return, he will go:

Unto the Dwelling whose tenants are ever bereft of the daylight,
Where for their food is the dust, and the mud is their sustenance: bird-
*   like*
Wear they a garment of feathers; and sitting there in the darkness,
Never the light will they see.

The rest of the epic is sad, rather strange, and unexpected.

Gilgamesh, in spite of his previous heroics, is appalled at Enkidu's death. He not only mourns a friend, he is struck for the first time by the terrible truth of his own mortality. He spends the rest of the story seeking the gift of immortality. Shortly, he interviews various immortals and ex-mortals, including Uta-Nipishtim, and makes attempts to achieve his aim. He is discouraged by discovering that he cannot as it were pass the preliminary test for godhood, which is to stay awake indefinitely. He reaches within measurable distance of achieving his aim by a successful journey to the bottom of the sea in search of a plant that will make him young again—only to have it stolen from him by a serpent. Finally, in sorrow he summons up the shade of Enkidu—who can do no more for him than tell of the wretched lot of those who must die, especially those without benefit of full ceremonious burial. He catechizes Gilgamesh thus:

> *"Then the hero slain in fight,*
> *Didst thou see him?" "Aye, I saw:*
> *Father, mother raise his head,*
> *O'er him wife in bitter woe."*
> *"He whose corpse in desert lieth,*
> *Hast thou seen him?" "Aye, I saw;*
> *Not in earth doth rest his spirit."*
> *"He whose ghost hath none to tend,*
> *Didst thou see him?" "Aye, I saw,*
> *Lees of cup, and broken bread*
> *Thrown into the street he eateth."*

On this sad, enigmatic, inconclusive note the poem abruptly ends.

In the meantime, however, we have had the legend of the Flood as told by Uta-Nipishtim. This Sumerian Noah has, in the story, been made immortal as reward for his pains, and seems to be doing not much more than to tell Gilgamesh how at least he managed to gain the prize himself—though he does make some amends, for it is he who tells Gilgamesh where to find the youth-giving plant. It was discovery of this part of the poem telling the story of the Flood that caused the greatest stir at the time, the *Daily Telegraph* offering £1,000 for a search for further evidence. We shall, however, not gain much greater intimation of the lives and thoughts of those times by quoting further. The story coincides remarkably, though not completely, with the Bible story. In one significant aspect does it differ. It is no single god of righteousness who is trying the world for its sins. The gods in company plan the disaster, and Ea, the Water God, to whom in normal times men pray for beneficent rain, divulges the secret to his mortal favourite. And when the deluge does come it is not only Uta-Nipishtim and his like who are terrified but the lesser gods also. They crouch in the outskirts of Heaven, "cowering like curs". Ishtar shrieks, but this time showing signs of grace in that she bewails her rashness in having agreed with the others that mortals should suffer the disaster.

It would be tedious to seek to list all the conclusions that we can draw from this strange, naïve, sad, though sometimes rollicking poem. Of interest is the fact that the pair's great adventure is to fetch cedar-wood. Raw materials are even more absent from the land of the two

Sumerian hero, probably Gilgamesh, showing strength and superiority

rivers than that of the Nile; and cedarwood for building (as also apparently, from this poem, its resin for incense) was in universal demand in the ancient East. Here appears the importance of trade, and also the dangers and heroic excitements of trade: the obvious parallel is the story of Jason and the golden fleece. Of equal interest is the feeling towards the gods that the whole poem shows. It is an ambivalence, not by any means a simple and wholehearted worship. Sacrifice, supplication is, of course, made; but part of the heroes' claim to heroism comes from their ability to defy the gods—which defiance, however, does them no good at all. Once again we are reminded of the stories of the archaic Greeks, also a little of the story of Job. Perhaps here is shown a universal feeling of the peoples of primitive civilizations.

They create not only jealous gods but gods of whom, because they combine human frailties and cruelties with arbitrary and unlimited power, *they* are jealous. Mortals, therefore, who dare to compete with these gods—criticize them, cross them—are hailed as heroes. Yet everyone knows that the dice are loaded against the mortal, that he has not a chance of a happy issue to his rebellion—except possibly to join, as a belated and grudging reward, the ranks of those against whom he has rebelled. The gods are omnipotent. The best and safest line of conduct is to placate and worship them. . . .

The piety of the Sumerians is shown by the archaeological evidence. The outstanding monument of their city-kingdoms is always the temple, the Ziggurat, the "Tower of Babel". Here again the legend centres round the idea of man's presumptuous pride, at least the biblical legend; but the building of these artificial mountains must

Reconstruction of a ziggurat

rather have been an action of supplication, of worship by a people who had come to a flat land and who by nature thought with the psalmist: "I will lift up mine eyes to the hills, from whence cometh my help." The Ziggurat must have been to the Sumerians what a combination of Buckingham Palace, the Tomb of the Unknown Soldier and Westminster Abbey would be to us. Hither went the great possessions. And where the modern crowd cheers restrainedly or stands in well-ordered silence, waves a hat or wipes surreptitiously a moist eye, the Sumerians surely let their emotions have full and glorious play. As evidence of this there is the invitation of the courtesan girl held out to her uncouth yokel of a lover:

*Enkidu, come then to Erech, the high-walled, where people array them
Gorgeous in festal attire, and each day the day is a revel,
Eunuch-priests clashing their cymbals, and dancing girls . . .*

5

*. . . flown with their wantoning, gleeful, and keeping the nobles
Out of their beds.*

Perhaps the girl pardonably exaggerated, and in any case the trans-
lator has to say that the rendering of the last two lines must be
incomplete and may not be exact. But over all we can legitimately
conjure up a picture of a very ceremony-conscious people and uninhibited at that. Often the emotions must have been those of awe rather
than abandon. The prime purpose of the Ziggurat was the consumma-
tion of the yearly ceremony whereat a human mating, or a human-
divine mating, set going magically and successfully the seasonal
fecundity of Nature. Whether the human actors, king and queen or
surrogate king and queen, or bride of the god, were put to death when
their service to hungry humanity was accomplished, we do not know—
and if we do not know we should not assume so. Yet there are the great
death pits of the Cemetery of Ur. If crowds watched those ceremonies,
as they watched the processions to the Ziggurat and the symbolic
ceremonies enacted upon its peak, then there must have been times not
of clashing of cymbals but of terrible and bursting silence, when the
emotions of the onlookers were an almost overpowering mixture, not
entirely admirable, of fascination, thankfulness—for mercies given and
for not being themselves a victim—and thrilled awareness of belonging
to a community of worship and common destiny.

For the rest, the Sumerians, in the time of their established prosperity
at the beginning of the Third Millennium, must have belonged to a
lusty, even pleasure-loving, busy society where religious and superstitious beliefs permeated and were not separable from everyday life, a
society already divided into classes of peasant, artisan, priest and
aristocrat, and busy in a variety of activities that centred round the
household and storehouse of god's tenant-farmer, the king, as naturally
and practically as the life of an English county town of a few generations ago centred round its market place or of a cathedral city about its
close—with the difference here that close and market place were pretty
well the same thing.

CHAPTER VII

The Old Kingdom

THE early Egyptians were not much like their disillusioned descendants, oft-defeated, tradition-bound, bewildered and magic-ridden, whom the Greeks regarded with a mixture of scorn and reluctant admiration, not even much like their descendants of something approaching a thousand years earlier from whom the Hebrews fled with possibly some ingratitude but no doubt much justifiable hatred. They were the same people racially but not spiritually, just as the French were different in 1789 from what they were in 1815 or the Romans of 400 B.C. differed from those of A.D. 400. Because Western historians for a long time derived their knowledge of the ancient inhabitants of the Nile valley almost entirely from the mostly unfavourable reports of the Greeks and Jews we are inclined to do them less than justice.

The Egyptians of the Third Millennium may best be regarded in terms of their achievements. It is a millennium which begins with the early pyramid-builders of the Third Dynasty,* covers the whole span of what is known as the Old Kingdom (Dynasties IV to VI), suffers the chaos and anarchy of the "First Intermediate Period", but revives just before the thousand years are out with the beginning of the Middle Kingdom. The outstanding early achievement is the pyramids themselves. They evolve by traceable steps from primitive neolithic inhumations with a heap of sand above them—the desert equivalent, we might say, of our own long barrows—and by the end of the Old Kingdom they have ceased to be made. They are tombs, possibly sometimes cenotaphs, no more mysterious or inexplicable than any other great monument to the illustrious or beloved dead—and they are outstanding feats of architecture, the first great monuments of hewn stone. The people of Egypt, the people who built them, were undoubtedly proud of them: the architect of one of the earliest, Imhotep, they raised in

*Egyptian history is divided into dynasties, and the wider division of kingdoms and periods, after the arrangement of the Ptolemaic historian, Manetho. Manetho's dates have long been discarded, but even now the dates for dynasties before the eighteenth vary from authority to authority.

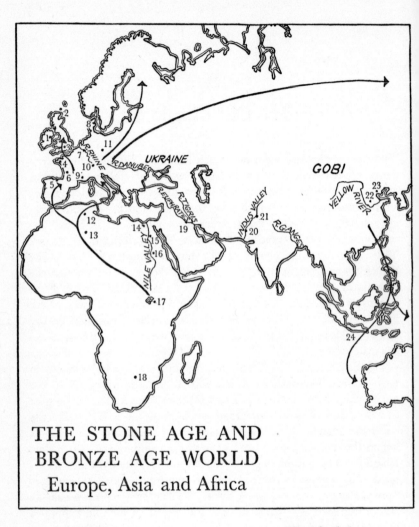

THE STONE AGE AND
BRONZE AGE WORLD
Europe, Asia and Africa

KEY

1	New Grange	7	Neanderthal
2	Skara Brae	8	Barkaer
3	Stonehenge	9	Azilian
4	Carnac	10	Lake Dwellings
5	Altamira	11	Predmost
6	Perigord	12	Capsian
		13	Tassili
		14	Merimde

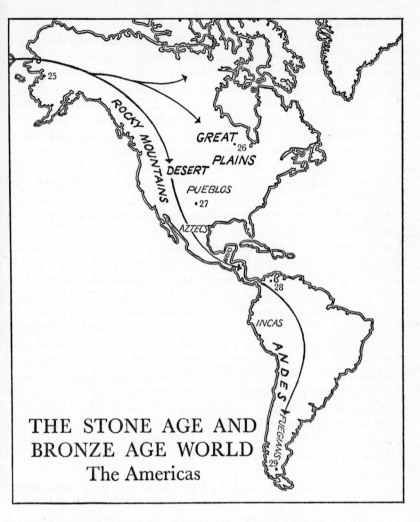

THE STONE AGE AND
BRONZE AGE WORLD
The Americas

succeeding generations to the status of sage and father of invention, a kind of combination of what Daedalus was to the Greeks and Solomon to the Jews. Impressive statistics have always been quoted since the time of Herodotus: the Great Pyramid of Cheops or Khufu, for instance, covers thirteen acres and contains about two and a third million blocks of average weight of $2\frac{1}{2}$ tons. One figure that the industrious but not always sufficiently critical Greek gives us, however, we should not believe: that the job employed a hundred thousand men for twenty years. At least we should not envisage twenty solid years of work, for, however powerful the Pharaoh, however well organized his economy, that would be impossible. From late July to October or November little work can be done by the Egyptian peasant, since he is waiting for the flooding of the Nile to recede. It was no doubt in these months of the year that the gangs of labour were employed, much more a matter of "public assistance" than of the cruel exploitation of the masses. The engraved records of the men's rations, shown to Herodotus by the priests, impressed him by their lavishness, but for the rest he accepted what he was told. And, since Cheops had been very unpopular with the priests of his own time, instituting the first recorded curtailment of their powers and impositions, what the later-day priests told was still in the tradition of being unkind to Cheops. The Egyptians of the time, both high and low, must have been not only proud of the achievement but practically anxious that it should succeed. For here was a monument that would protect their ruler and ensure his ascent to the home of the gods, where he as a god would, in fair exchange for loving services rendered, exert his powers for the benefit of the mortals he had left behind. The pyramid texts that have been found exult in his translation, in language naïve but striking:

A ramp to the sky is built for him, that he may go up to the sky thereon.

He rushes at the sky as a heron, he hath kissed the sky as a hawk, he hath leapt skyward as a grasshopper.

And in the sky he will accompany Rē, the Sun God, in his beneficent journey across the firmament:

He flieth as a bird, and he settleth as a beetle on an empty seat that is in the ship of Rē.

Often the songs and prophecies are far less humble in sentiment:

He sitteth down beside him, for Rē suffereth him not to seat himself on the ground, knowing that he is greater than he (Rē). He is more glorified than the Glorified Ones, more excellent than the Excellent Ones, more enduring than the Enduring Ones. . . .

There is strife in heaven, we see a new thing. . . . He seizeth the sky, he cleaveth its metal. . . . The gods are afraid of him, for he is older than the Great One. . . . Cry aloud to him in joy, he hath captured the horizon.

His *kas* (vital forces) are about him . . . his serpents are on his brow. . . . He is the Bull of the Sky. . . .

So the Egyptian king, more fortunate than the Sumerian hero, achieves immortality, not to say pugnacious immortality, and continues his good works, still the god and father of his people. In life the hawk will be his emblem and on his brow he will wear the serpent, the *ureus* emblem, spitting venom and fire at his enemies. There were weak and foolish Pharaohs, and all were autocratic; but there were few who were wicked or who did not have the well-being of their people at heart. If Egypt depended upon the Nile she also depended upon her king—in one of his many aspects and impersonations, indeed, he *was* the Nile. And this was a truth that the Egyptians knew.

So, in the achievement of the pyramids, we have poetry and emotion and superstition, as well as the skill of the builder and the engineer. But the Egyptians were always practically-minded, and like most primitive peoples capable of mixing what we should regard as a wholly modern, reasonable and scientific outlook quite inextricably with a superstitious one. Their practice of mummification, for instance, which began in these early times, led them to an anatomical knowledge that was a lesson to the later Greeks, though to what extent the Egyptians put their knowledge to sound pathological uses is not certain. It is certain that their knowledge of herbs and drugs became extensive.

It is obvious that their increasingly complex bureaucracy and civilization would be likely to create a need for measurements in space and time, and well known that some quite striking advances in mathematics were made. The Egyptians share honours here with the Sumerians, equal perhaps in astronomy, not so good at arithmetic, better at geometry. Egyptians did not achieve proper multiplication tables and did not recognize any fraction that had anything but unity in the numerator, $\frac{3}{4}$ being $\frac{1}{2} + \frac{1}{4}$; they knew, however, the somewhat complicated formula for calculating the volume of a truncated pyramid; at $\dfrac{16^2}{9^2}$ they were nearer to a true estimation of π, ratio of the circle's circumference to its diameter, than the Sumerian's rather poor effort of 3. The moon is a useful and easy time-measurer for mankind, the sun also useful but less easy. The Egyptians early marked the length of the year as 365 days, and proceeded for convenience to divide this into twelve months of thirty days, with five odd days over, and the months into three weeks of ten days each—a length of week which, incidentally, H. G. Wells once advocated with some passion, partly for a hedonistic reason which would have pleased the Egyptian common man, that it would conveniently and reasonably afford a long week-end. They soon got closer to the truth, of $365\frac{1}{4}$ days, by the observation of that significant heliacal rising of Sirius, the Dog Star, which presaged the flooding of the Nile. Not only so, but they were soon to realize the discrepancy and to calculate the gradually widening gap between dating by this calculation and by a 365-day year—a calculation that enabled modern history's earliest absolutely accurate date, in the reign of Rameses III, to be achieved. Day and night the Egyptians divided into twelve hours each, hours, however, not of standard duration but varying in length with the length of day and night, an awkwardness that does not seem to have incommoded them but only to have inspired them to the invention of an ingenious elaboration of the water-clock. The clever men of Egypt, however, spoil their reputation for us as scientists by making a mystery of their knowledge, so that the foretelling of the yearly rising of the Nile was regarded not as a triumph of science but of magical power. Perhaps in some way they even so regarded it themselves: astrology was to them no more than a quite actual extension of astronomical knowledge.

It is rather the fashion amongst the popularizers of prehistory to startle with such technically detailed statements as that a culture owes its success to "the palaeolithic equivalent of the spoke-shave" or "the force-draught charcoal-fed furnace". We will at least go so far as to say that early Egypt owed a great deal to the furnace and the wheel and the sail.

The ploughshare was still of wood and the hoe of wood or flint; but the metals copper and gold entered much into the lives of the aristocrat and the man who served him, the craftsman. These men knew how to smelt copper—they called it causing it to swim—and to cast it; to smelt gold, to beat it into thin sheets, to solder it and fashion it to produce crowns and diadems and the like, more beautiful even than the Sumerian. Pottery became much less clumsy by reason of two of the three basic inventions mentioned above, better firing in kilns of much greater heat, and the potter's wheel. The Egyptians, however, loved, in particular, stone, and were not dismayed by the

"Gracious living": sport for the Egyptian nobleman

difficulties in using it, whether to make bowls or statues or pyramids: eight foot long copper saws have been found, and the statue of Chephren, successor to Cheops, was made of the excessively hard diorite. As a contrast, the women could weave linen which, compared to the first linen of their neolithic ancestors, was as gossamer to a piece of sacking. There were cabinet-makers, upholsterers and fine workers in leather; there was already being created for the aristocracy, the members of the great household of the king and of the lesser house-holds of his state officers and governors, a kind of living that was to culminate in the luxury of the New Kingdom and which perhaps really deserved the presently overworked epithet of "gracious". In this era was learnt the art of gumming strips of reed together, first one way and then at right angles, to form papyrus, the forerunner of paper; here was the chance for the artist-writer to excel himself, firstly in beauty and then, with the later shorthand hieratic and demotic scripts, in speed.

For the man who did not possess a boat of some sort the early Egyptians had a special word—as our fathers used to talk of those possessing not a penny to bless themselves with and as our children may have a word for the person who does not own a television set. The Nile possessed the amiable attribute of flowing against the way of the prevailing wind; and so with a sail a man might travel in most seasons both up and down the river with little effort. Not only this, but by the time of the Old Kingdom it was not only ships from some foreign country of rounded hills that were trading with Egypt. Native ships had dared to sail beyond the Delta, to Crete and Cyprus and the eastern shores of the Mediterranean, where such towns of commerce and interchange of skills and learning as cedar-exporting Byblos were growing up.

Not all was idyllic however. Though surely the most peaceable of the early peoples, the Egyptians were not without their barbaric ruthlessness. The pyramid texts, exulting over the impending heavenly success of their dead Pharaoh, can turn from the poetic fancy of "he hath kissed the sky as a hawk" to the savagery and primordial thinking of,

> He hath broken up the backbones and the spinal marrow, he hath taken away the hearts of the gods. . . . He feedeth on the lungs of the Wise Ones; he is satisfied with living on hearts and their magic. . . . Lo, their soul is in his belly. . . .

Then it is apparent that some of their caravan treks in search of trade were almost like military and punitive expeditions. The Egyptians were finding, as all societies that progress beyond primal simplicity must find, that the taboos and observances and priestly sanctions that can peaceably bind a small community together are of little use where other communities are met. There was a man named Uni, a courtier of the Sixth Dynasty, who was sent on no less than five military expeditions. He seems to have been a man of tact and character, having earlier sat in judgement over a very delicate matter of the Pharaoh's—"Never before had one like me," he boasts, "heard the secrets of the royal harem." His military discipline, he asserts, was exemplary: not one of his men "plundered food or sandals from the wayfarer, not one thereof took bread from any town, not one thereof took a goat from any person". Nevertheless, his Triumph-Song on his return begins:

This army returned in safety,
It had hacked up the land of the sand-dwellers;

and ends:

This army returned in safety.
It had seized multitudes of living captives.

Here was a purely military expedition, though no doubt for the protection of trade. There were also professional caravan leaders, and their job and status were both important. One by the name of Harkhuf, also in the Sixth Dynasty, writes:

His Majesty sent me a third time to Yam [in the south]. I found the chief of Yam had gone to the land of Temah, to smite Temah as far as the western corner of heaven. I went after him to the land of Temah and I pacified him.

Though the end was peace it does not sound very much as if the means were so peaceful. Harkhuf's king was Pepi (or Phiops) II, the last of the Pharaohs of the Old Kingdom before the break up and the time of chaos. Pepi II reigned for the immensely long period of over ninety years. A small boy at this time, he sent this caravan leader a long letter, a mixture of regal pomposity and childish enthusiasm, giving instructions how a certain dancing dwarf from the Sudan should be brought home with the utmost care so that it might arrive intact for the Pharaoh's delectation. Pepi II proved in his later years a weak king and his reign lasted much too long. Peaceful prosperity, supported by successful foreign trade, could not be made to last, for there was trouble from within.

We come to the first known social revolution and the first described disintegration of a civilization. The experience for us is impressive and disconcerting. Judging by the records, the experience for those who actually suffered in this long anarchy of over two centuries must have been traumatic.

It was a failure of over-complicated, over-ambitious, perhaps repressive, and finally weak government. Egypt had been divided into nomes or administrative districts, essentially self-contained areas of river-drainage and irrigation. At the nome's head was a nomarch—it is indicative of the debt that Greece owed to Egypt and the interest that the younger civilization was to take in the older that these words we use are Greek—and the nomarch was a very powerful person. An aristocrat, educated very likely in the same school as the Pharaoh's sons, if he was not one himself, he went forth to take over the reins of local government as landed gentleman and *ex-officio* high priest. His life was pleasant and well-ordered, as is shown by the many tomb paintings that have survived. So, too, appear the lives of his people on his great estate and in the villages around, the farm workers parading their beasts for the master's inspection, the carpenters and goldsmiths busy in his workshops—pleasant, that is to say, so long as they are content with well-ordered uneventfulness and hard work in that state to which it has pleased the Pharaoh to call them. In particular, those nomarchs on the periphery of the country, in the south towards Nubia, for instance, where Egypt was steadily pushing out her frontiers, possessed great power. Their retainers tended to become private armies; the written messages of the distant king tended to be increasingly disregarded. It was a disturbing sign of the times that the office of nomarch tended to become hereditary. It was a sign, too, that the nomarchs in their role of high priests made increasing demands on the Pharaoh for grants of land and wealth for the temple hierarchies, demands which the aged and increasingly pious Pepi II, an earlier Edward the Confessor, met.

Then, at the end of Pepi's long reign, came the collapse. We have only preserved to us a long and bitter lament called "The Admonitions of a Prophet" or "of a Sage", and the negative evidence of silence and cessation; cessation of works of art, of tombs and tomb pictures and monuments. It must have been an uprising of the people, followed as a result by invasion from without. By now there tended to be in the Middle East two different kinds of people, the settled agriculturist and the congenitally unsettled herdsman. The latter, who was typically the bedouin Semite, surrounded the former, always unconsciously pressing inwards, vaguely jealous of the ease and luxuries that he saw but which he would only doubtfully enjoy when he got them. When the ramparts were weak, these people flowed inwards. It was a recurring phenomenon and here is its first known incidence: not in this case a military invasion but in its methods and effect hardly less drastic or bloody.

"Nay, but the plunderers are everywhere," laments the Sage, "the stranger people from without are come into Egypt. Nay, but the face is pale, the bowman is ready. The wrong-doer is everywhere." Even the most peaceful professions are in revolt, the confectioners and the brewers—"the bird catchers have made themselves ready for battle". The yearly flooding of the river is neglected, famine stalks the land, and plague. The dead are buried in the river and the river "is blood". "Nay, but gates, columns and walls are consumed with fire." "Squalor is throughout the land; there is none whose clothes are white in these times."

It is the reversal of the established order of things that the Sage continually laments. "Nay, but the land turneth round as a potter's wheel"—the simile of "revolution" has been invented early. "The robber possesseth riches. . . . Nay, but poor men now possess fine things. He who once made for himself no sandals now possesseth riches. . . . Ladies are like slave-girls . . . all female slaves are free with their tongues; when their mistresses speak it is irksome to the servants. . . . He that once begged [for the rich man's] dregs now possesseth beer that bowls him over. . . . He that never built for himself a boat now possesseth ships. . . ." However, this is more than an attempt by the underdog to come out on top; it is not successful revolution but an attempt at revolution that leads to anarchy. "Nay, but the public offices are opened, and their lists (of everyone's status) are taken away." "Nay, but the magic spells are divulged and are now ineffectual." "Men sit in the bushes until the benighted [traveller] cometh." Tomb robbery—a chronic disease of the body politic of Egypt in bad times— is rife and even the Pharaoh's body is not safe. There recur vivid phrases that show the writer's horror at the times he lives in. "Nay, but the crocodiles are glutted with what they have carried off; men go to them of their own accord. . . . Nay, but laughter hath perished and is no longer made. . . . Little children say, 'He ought never to have caused me to live.' "*

So this euphemistically called "First Intermediate Period" in Egypt's long history. Egypt climbed out of her trouble. There was much grouping and regrouping of the nomarchs, who jockeyed for position

*These quotations are taken from the English translation of *The Literature of the Ancient Egyptians* by Adolf Erman (Methuen, 1927).

and power or genuinely tried to re-establish order. The Two Kingdoms fell apart and for a while the upper, the Delta, kingdom gained nominal ascendancy. But it was always the lower that was the more virile. At length, about sixty years before the end of the Third Millennium, a general who was to become crowned over a reunited kingdom as Mentuhotep II defeated the Northerners and established the "Middle Kingdom" and the Eleventh Dynasty at his southern capital of Thebes.

CHAPTER VIII

Sumer and Akkad

THE Third Millennium is predominately the copper and bronze age of Egypt and Sumeria, with neither civilization having as yet much effect upon the other. It is also the age that sees the birth of other civilizations, as example in Crete and the Indus valley. It is the age of the spread of the Bronze culture to the outer fringes, so that by its end the influence is even about to cross the English Channel, a somewhat strange missionary influence, as will be seen in the following chapter. This chapter will consider the rest of the Sumerian story, which ends for good when a fresh tide of nomadic Semites sweeps into the country at just about the start of the next Millennium, the stirred and stirring Second.

Sumeria suffered as did Egypt from the less civilized peoples of the hill country and the desert without. She suffered more and she suffered in a different way. From the beginning she had the Semites in her midst, that is in her northern midst.

These were the Akkadians, perhaps a more virile and certainly a more stern and warlike people. For many centuries they accepted, willingly or otherwise, the tutelage of the more civilized Sumerians, seeming to become, if not much more than superficially, absorbed. The country, from the waters of the Persian Gulf to the place where the twin rivers most nearly meet, became known as the Land of Sumer and Akkad, and the ruler—at such times as he was able to regard himself as ruler of the whole—as "The Shepherd of the Black-Headed People": either the two races were mingling or else recognized themselves as equally dark.

The land's perpetual trouble was its inability to follow Egypt's example and become something more than temporarily and superficially united: the struggle was not only between Semite and Sumerian, it was between city and city.

At the beginning of our period Ur, after the time of the shaft graves and Queen Shub-ad, was losing her status as the most important city. There may have been trouble from Elam in the east; the city of Mari, right up the Euphrates where now lies the border between Iraq and Syria, is recorded as supplying a Sumerian dynasty. Then Kish, not so far north but in the Akkadian part of the country, comes to the front, with no blue-blooded king but a queen by the name of Ku-Ban, who by repute started her life as a wine-seller or brothel-keeper—perhaps the two trades were usually combined. But though the Semitic element is losing its inferior status its time has not yet come to usurp control. Power shifts south again, to the city of Lagash. And now full-

King Ur-Nina and his family

scale war and marching armies and military campaigns and warrior kings come into the picture. First under King Ur-Nina there is consolidation and prosperity and fortification—temples, canals, city walls—and then his grandson, Eannatum, goes to war.

Man, they say, is the only animal that destroys his own species. It is a criticism of no significance, since no animal has the capacity, the brains or organization, to do a very great many things, good and bad, that man does—man is also the only animal to electrocute himself or paint the Mona Lisa. Nevertheless, the fact is a shameful one. That being so, we must seek to view war objectively. It did not arrive early in man's history; but its arrival was inevitable directly the self-contained tribe, wherein the effective sanction was accepted tradition, began to clash with other tribes, whose interests were opposed, whose state of cultural advance was different. By the time of Eannatum there had been reached the stage where rulers could talk—whether they exactly did so is another matter—in terms of "keeping the way open for trade" and of "inalienable rights of access", even of "empire" and of "spreading our superior culture". And the truth is that a great deal of culture, acceptable at least if not superior, was in fact spread by war.

Lagash's emblem of power

The symbols, the "arms", of embattled Lagash embody the lion and the eagle, emblems of ferocity and power, the use of which no conqueror or conquering nation could ever after resist. King Eannatum inherited the armed chariot—which goes back to the shaft graves of Ur, though asses and not horses are yoked to the shaft—and invented, or so it appears, the phalanx or close rank of infantry. The famous "Stele of the Vultures", now in the Louvre, shows him, wearing the curious wig-helmet of his times, and leading the solid irresistibility of his men, closed in behind their shields and with their spears pointing forwards. Eannatum starts with the city of Umma a little higher up the Tigris, which has dared to be difficult over water supplies, then conquers Ur

and once-famous Erech, and finally distant and northern Kish: Sumer
and Akkad are united. Eannatum then dies fighting the King of Umma
in revolt. Later we find the last of his line having to throw off allegiance
to a resurgent Kish but then possessing sufficient authority to restrain
the greed of the priests and to protect such of his "black-headed people"
who were in the position of Naboth and owned possessions that richer
men coveted. He falls finally to the revengeful men of Umma. "They

"Stele of the Vultures"

have carried away the silver and the precious stones," laments a priest
of Lagash, "and have destroyed the statues. . . . As for the conqueror,
may his goddess bear this sin upon her head." He, however, goes from
strength to strength, transferring his seat of power to a subjugated
Erech and making finally the boast that his edict runs from "the Lower
Sea to the Upper", from the Persian Gulf to the Mediterranean. There
is no evidence to substantiate this boast however.

It is at this stage that the Sumerian story of ups and downs, which tends to become monotonous, takes on a new aspect. We have already reached beyond the half-way mark of the millennium, which probably shows that this quick resumé is liable to give a distorted picture and that there is plenty of time for long peaceful periods between major wars. There comes now the real upsurge of the Semitic Akkadians.

In contemporary Kish, King Ur-Ilbaba is ruling—his name is euphonious but unimportant. He has a gardener, promoted to cup-bearer by the name of Sargon.

Sargon is a name to conjure with. Later, fierce Assyrian kings took on his name in the hope of reviving his glory. It moved our own H. G. Wells to return from history-writing to fiction to create in *Christine Alberta's Father* the character of the little man, somewhat turned in the head, who sees himself as a reincarnation of the superb hero. Legends clustered round Sargon, including one that was to become a favourite, that his poor and humble mother had set him as a babe upon the river of fortune floating in an ark of bulrushes stoppered with pitch.

Sargon revolted and usurped the throne of his king. Here, we may interpret, was an uprising of the people such as a little later was to come in Egypt but, because better led, much more successful. Its end was a race to power and very much the usual wielding of it. But it was a magnificent wielding. Sargon, having first made himself safe in the north, turns and subdues all Sumeria. Then he subjugates the Elamites to the east. Then north-east, into the Zagros mountains to subdue the fierce and primitive Gutians, then a turn left and an even deeper push, right across the Taurus mountains into Asia Minor. Annals of his exploits have been found amongst the Hittites and even amongst the Egyptians, though only his fame and not his army penetrated there. There were stories even that he invaded and subdued Cyprus. Here is no less than the first empire carved out by conquest. Here are the first, or at least the first certainly established, campaigning armies, professional soldiery who do not see their home for years. Here, too, is the prototype of the great conquering oriental potentate: decorated, curled, bejewelled; holding state amongst his bored and wary courtiers, with his slaves and concubines, his golden drinking goblets, and his dice and gaming boards, then going personally to war, to slay and have the captives brought in chains before him—arrogant, ruthless, greedy of controlling more and more the lives of men so that he may, according to his lights, benefit them in the mass, but whose fates as individuals are to him as nothing. . . .

The practical thing to remember is that Sargon was a Semite, leading the Semitic element into power and ensuring that, with unimportant breaks, the Land of the Two Rivers will be Semitic for the rest of its days of importance.

Yet Sargon was kind to the conquered Sumerian race and to their susceptibilities. He allows them to worship in their old and accustomed ways; indeed, he goes out of his way to respect tradition. Though he builds himself a new capital in the north, Agade, Ur is allowed to remain a religious centre. When the conquered conqueror of Lagash is brought before him in chains it is in front of Enlil, the head of the Sumerian pantheon that the symbolic transfer of power is effected—as Napoleon crowned himself in a cathedral. Reaching the Persian Gulf, Sargon performs the age-old ritual of washing his arms in the sea. Much of this is no doubt what we should call propaganda, impressing and placating the common people. But it is also the half unwilling but ungainsayable respect of the lately uncivilized for the civilization of the weaker and less virile people whom they have overcome. Here is a recurring, and fortunate, phenomenon of history. Nor was Sargon unmindful of the material welfare of his people. Lebanon was made to yield up its cedar—no fear of guardian monsters there now—and the Taurus Mountains its silver; from Asia Minor he brought back specimens of fig and vine and rosetree—and had the fact duly recorded.

Yet Sargon's life ended in revolt and assassination. The revolt was Sumerian; but help was given from the north, from the land of Subartu, later to be known as Assyria, and from the previously unheard of town of Babylon. The one is conquered and the other is sacked. But then comes Sargon's assassination by his courtiers. They were said to have done the deed, with unconscious symbolism, "by the aid of their seals", those beautifully carved equivalent of our signet ring which for many ages had been the artistic pride and distinction of Sumeria. The courtiers are believed to have worn their seals, attached to a long pin, in their hair—quietus with a bare bodkin in fact.

Four kings follow Sargon, the most famous of whom is Naram-Sin. He leaves a stele of himself, semitically bearded, helmeted magnificently like a later-day Viking, and conquering some miserable mountain tribe. His predecessor boasts in figures: 5,460 men killed and 8,040 men, including the King of Ur, taken prisoner. It is a long tale of struggle to keep intact the empire gained and to subjugate the defeated peoples, both within and without the land of Sumer-Akkad. The effort finally fails: after the fifth name in the dynasty comes the chronicler's despairing or exasperated cry: "Who was king, who was not king?" Inevitably, as foreign bees will rob a sick or unguarded hive, peoples from outside come in to fill the political vacuum: retribution comes from the previously conquered hillmen of the Zagros mountains, the Gutians.

The Gutians were primitive, "they knew not kingship". There follows a century or more of anarchy, such as Egypt suffered at about the same time.

But the greatness of Sumeria is not over yet. There is a final flare of real brilliance, before the light goes out. It comes from the Sumerian and not the Akkadian part of the land, once-warlike Lagash and once-prosperous Ur.

The Gutian overlords seem to have been better at fighting than administration. Towards the end of their rule they appear to have given the local native governors wide power. Those of Lagash made use of them not only in a practical manner to increase trade but also to restore the spiritual awareness of their compatriots by rebuilding temples and reviving rituals. Gudea, the greatest of these governors, gains for himself a place in native history something akin to England's Alfred the Great— and the number of fine statues of himself that he leaves behind help considerably to this end. It is not from Lagash, however, that there comes revolt, but from Erech, daring once more to remember its past heroes. Gutium, "the viper of the hills, he who was the enemy of the gods", who has taken away the kingship of Sumer to the mountains, is destroyed in battle.

The beneficent Gudea

None the less the sceptre of regained power does not remain with Erech but passes to Ur. Ur's last dynasty, the Third, is its greatest.

Great names recur on the monuments: Ur-Nammu, Dungi, Ibi-Sin, the last a Semitic one, which shows perhaps that in the face of external enmity the two racial elements of the land have forgotten their old hatreds. With the second of these there was added to the tale of increased prosperity the old familiar tale of campaigns and conquests. Elam and Assyria were both made to pay tribute. With the control of routes and an efficient civil service there seemed in fact to have arrived not only a prosperous time but a stable one. Dungi was not making the Egyptian Pharaohs' mistake of allowing too great an autonomy on the part of his satraps and governors. He combined efficiency with popularity: he was deified in his lifetime and the people named their children after him, *Dungi-abi*, God-is-my-father.

Ibi-Sin was as unfortunate a king as Harold of England. He was faced with invasion from two opposed quarters, one from the south-east and always to be expected, from the traditional enemy, the Elamites; the other from the north-west, and likely to have been a surprise. Mari, on the farther reaches of the Euphrates, the city that Sargon had once invested, had now climbed back to power and supported a dynasty who were building themselves a palace comparable to a later Knossos in complexity and size. From out of this stronghold issued one Ishbi-Ira. He overran Akkad while the Elamites overran Sumer. It was done with savagery.

> Whereunto, Oh Sumer, did they change thee?
> The sacred dynasty from the temple they exiled,
> They demolished the city, they demolished the temple.
> They seized the rulership of the land.

> Enlil directed his eyes towards a strange land.

Archaeological evidence bears out that of the written lament. The Sumerians had lost their power and their confidence. Their civilization, in many respects the earliest of the world's civilizations, was, so early, at an end.

"We have outgrown," writes Sir Leonard Woolley,* "the phase where all the arts were traced to Greece and Greece was thought to have sprung, like Pallas, full-grown from the brain of the Olympian Zeus; we have learnt how that flower of genius drew its sap from Lydians and Hittites, from Phoenicia and Crete, from Babylon and Egypt. But the roots go farther back: behind all these lies Sumer." Much more so than the Old Kingdom of Egypt, Sumeria spread her

*The Sumerians (O.U.P., 1928).

culture by conquest. Her language now dies, but not her literature, which is respectfully translated by those who follow. Her cuneiform script is taken over intact and adapted to a language which it does not fit. Its gods are merely given other names. For both good and ill no doubt, the Sumerian legacy is extensive.

CHAPTER IX

Spread to the Outskirts

THE spread of the glow of civilization that had ignited itself in the lands around the Eastern Mediterranean must have been a continuous process throughout the Third Millennium. It has, however, its intensifications at the beginning and the end of this long period. The causes of them are very different though each is based on a lack. The first is the lack of knowledge of good farming methods, the second is lack of metal.

It must be remembered that in tracing the history of the millennium other than in Egypt and Sumeria we still have no written records to help us. Crete's "Linear A" script may go back to beyond 2000 B.C., but in the first place it has not been deciphered and in the second, since it is sparser and more primitive than "Linear B", which itself produces little beyond store accounts and nominal rolls, it is not likely to tell us much if it is deciphered. Nevertheless, the careful categorizing and comparing of the archaeologists' finds does give a much clearer and more authentic picture than would have been believed possible even fifty years ago. Sometimes the tracing of similarities in pottery fashion from place to place has been very much like indulging in a paper-chase, and the fact that the clues were laid out not minutes ago but millennia does not make them the less valid. There is one danger, the danger of presenting a wrongly balanced picture, of affording to a people undue or too little importance. Where there are written records the first of these can hardly happen: the very possession of such a record pre-supposes an advanced and significant culture. But the accidents of preservation or of inability to excavate are a different matter: there may be peoples quite unknown to us who contributed more to our inheritance than others known by a wealth of unearthed monuments and grave goods and works of art. It can only be said that this is not now likely. The archaeologists' picture is pretty clear, its outlines are agreed upon, and the future is only likely to add a highlight here, a minor excision there. And the picture probably owes its truth not only to the careful collection of facts but also to the even wilder guesses of the enthusiasts, guesses that are corrected with contumely but which nevertheless act as a sort of leaven to the basic but rather heavy dough which is the product of the orthodox expert.

Two inspired guessers, now largely considered to be discredited, are those champions of the "Diffusionist" school of forty years ago, W. J. Perry and Sir Grafton Elliot Smith. They attributed the spread of civilization almost entirely to one source, Egypt, and pictured a diffusion of metal-hungry, sun-worshipping enthusiasts galvanizing and proselytizing the world. Their deductions have been proved often unjustified, their tracings of similarities over-optimistic, their elevation of Egypt to the rank of sole benefactor fantastic. None the less, the victory really rests with them. Their basic idea of *diffusion*, duly widened and watered down no doubt, does remain as very largely accepted. It is a fact—a surprising fact; it need not have been so—that to some degree the whole world, to a very great degree Europe, owe their Neolithic and their Bronze Age progress to the Middle East.

They owe it fundamentally to Egypt and Sumeria, to which we have circumspectly but reasonably afforded a tied top place. But this debt is really only second-hand. The actual people who spread outwards—and ideas and techniques cannot spread without people—were the more restless ones, ones that were already affected by the two great centres but who had not inherited the good fortune of their peoples and so had less inducement to stay put.

We have already said that the islands of the Mediterranean show no sign of being inhabited by palaeolithic men. The same applies, though less certainly, to Greece. The first neolithic farmers came to all these lands, it seems likely, from Asia Minor or at any rate Western Asia. They settled down to a village life that, by the very fact that it was settled, presupposes a sufficient knowledge of agriculture to be able to keep their lands permanently fertile and not to exhaust them. True to neolithic type, their villages are not fortified. As the Third Millennium dawns it is Crete, together with the islands of the Cyclades streaming out from the Peloponnese towards Crete, that show the greatest progress: houses rather than huts, seals with possibly hieroglyphic signs on them, stone vases, some copper and jewellery, the marble of Paros and the obsidian of Melos used. Sicily, Italy and Spain receive their influence and no doubt their human infiltration from the East, though here there have already existed mesolithic and palaeolithic inhabitants. In Spain an entering stream from the east seems to meet a stream crossing from the south.

It is this latter stream that is of immediate interest to us, since it is one of four that have been traced as penetrating right up into central and northern Europe.

It must have crossed from the north coast of Africa; it must have originated—judging by its pottery, which is found in origin at the site of Merimde, north of the Fayum—on the desert margins of the Nile. "Stream" is the right word only if we regard this matter with the god-like contemplation to which a thousand ages are but as an evening gone. The stay on the North African coast may have been a long one before taking the plunge across the Mediterranean. Even then it was not a continuous movement but a matter of settling down and then of uprooting when the soil was exhausted. Nor was there always advance in a steady direction: a site has been found that shows a re-occupation, after the lapse of a few generations. Nevertheless, looked at from sufficient distance, it is a steady movement and a surprisingly great one. Up through France, and then splitting, it ends finally in two very different environments, the lakes of Switzerland and the rolling downlands of England.

This is not to suggest that the Lake Dwellers of Switzerland or the Windmill Hill people, as they have been called, had much in common or any knowledge of each other by the time they reached their final destination. But they were the first of northern and central Europe's farmers and they were bringing from the margins of the Nile the revolutionary neolithic techniques.

To examine their cultures in detail would be to repeat much that is in Chapter III: their relics can be seen in the Museum of Avebury or prolifically in the museums of Switzerland and around—in this instance there was even at one time, so great was the demand, a good trade in forgeries. Each set illustrates a distinctive way of living.

It remains in dispute whether the Swiss villages were built out over swamps or lakes. But remains of boats have been found and at least at times there must have been water below and not reeds and mud. It must have been a good life, with the peace and security of the cluster of thatched, clay-floored, strongly supported timber huts at the end of its guarded causeway, with the strips of cultivation along the shore, with the forest behind for hunting. A paradise perhaps for children, who, if they were like their modern counterparts in the East Indies, would have very early learnt to swim. The Swiss lake dwellings lasted on into the Bronze Age. But many show traces of being rebuilt after fire, and more than once: fire, unexpectedly, seems to have been the great and no doubt terrifying danger—in the dry season in particular perhaps, when the water had drained away.

The Windmill Hill people settled on the downlands of a much-forested England. Typically we may imagine them, cowboys rather than agriculturists, driving their cattle in the autumn to the yearly round-up. There, in what have been called the causewayed camps—for instance, the earlier, almost obliterated double circle of Maiden Castle, in contrast to its much later and much greater fortification of immediately pre-Roman times—the cattle stood corralled in the centre while their owners, surely praying for fine weather and probably in that millennium more often getting it, lived for a while and disported themselves in the wide surrounding ditches. It was the time for the salting down of meat for the winter, a time no doubt of branding and buying and selling, and a time, too, of feasting, of love-making, of the observance of ceremonies. If the gods of these people showed any vestiges of their Nilotic origin they would in greater likelihood have been the earth-gods of the earlier and simpler Egyptians and pre-Egyptians, the universal Earth Mother of fertility, rather than the Sun God of later times. Both the Hill People and the Lake People, together with the groups that they had left behind on their long trek—they are called sometimes, generically, the Westerners, with a distinctive pottery called Cortaillod—were to enjoy many centuries, if not of progress, at least of peace. While young Pepi II worried about his dancing dwarf and the ageing Sargon about his suspected assassins, before the Westerners themselves were to be disturbed by the trading caravans of the Beaker People or the nosing prows of the ships of the earnest and perhaps fanatic Megalith Builders, there passed in backward Europe long centuries of barbaric neolithic stability.

Meanwhile, another stream of migrant people with a type of pottery evolved, it would seem, from that excellent container, the dried gourd, moved across from Asia Minor. These have been called the Danubians, for it was up the Danube that they spread, and, by comparison, quickly. At the site of present-day Belgrade they had before them the wide plains of Hungary made in the past potentially fertile by the *loess* dust of the Ice Age. They took advantage of that fertility—a sort of final benediction, one might say, of the palaeolithic hunters who had passed that way to ultimate extinction—and, reaching at length the Rhine, passed down it, struck north again, and finished up in Jutland. Here, at the site of Barkaer, these people had built a village on a little island in a lake. A long row of small huts, all alike, on each side of a cobbled street was discovered—an egalitarian rather than an aristocratic society? A tough society, too, no doubt, with fine, strong, polished stone axes, with which the modern discoverers were able to cut down an eight-inch tree in eight minutes. Here are the outer pioneers of the Neolithic Age. They must have come from a society that already knew metal. Here, such a knowledge is only evident to us, however, by the find of two small copper pendants. Amber beads there are, evidence of a trade that will increase: exchange of copper and bronze, gradually to be used for more practical purposes, from the civilized and sophisticated, for amber and jet and suchlike potential things of beauty from the primitives.

The great metal traders and prospectors, the Beaker People, arrive after the Megalith Builders, rather as in recent African history the trader arrived after the missionary.

This likening of the builders of the megalithic monuments to missionaries, which may seem to beg the question of the purpose behind the migrations of these strange people, tentatively follows an idea of the aforementioned diffusionists and wholly subscribes to an idea put forward by Geoffrey Bibby in his book on the archaeology of northern Europe, *The Testimony of the Spade*, backed up to some extent by O. G. S. Crawford's *The Eye Goddess*. It is an interpretation that appeals to the present writer, not only as highly reasonable but also as one fitting the conception that all early civilizations were governed much more by religious outlooks than by economic.

The facts about the Megalith Builders are these. They raised, as their name implies, monuments of great stones. These were either in the form of standing stones, placed in long avenues as at Carnac in Brittany or in circles as at Stonehenge, obviously for some ritual purpose, or else in the form of a mausoleum, typically covered with earth—the tumulus or barrow and the dolmen. These monuments, showing great similarity both of construction and of ornament, are found of oldest date in the Mediterranean and spreading eastwards to India and more particularly westwards and northwards around Europe. They, the European ones at least, always lie near to the coast or to navigable rivers. If these monuments were spread by a single people—and any other explanation is very difficult to justify—then these people were sailor-adventurers.

They were not metal seekers. For, though the customary grave goods were left beside the dead man in his tomb, yet they very seldom included anything of metal. They were *not* a great mass of people on the move, arriving and settling and supplanting the original inhabitants. There is one particularly significant fact: though the architecture of the megalithic tumuli is the same the grave goods vary—by and large, they are the grave goods of the original inhabitants of the hinterland.

Here then, more than anything else, is manifested the spread of an *idea*. The tombs, it could be said, bear a distant but basic resemblance to the Egyptian pyramid: bury the great one in a replica of his earthly house and then build a lasting monument about him. A closer relationship is to the Tholos or domed-vault tomb which at this time is beginning to appear in the lands around the Aegean, a great beehive-shaped tomb, led into by a steeply walled causeway that is filled with earth after a burial and cleared again at the next interment. The typical megalithic barrow around the coastlands of north-west Europe is built on exactly the same principle, a chamber led into by a passage and covered with a mound of earth or stones, which, however, will not prevent the reopening of the chamber for successive burials. It will be, always, the tomb of a great family, as great locally perhaps as the family of Atreus which Homer immortalized and whose remains must once have lain in the tholos tombs at Mycenae.

What is the great idea behind this megalith building? Perhaps nothing more than ancestor-worship, which is not a new idea, though here there may have been very firmly held ideas as to how exactly that worship should be observed. On the other hand, the temples, as opposed to the tombs, and as is well known, show by their orientation some sign of a sun worship or at least a preoccupation with an accurate marking of the seasons. The decorations as well as the architecture may help to give a clue. We are taken now not to the Aegean but farther eastwards and into the upper reaches of the Euphrates. Often in the carvings of the stones used in the great barrow passage graves—at New Grange in Ireland as an outstanding example—there occurs scroll-like carving that has been traced in its similarity (in the late Mr. Crawford's book as already mentioned) to most curious "eye-goddesses" that occur in great numbers as votive offerings in the temple excavated at Brak. There is here the same sort of slavish copying, ending in the unintelligible, as was shown in the Azilian pebble-painting. And what is the significance here? It must surely be an idea of the *all-seeing* eye. Of the departed ancestor? Of, again, the sun?

Speculation, though fascinating, must be curbed. The irreducible, indisputable fact is that, on each side of the ending of the Second Millennium, people were moving across the face of the world, spreading a way of building and a way of burial, each of which must have been an emanation of a way of thought. Hence the use of the term "missionary" is justified. Not, of course, that it must be interpreted too strictly. These people hardly travelled *because* they were missionaries; rather they were missionaries when they had ceased their travelling. They must have been forceful people, gaining an ascendancy either moral or physical or both, not necessarily wherever they went but in a great many places. If the Westerners and Danubians, long before, had exported the ways of farming, the Megalith Builders exported new ways of religion. They must have been spectacular and exciting ways, the procession to the long barrow or stone circle having much in common with the procession to the shaft grave or the pyramid or the Ziggurat. . . .

By comparison the Beaker People are unmysterious. They are known by and named after their distinctive, bold and beautiful beakers or tankards. It has been suggested, not unreasonably, that such fine containers were made for something worth containing and that their owners carried with them the art of making good beer. More importantly, these people carried with them the art of making tools and weapons and ornaments of copper and bronze. They traded, they prospected, they often settled. They came from a country of considerable copper, Spain, and they travelled—apart from crossing the English Channel—largely by land, by ox-wagon. It is curious how slowly the use of metal spread through Europe: taking time to root in Spain, it had not reached the British Isles until after the turn of the Second Millennium into the First. Copper and bronze were, presumably, for a long time much too expensive a commodity for the poor neolithic farmer, who had nothing worth while to give in exchange. Alternatively it was, once more, a matter of human conservatism: flint was the traditional medium and not to be despised. Even the Beaker People themselves used it for their arrowheads. They also had another and unexpected use for it. They often left behind in their graves beautifully made rectangular plates, thin and curved, four inches or so long, of polished stone or sometimes of bone or baked clay. It was not until one of these was found resting on the wrist-bones of a skeleton that its use was realized. In each of its corner-holes was a small gold-headed stud. It had been used, riveted to a leather strap, as a wrist-guard against the snap of the bow-string. The Beaker People, as well as traders and tinkers, may have been both great drinkers and great hunters.

So the four main streams of diffusion of culture into Europe, the Westerners and the Danubians bringing the knowledge of cattle-ranching and farming, the Megalith Builders a way of thought and of building, the Beaker People the use of metal. To the use of metal, Crete, as it were on one of the inner circles of diffusion, owes much of her initial greatness, so that in the ensuing millennium she herself took on importance as a great centre of civilization. We will take a look at Crete as she begins to grow to maturity, before turning to the last of the early "outposts", the civilization of the Indus valley.

The Cretan bull. An example of artistic skill that later spread to the mainland

The ores of copper, though by no means unknown around the original centres of civilization, were more plentiful in the islands and on the northern and western shores of the Mediterranean. East Crete had its supplies, Spain and Portugal, and, outstandingly, Cyprus. Tin, the necessary hardening element for the making of bronze, was rarer: Etruria, Gaul, Spain, the British Isles (Cornwall) and Bohemia (the Erzgebirge) were the sources of supply, gradually becoming known through the second half of the Third Millennium. The Bohemian supply would come by caravan to the shores of the Adriatic. Thence its sea route would meet the sea route from the West in the Ionian Sea. "Half-way between Cyprus the Copper Island, and the sea by which the tin came, opposite the Cyclades, equidistant from Egypt and the Troad [the hinterland of Troy, now also becoming prosperous], Crete was wonderfully placed to attract the Manufacture of Bronze and to distribute its products."

So writes Gustav Glotz in his book, *The Aegean Civilization,** adding that Knossos on the north coast of Crete is the same distance from Troy as Zakro on the east coast is distant from the mouth of the Nile. Crete was in a central and strategic position. She rose to the opportunity and increased what the *Odyssey* calls her dark-prowed ships, and thrived on trade. Just as the mud-flat lands of Egypt and Sumeria were not self-sufficient and needed, if their populations were to increase and their civilizations develop, to become traders and importers, so and even more so must have been the rugged and mountainous land of Crete. And Crete was an island; trade meant, therefore, fleets not of caravans but of ships. There arrives that resounding word, "thalassocracy", a society dependent upon sea power. Crete became such round about 2400 B.C., and ceased to be so very suddenly at 1400 B.C.

The Cretan rise to wealth takes its time. But by 2100 B.C.—which date marks under Sir Arthur Evans's chronology† the change from the Early to the Middle Minoan Period—prosperity is established. With wealth comes, as perhaps could be expected, a concentration of power. So far the towns of the east and the south and the north seem to have had equal importance; so far there have been no grand, labyrinthine palaces. But as the Third Millennium comes to an end Knossos, facing north, and Phaistos, facing south, rise to power and there begin to be built dwellings suitable to the opulence of their princes. The distinctive civilization of Crete is about to unfold its highly decorative blossom.

Lastly the rise of the civilization of the Indus valley, of the exotically named peoples of Harappa and Mohenjo-Daro. Their discovery is recent, in the twenties of this century.

Here one thing must be made clear from the start. To treat the Indus civilization as one of the "outskirts" is a little unfair to it. It is certainly not to be compared with the primitive Barkaer or Windmill Hill cultures. But so long as that fact is remembered, the inclusion is justified. The Indus civilization appears suddenly at the beginning of the twenty-fifth century B.C., by which time Sumer and Egypt had already existed for at least a thousand years. "It is legitimate," says Sir Mortimer Wheeler, an authority on these parts, "to affirm that the *idea* of civilization came to the land of the Indus from the land of the Twin Rivers"—going on, however, to stress the essential self-sufficiency of

---

*In the *History of Civilization* series (Kegan Paul, 1925).
† Challenged but not discredited.

each.* Concrete evidence of connection between the two is only apparent a couple of centuries after the Indus civilization's beginning, at the time of Sumeria's Sargon.

Harappa and Mohenjo-Daro are preceded by a chalcolithic and neolithic stage, which stages, however, are apparent almost wholly in the hills and highland to the west of the great valley, in part of the upland mass that extends to the land of Elam that overlooked in a similar way the valley of the Twin Rivers. It is exactly the old story of Sumer and of Egypt repeated. The tribes of the hills have, to use a phrase of Sir Mortimer Wheeler, reached in their particular environment, "their cultural optimum": they will not progress until they are moved to change their environment. With no doubt some contacts and influences from without and upon one another—perhaps at yearly fairs and round-ups as with the Windmill Hill people—the mountain tribes yet remain independent and primitive, and are likely to remain so until some of them, forced by economic necessity or inspired by example, take as it were the plunge. The great river-plain of the Indus and its tributaries lies below them, in this instance probably more jungle than reeded mud-flats but certainly more inviting than in its present-day arid and salt-encrusted state. Those people who go down there and set up a new civilization will have to work hard in order to seize the beneficence of nature and will have to submit to control and organization of their lives if they are to do so. Suddenly they are inspired to make the effort as others have made it before them. Their success is immediate and spectacular. And the reason for this may be that by all the evidence they allow themselves to a greater extent than any other early civilization to be regimented.

In avoiding unfairness we must not overstress the importance of these people that are now known as the Harappans. Their very name is significant: they made so little impact upon contemporary records that we have had to call them after the modern name of the site of one of their cities—as if we were to call the Egyptians the Luxorites. Compared with the massive displays of works of art left behind by Egypt, or even by Sumeria, their relics are scanty. Their script appears as something copied rather than evolved locally and if ever deciphered is not likely to provide more than a few proper names or names of weights and tallies. Only their seals show a skill that rivals the Sumerian, influencing as well as being influenced by the original

*See his *The Indus Civilization* (C.U.P., 1953) and also his *India and Pakistan* (Thames and Hudson, 1959).

practisers of that art. No imposing monuments, heart-lifting manifestations of a passionately held religion, have been discovered.

The Harappans did, however, in a few hundred years spread a civilization along the Indus and its tributaries over an area larger than ancient Egypt. And they did build, tremendously.

They built modernly, not with mere sun-dried lumps of clay but with kiln-fired bricks. They were ahead of even the Minoans in their drainage and plumbing. They were, indeed, a clean people, coupling no doubt, as does the present-day Indian, cleansing with the ritual of religion. One of the principal buildings of Mohenjo-Daro is a Great Bath or Tank, 39 feet by 23 feet by 8 feet deep and lined with bricks set watertight in bitumen. The other outstanding buildings both at Mohenjo-Daro and at Harappa show more than anything else a grim public efficiency. Both towns possessed a large public granary; and Harappa built also a series of corn-grinding platforms showing apparently that not only was grain stored centrally but its preparation was also a public and regimented affair. Both towns—particularly Mohenjo-Daro, which is better preserved —show streets of identical box-like houses, what Sir Mortimer Wheeler has called "coolie lines".

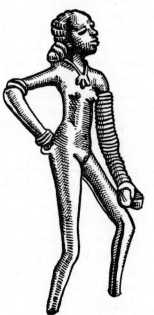

This aspect of the towns increases as time goes on. Towards their end, many of the bigger houses become divided into tenements and—a process with which we ourselves are familiar—slums are created. The end, in the middle of the next, the Second, Millennium, will be sudden, and violent. But the decline is long and slow. The enemy is not from without, nor judging by the comparative rarity of fortifications or weapons was one expected. Perhaps the task of coping with the vagaries of a river less dependable than the Nile exhausted the people; perhaps regimentation exhausted them—it did not sufficiently exacerbate them, for there is no sign of revolt. The relics left behind, other than buildings, do not give a very happy picture. There is evidence of an

The Mohenjo-Daro
dancing girl

efficient system of weights and measures. Clay votive offerings give an impression of grotesqueness or of being produced cheaply and crudely for the multitude. A seal shows a horned god or goddess, sitting in a Buddha-like attitude and looking reasonably benign, but what statues there are—whether of kings or priests or gods it is impossible to tell— show a kind of sneering inhumanity. The only emblem of light-heartedness left behind is the bronze figure of the relaxed and graceful dancing girl—and here the pleasure may have been exclusively upper class. . . .

In this chapter there has been rather much of surmise. The picture may alter a little, will certainly become more detailed, as archaeology and anthropology and philology progress. But whether or not the eye-obsessed people of Brak did influence the Megalith Builders, or the Harappans owed much or little to Sumeria, whether or not we are correct in our dating of Crete's beginnings or the Beaker People's peregrinations, all that is of little importance compared with the facts that such peoples did exist and that they have left behind sufficient material for us to base upon it reasonable guesses at how they pro-gressed and behaved and thought. At any rate, in the Third Millennium before Christ, in the earlier ages of copper and bronze, men did undoubtedly progress, and with few setbacks.

CHAPTER X

Imperial Peoples

WE come now to tell of empires and very soon of the clash of empires.

We enter the Second Millennium B.C. And if it was a good generalization to speak of the Third as on the whole—and with obvious exceptions—a peaceful millennium, then it is perhaps even better to speak of the Second as one of change and increasing violence. The scene is once more the central one of the Eastern Mediterranean and the lands around it. But now the influences of one part upon another are greater. So also begin to be greater the influences from outside, the noises off.

The empires we shall consider, in this and the following chapters, are in turn the Babylonian, the Hittite, the Egyptian, and then the Minoan and the Mycenaean. The Babylonian is successful if short-lived, the fabulous city's earlier golden age before Nebuchadnezzar's greater age some thousand years later. The Hittite gets off to a false start. The Egyptian is delayed, and unexpected; it is surprising that such a protected land and such a peaceable people should come to produce an empire at all. The Minoan is a brilliant product and comparatively short-lived also. As for the Mycenaean, how far are we justified in giving the efforts of these horsey, swashbuckling Northerners the title of empire builders is as yet not quite clear; what recent archaeology and philology have made clear, however, is that the peoples over whom Agamemnon was once king did produce, before the dark ages at the end of the millennium came upon them, a more powerful and a more sophisticated civilization than had been imagined.

The sound of the name Babylon is much more modern than the sound of Ur; it helps us, therefore, to realize the fact of change in that, as the Third Millennium slides into the Second, Ur and the other great Sumerian–Akkadian cities disappear from the scene and Babylon gradually takes their place.

We have already seen how in the reign of the unfortunate Ibi-sin the poet was lamenting the incoming "deluge of the Elamites". These people, whose capital was Susa, had received help from the Amorites, whose very name, Amurru, means Western. These came from Syria and Canaan, perhaps originally from Arabia. While the glory of Sumeria was slowly seeping away and kings under sufferance from the Elamites pretended to rule from the townships of Isin and Larsa, the Amorites we must believe were slowly building up their strength. A new and wholly Semitic power was about to arrive in the Land of the Two Rivers; and it would be based on Babylon.

Babylon was not a new city, only its greatness. And that greatness, since it was commercial and cultural more than military, was to survive disasters, ignore conquerors and outlast dynasties. The site of the city is near to the modern town of Hillah (partly built of its ancient bricks) some sixty miles south of Baghdad, and on the east bank of the Euphrates where that river approaches near to the Tigris. It was a central position, commanding trade routes both by water and by land; and it was within an ancient religious area of the Sumerians.

That, it would now seem, is the new order of importance, trade first and religion second, though religion is certainly still a good and powerful second. The "great household" economy seems to be fading. In modern, but applicable, terms, a middle class is appearing: merchants, civil servants, skilled artisans, professional soldiers. They possess purchasing power; and so, therefore, production can be not for the closed circuit of the king-god's household but "for the market". Money has come upon the scene, the handy and transportable means of exchange: no longer the sheep or the cow but the standardized weight of precious metal. Admittedly there is as yet no small change, no coinage, though even this convenience was not far distant in that coils of silver wire were used, from which one could snip off a convenient length.

We must not imagine, however, that the merchant of early Babylon, or for that matter his brother across on the Mediterranean coast, or in Crete or Egypt or the Indus valley, was a free agent. Far from it. The very wealth that he was creating was giving greater power to his king, who still had the sanction of religion behind him, who increasingly exercised the power of armed force. No doubt the first kings of this new Amorite dynasty were great men, names known from the cuneiform records though not names remembered; but the sixth in the line is the greatest, and if, as happens with great names, he accretes to himself some of the fame of his predecessors we need not worry too much on that account. The reign of Hammurabi focuses the might and glory of the first golden age of Babylon. He ruled for over forty years in the eighteenth century B.C.

There is nothing very heroic about Hammurabi, he does not rise romantically like Sargon from lowly beginnings. He inherits his glory and increases it; he is, essentially, efficient. We have besides his laws many of his letters, and we gain the impression of a supremely busy man, even of a man who has not learnt to delegate his authority or, more probable perhaps, a king who loves to pose as a benevolent guardian of his people and one for whose notice no incident is too small. We may imagine him doing business, with his confidential secretary by his side ready with his stylus and clay tablet, with messengers constantly bringing in news and reports from the cities and outposts of his empire. Here there is a question of temple property, here an official guilty of bribery who needs to be punished. The Euphrates between Ur and Larsa has become obstructed and the local governor is commanded to clear the channel at the earliest possible moment. The king's wise men, not so wise this time, let him know that their calculation of the seasons has slipped more than a little, and he writes a circular letter to his governors: "Since the year has a deficiency, let the month which is now beginning be registered as a second month of Elul"— though this does not mean that taxes due next month are to be deferred. Hammurabi is making full use of the power and control that the invention of writing is giving him. Yet the great man must know also how to stoop. There is the case of the chief of the temple bakers who has to attend a religious feast at Ur just when he has an important law suit coming on. The king duly postpones the law suit.*

Most primitive civilizations, particularly perhaps the Semitic, have been litigious, and this civilization was no exception. The people did at least have an up-to-date code of laws, however, on which to base their disputes: it is Hammurabi's legal code that has done most to make him famous. Like all good law-givers he had not failed to incorporate earlier codes and customs; and like other early law-givers he had not omitted to make it clear that he was but passing on the rules that came straight to him from his god. The stele on which are inscribed his laws shows King Hammurabi receiving his staff of authority from the god recently promoted to head of the Babylonian pantheon, Marduk. It is a significant illustration of the times that this stele, now in the Louvre, was found not at Babylon but at Susa of the Elamites, whither it had been carried off in conquest.

*From *Ancient Times* by J. H. Breasted. (Ginn, 1916).

The code begins by stressing the importance and sanctity of witnesses. It goes on to cover theft, the duty of officials, agriculture, contracts and loans and debts, the family, penalties for assault, the duties of doctors and architects and builders, property and slaves. It is modern in its insistence upon proper evidence; it is ancient in the ferocity of some of its penalties and its insistence upon "an eye for an eye and a tooth for a tooth". Some of the punishments have a sort of naïve, startling, and horrible appropriateness: those guilty of incest are to be drowned after

King Hammurabi receives his staff of authority from
the god

being bound together; a son who strikes his parents may have his hand cut off (so too may a careless surgeon); a wet nurse who secretly takes a second nursling may lose her breasts. Women's rights are protected, however, as they have not been before. The code tends to favour the creditor rather than the debtor, for interest rates are allowed up to 33 per cent. What tells us most of the society in which these laws were framed is the fact that three castes or classes are recognized: aristocrats or patricians (amelu), which included all government officials, priests and professional soldiers; the burghers or commoners (mushkinu) which included merchants, shopkeepers, schoolmasters, artisans, farmers and labourers; and finally slaves. As with our own Anglo-Saxon laws, it cost very little to be convicted of harming a slave but a great deal to harm a patrician. But there is added and surprising fairness about these distinctions: the *amelu* on the other hand had often to pay more than the *mushkinu* for perpetrating the same crime—a matter of *noblesse oblige*. Sir Leonard Woolley sees in this the importance of the aristocratic class as defenders of the state: they must have not only their rights but their stricter discipline.

This fact constitutes a useful reminder to us, contemplating as we are evidence of an ordered and settled and sophisticated way of life. Such is not the whole picture. This Amorite civilization of Hammurabi and his dynasty is a military empire based on conquest. Riches can best be obtained by control of trade routes; and such control can only be won and kept by force of arms. Hammurabi, for all his occasional championing of the poor and the oppressed, for all his executive efficiency, was quite capable of being the ruthless conqueror. He had, too, to fight for his kingdom: not until half-way through his reign had he wrested the city of Larsa in the south from the Elamites; and then in the thirty-third year of his reign trouble came from Mari in the north. Sargon is believed to have invested that city; but, in a way that Mesopotamian cities had, it rose again and was imposing and prosperous in the last days of Sumerian pre-Amorite power. Hammurabi conquered Mari. When it dared to stir in revolt two years later he caused it and its magnificent palace to be pillaged and burnt.

Against Hammurabi's successor came once more revolt from the south. It seems to have met with some success, but only temporarily. At the end of the eighteenth century the great city of Ur was destroyed, to hang on in meanness and squalor until an effort was made to resuscitate it a couple of centuries later. Then, just about 1600 B.C., came not revolt but invasion. Under their king, Mursilis the First, the Hittites entered Babylon. It was by no means the end of the city, but it was of its Amorite greatness.

And who were the Hittites? From the facts that the discovery of their importance has been recent whilst the Old Testament does little other than mention them casually and patronizingly as one of the tribes of Canaan, they remain for most of us a mysterious people. They appear in their self-portraits and their portraits by the Egyptians as a large-nosed but not a Semitic-looking people. Their language has definite Aryan affinities. Were they "Aryans" then? The only possible answer to that question is to say that it is an improper one. Once in the steppe countries of Europe and Asia, north of the Black and the Caspian Seas, there must have been an original Aryan-speaking tribe. But language can and does cut across race; and by the time the Aryan language speakers appear in history their racial characteristics are varied. The Hittites themselves when they appear on the pages of history already seem a mixture, an Aryan-speaking aristocracy perhaps superimposed on a different indigenous people. The more one studies ancient history the more one becomes convinced that to try to ascribe racial definitions

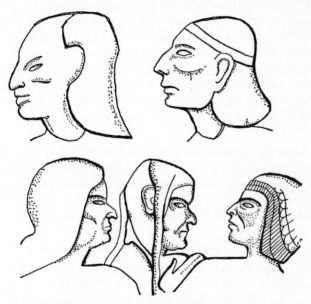

Hittites, as portrayed by the Egyptians

and differentiations is a snare: ancient peoples must simply be accepted and studied as they are, with no labels attached purely for the sake of attaching labels. Two things are really significant about the Hittites. One is that they *were* Aryan-speaking. The other is that their home is a home of mountains. For some time now, and for some time to come, power is leaving the people of the plains, the originators and developers of husbandry and the city and the settled way of life, for the hardier peoples of the uplands and the mountains. The Hittites are a case in point.

We find them established in the highland plateau of Anatolia, that is to say, Asia Minor. The scenery of their home is rugged, the valleys are well wooded, but the limestone-studded heights are bleak and windy: people from the steppes could thrive on them, but peoples from the Twin River valleys certainly could not. We hear of the Hittites first from the letters of certain merchants from Assur—we will not call them Assyrians for the nation of Assyria is not yet. These, in the years around 1900 B.C., were sojourning and going about their business in the Hittite country. They speak of many princes and palaces and of one great prince: there is as yet, one imagines, no more than a loose confederation of tribes with one aristocrat-ruler exercising or at least claiming suzerainty over the rest. The merchants' letters cease—perhaps they had to retire—and we learn, from later annals, that a certain king Anittas is fighting his way to the top. He destroys the town of Hattusas in the process. Next comes one, Labarnas; and he is the real founder of the Hittite Kingdom, the great man from whom later kings claim their lineage as Kings Atreus and Aegeus were claimed as ancestors by the early Greeks.

> Formerly Labarnas was king; and then his sons, his brothers, his connexions by marriage and his blood-relations were united. And the land was small; but wherever he marched to battle, he subdued the lands of his enemies with might. He destroyed the lands and made them powerless, and he made the seas his frontiers.

His son, Hattusilis I, continued the good work. He transferred his capital back to the old and previously destroyed site of Hattusas.* He becomes more adventurous, and issuing forth from his mountain fastness, over the formidable Taurus range, he and his army struck south and east. They invested Yamhad, the modern Aleppo. Aleppo later revolted, by which time Mursilis I, an adopted son, was on the throne. It was Mursilis who not only reconquered Aleppo but penetrated down to the middle reaches of the Euphrates and to Babylon. We have come to around about the year 1600 B.C. and to the end of the Amorite hegemony and of the Hammurabi era in Babylon. Mursilis had made a brilliant raid; and when he retired, leaving a

---

*We should really perhaps call the Hittites the Hattites or, as the Egyptians did, the Khattites, though this "Kh" is really no more than a sort of over-aspirated "H". In any case, it was probably only the most ancient inhabitants who called themselves by any such name; the Aryan-speaking conquerors must have called themselves something else, though no one knows what.

vacuum, a people called the Kassites filled it and Babylon fell out of the run of history for something like a thousand years.

Now this conquest of the city of Babylon can have been no more than a raid, a penetration as ineffective perhaps as Napoleon's into Russia, though rather more successful. It looks as if the Hittites in the pride of their early success have over-reached themselves. They seem at this time to have suffered from one disability in particular, which they shared incidentally with our own Saxon ancestors—and since both must have come from those ancient and original Aryan-speakers, the similarity may have some significance. It is that their royal succession was theoretically elective but in practice a matter of intrigue. and dispute. This was something indeed of which the Royal House was acutely aware: the annals we quoted show a desire to point the moral of an earlier unity, and we have, too, the records of a speech by the great King Hattusilis I himself, telling how he first brought up his nephew to be the Prince Regent and then thought better of it:

> . . . Well! No one will (in future) bring up the child of his sister as his foster-son! The word of the king he has not laid to heart, but the word of his mother, the serpent, he has laid to heart. . . . Enough! He is my son no more! Then his mother bellowed like an ox. 'They have torn asunder the womb in my living body! They have ruined him, and you will kill him!' But have I, the king, done any evil? . . .*

There is something remarkably human about this appeal, recorded —perhaps taken down verbatim?—as an address by the king to "the fighting men of the Assembly and the dignitaries", something reminiscent of the outspokenness in another assembly, when Achilles rated King Agamemnon for his overweening pride and retired to nurse his famous wrath. The schemes and appeals of King Hattusilis achieved by no means full success: Mursilis, whom he adopted in the stead of his nephew, ended by being murdered in a palace intrigue. The usurper and his successors then lost most of the territory won by the arms of the three successful early kings. . . .

The true greatness of the Hittites comes about 1460 B.C., and lasts for something over 250 years. That is a subject for a later chapter; and all we need to do here, so far as Hittite history is concerned, is to connect their first and rather false start with their subsequent success.

---

*This and the following quotations are taken from O. R. Gurney's *The Hittites* (Penguin Books, 1952).

After the murder of King Mursilis they suffered disaster from a people called the Hurrians and came up against the might and expert horsemanship of the Mitanni, of both of whom more later. It is sufficient to say that in the face of enemies and great difficulties they managed to survive and finally to consolidate themselves. They evolved in the process better rules for their kingly succession, whilst their rulers, like Hammurabi of Babylon, produced a system of justice and a code of laws.

It would be tedious to quote from these laws at length. The code has many similarities with that of Hammurabi. What is more interesting, however, are the differences. For the Hittite laws give on the whole a picture of a more enlightened people; from our modern viewpoint they show an advance.

There is, for instance, much more stress on restitution and compensation for a crime committed and less on retribution. The only capital offences are for rape, unnatural sexual intercourse, defiance of the authority of the state, and disobedience on the part of a slave. It is slaves only who ever suffer a sentence of mutilation. As with the Anglo-Saxon "weregilt" there is a scale of charges for ways of causing bodily harm, twenty shekels (roughly the value of twenty sheep) for breaking a

An armed Hittite—king or god

man's arm or leg, for instance. Slaves are half-price, which is in reality a great advance, the masters no longer being able to do entirely what they like with them. One rule is curious: "If anyone kills a man or woman in quarrel, he buries him and gives four persons, men or women, and he (the victim's heir) lets him go home." The expression "persons" is that generally used for slaves. Were they slain then at the tomb of the murdered man? No one is going to pretend that to be even a Hittite slave was a happy fate.

The other point about this law is that there is something of restitution in it but nothing of punishment. The Hittite law in fact does not yet presume to control the private enmities and the blood feuds of men but only to regulate. Indeed, it makes this abnegation specific:

The rule of blood is as follows. Whoever commits a deed of blood, whatever the 'lord of blood' (i.e. the next of kin) says—if he says, 'Let him die', he shall die; but if he says, 'Let him make restitution,' he shall make restitution: the king shall have no say in it.

The Hittites show themselves, in fact, as a tough and fierce and independent people, but perhaps more openly magnanimous and less darkly cruel than some of their neighbours.

These laws date mostly from the first part of the fifteenth century B.C.; and by the middle of it the Hittite kings were feeling strong enough to make their second and much more successful attempt at empire building. They started in exactly the same way as before, by attacking and investing Aleppo. But now there is a difference. Another power is present: the Hittites, it seems likely, were acting in alliance with a resurgent Egypt. . . .

In Egypt there will be some time to go before its rulers are moved to think of empire or, as one Pharaoh put it, of "extending the boundaries". The country, having recovered from the earlier of its two so mildly called Intermediate Periods, was first to enjoy the prosperity of its Middle Kingdom and then suffer its second Intermediate Period, in which it knew the unhappiness of alien rule. First we must look at this double stretch of history, which will take us to the year 1575 B.C.

Egypt's Middle Kingdom has sometimes been called an empire. But the title is not yet justified. Later generations accorded to one of its Pharaohs, Sesostris III (un-Greek name, Senwosre), the role of a conquering hero. But again he does not deserve it. This is not to say that Sesostris was anything but a great and powerful monarch: under him there is foreign penetration, there are military expeditions. But these appear as more a matter of necessity and the country's self-preservation than of ambition and power bursting out at the seams. It is outpost forts that are more typical of the period. Egypt after her first period of chaos is a different Egypt, hating and fearing the foreigner and in particular the nomadic Asiatic, the "sand-farer" as she calls him. "He has been fighting," declared one writer, of the South Palestinian warrior of Aam, "since the time of Horus, but he never conquers, nor is he ever conquered"—a statement as optimistic in its first part as regretful in its second.

Egypt was very prosperous, however. As the Third Millennium ends a Theban dynasty at last gains full control, and peace and well-organized government return to the land. It is, in fact, highly organized government. The local governors, the once over-powerful nomarchs, are at least not deprived of their prestige or their glory or their status, though they are deprived of their autocracy. The Egypt of this time is a truly feudal country, and with one autocrat only, the Pharaoh. If Sargon I typifies the Eastern potentate, then the ruler of the Middle Kingdom, when Egypt has reached her maturity, is the typical mighty king god, hedged about with divinity, awe and sycophancy. Here, for instance, is described the approach of the noble Sinuhe, whose success story was the favourite reading of Egyptians for generations. At this juncture he is an old man, returning to be magnanimously pardoned for having incontinently fled the kingdom at his master's accession.

I touched the ground between the sphinxes with my forehead, and the royal children stood in the gateway and received me, and the Chamberlains, that conduct to the hall, set me on the way to the Privy Chamber. I found his majesty on his great throne in the golden gateway. When I had stretched myself on my belly, my wits forsook me in his presence, albeit this god addressed me kindly.

The Pharaoh's children enter and ceremoniously address the king-god and his consort holding out "their necklaces, their rattles, and their sistra":

"Thy hands be on the Beauteous One, O long-living King, on the ornament of the Lady of Heaven. May the Golden One give life to thy nose [the seat of breath and life], and the Mistress of the Stars join herself to thee. May the Upper Egyptian crown go down stream, and the Lower Egyptian crown go up stream, and be joined both together in the mouth of thy majesty. May the serpent be set on thy brow."

There is a good deal more of this before they allow themselves to plead for the kind reception of this returned wanderer and prodigal son, this "barbarian born in Egypt". But Sinuhe, who has been sojourning in that same land of Aam, and indeed highly successfully, has come back dressed as a bedouin, and it is a significant touch in the story that Pharaoh's children before their ceremonial hymn of praise have, with their mother, behaved much more humanly.

Said his majesty to the Queen: "See, this is Sinuhe, who hath come back as an Asiatic, a creature of the Bedouins." She uttered an exceeding loud cry, and the royal children shrieked out together. They said unto his majesty: "It is not he in sooth, O king, my lord!"

It apparently needed not only the king's word but a perfumed bath and some fine linen to make them believe the truth.*

This is a story to illustrate well not only the majesty of the Pharaoh but the state of sophisticated, rich and hierarchical civilization to which the Egyptians had reached and the contrast, of which they were perhaps exaggeratedly aware, between themselves and the peoples who ringed them round. The riches, the building activity, the artistic skill of the country, all are at this time increasing greatly. The builders, the architects, the artists, and also the rich for whom they cater, make great demands for material, so that the quasi-military, quasi-commercial expeditions penetrate north as far as the Orontes—near the banks of which a later Pharaoh will do great deeds—and south into Nubia and Ethiopia or the Land of Cush, whence will be extracted gold and ebony and ivory, and ostrich feathers and leopard skins and the tasselled tails of giraffes. Meanwhile the people will be law-abiding and will seek advancement, it seems, not by intrigue and violence but by hard work and the careful fostering of the regard of those in whose hands lies promotion. The laws of property and of inheritance become strict and detailed. The demands of the priesthood are regularized and elaborate—a certain temple superintendent is shown as due to receive daily not only eight jugs of beer but sixteen loaves of varying sizes. Though there is given a much greater impression of spaciousness and of creative ability than in the parallel civilization of the Harappans, still flourishing at this time, yet the Middle Kingdom Egyptians may have been nearly as closely regimented. The common people at this time developed their worship of the great trinity of gods, Osiris, Isis, and her infant Horus, mostly a friendly and homely trio. It is also significant that the falcon-headed war-god, Month or Mont, to be revived by the Pharaoh who later goes to war on the Orontes, becomes at present less in favour than the Theban (and human-headed) god of nature and fecundity, Amun, later to be allied to the Sun God to become Amun-Rē. From the nomes on the outskirts and the Maginot Line of the blockhouses, the officials keep a wary and protective eye, and report back to their Pharaoh: "All the affairs of the King's domain are safe and sound."

*Quotations taken from Adolf Erman's book of translations, previously referred to.

But then the Twelfth Dynasty peters out in the reign of a woman, denoting dynastic dispute, and in weakness. And if the comforting reports on the state of the realm continue they are not true, for weakness within always attracts the nomads from without. There comes now, in the shape of the so-called Second Intermediate Period, the rule of the Hyksos or Shepherd Kings.

"Shepherd Kings" is not the correct translation of the word *Hyksos*, which should be "chieftain of a foreign hill-country". It does not give an altogether wrong idea, nevertheless, for here were the flock-tending bedouin, the nomads again. Josephus, the Jewish historian of the first century A.D., wanted to see in the word's derivation the meaning "captive-shepherd", and that error, too, is not without significance. For the truth of the story of Joseph and his brethren may genuinely lie within this Hyksos invasion, which may even have been in part, or at its start, a humble and a peaceful invasion. Not much is known about these times in Egypt, and what is told about it by the Egyptians themselves may well give a false impression, for there is an obvious tendency to exaggerate the terror and misery so that the greatness of the ultimate liberators may be enhanced. It was a foreign domination indeed. But the Hyksos dynasty—there were probably six generations of it—seem to have been at pains to conciliate the native inhabitants and (like most barbarian invaders throughout history) to ape the greatness they had usurped, giving themselves names compounded of the Sun God Rē and adopting the use of the hieroglyphic writing. Nor does it seem that they ever fully conquered the Upper Kingdom.

Benefits they did leave behind, or at least new things, and two that were significant. These were bronze weapons and the horse-and-chariot, without either of which a peaceful Egypt, however, had managed so far very successfully to thrive.

The process of expulsion of the Hyksos may well have been more painful for the inhabitants than the invaders. Khamose is the first liberator. He possessed power around his native Thebes but no more—except ambition. He is described as complaining to his courtiers, "I should like to know what serves this strength of mine, when a chieftain is in Avaris (the Hyksos capital, in the Delta), and another in Cush, and I sit united with an Asiatic and a Nubian, each man in his possession of his slice of this Egypt." The courtiers, as do all Egyptian courtiers in the annals, thereby giving highlight to the Pharaoh's heroism, counsel caution: things are not so bad and why seek to disturb them? Khamose's reply is that they are wrong and he will fight—as he has already said, he will grapple with the Hyksos king "and rip open his belly".

Khamose does fight his enemy successfully. "When the earth became light I was upon him as it were a hawk. The time of perfuming the mouth [euphuism for lunch or breakfast] came and I overthrew him. I razed his wall, I slew his people and I caused his wife to go down to the river-bank" [as captive, presumably]. Soon Khamose is taunting an already half-beaten enemy. And then he boasts of his ruthless treatment of his own unheroic and too complacent people:

I razed their towns and burned their places, they being made into red ruins for ever on account of the damage which they did within this Egypt, and they made themselves serve the Asiatics and had forsaken Egypt their mistress.

This is a new sort of talk for an Egyptian Pharaoh, who had erstwhile preferred to boast of the blessings of peace that he had brought to his people. It is to be followed soon by that other new phrase, "extend the boundaries". In fact, if the first Intermediate Period left the Egyptian people shocked into a craving for peace and ordered government, then the second period left Egypt's ruling caste shamed into a craving for power and glory. There comes now the famous Eighteenth Dynasty of fighting Pharaohs, chieftains who leave behind legends of personal prowess—two of the Tuthmoses are fabulous bowmen just as a later Odysseus, whose ancestors were at this very time settling along the shores of Greece, was a fabulous bowman, whilst another, foreshadowing Achilles, is a tremendous athlete, rowing as strongly as two hundred men.

The great names of this dynasty are the above-mentioned Tuthmosis (once wrongly called Thothmes) and Amenophis (un-Greek equivalent, Amenhotep), three of the former and four of the latter. Most famous, perhaps, are Tuthmosis I and III and Amenophis II, III and IV, the last, however, famous by no means as a warrior but because he changed his name, significantly, to Akhneten. The span between the accession of the first Amenophis and the last apostate one is exactly two hundred years, 1550 to 1350, and Egyptian dates have by this period become certain to within a year or two. Between the warriors comes one who was content to gather fame at home, and she was a woman, Queen Hatshetsup, or to give her the slightly more meiufluous name that Sir Alan Gardiner insists is the more correct one,

Hashepsowe. Hashepsowe was a remarkable woman and it is a pity that because she does not noticeably appear on the international scene we cannot pay much attention to her. She was the first person that we hear of as wearing masculine dress: she assumed the full title, status and regalia of the Pharaoh, down to the little wooden imitation beard. She has two particular claims to our attention. The usual pharaonic boasting was focused in her reign upon deeds of architectural ostentation and her reference to the amount of gold she used, however discounted, shows that imperial Egypt was growing very rich indeed. The other point is that by managing to hang on to the throne for what should have been the first years of her son's reign she must have seriously cramped his style and set him all the more determinedly on a renewed course of conquest and military campaigning.

This son was Tuthmosis III (1490 to 1468). And it is to him (in his eighth campaign) that the Hittite king sent gifts and with whom he therefore probably allied himself when he set out to destroy Aleppo and to found the 250-year-long Hittite empire.

CHAPTER XI

Minoans and Mycenaeans

WHAT is happening, we must ask, on the northern arch of the Fertile Crescent that Hittite and Egyptian should meet there.

There is beginning a time of movement and increasing turmoil that finally and through the course of two crucial centuries, the fourteenth and thirteenth centuries B.C., affects the whole of the Eastern Mediterranean world. To understand this we must turn next to the civilization of Crete in its great days and to the rise to power of the Greek-speaking Mycenaeans. We shall find that at about the time of the fall of Aleppo the Cretan aristocracy are becoming Greek-speaking, a fact very surprising to historians when it was lately discovered and no doubt highly significant to the Minoans when it happened. That it cannot have been wholly unconnected with the end of their greatness which was little more than half a century ahead cannot have been apparent to them, any more than it can have been apparent to the defenders of Aleppo that their troubles and all the turmoil around them had its chief basic cause in the restlessness of that great parent Aryan-speaking stock one offshoot of which was Mycenaean. For a prosperous and pleasure-loving civilization that habitually looked to its original mentors in the south and east there was an ominous thunder on the left to which, however, their ears were as yet completely untuned.

That the Late Minoan civilization was a pleasure-loving one seems reasonably apparent. We may do them an injustice, however. For there is something about our knowledge that, with Sir Arthur Evans's dramatic discoveries and his brilliant exploitation of their significance still in our memory, we are likely to forget. It is simply that this knowledge is not large; compared with that of Egypt or Mesopotamia it may be called exiguous. The Minoans have left, or at least there has been discovered, practically no written records that tell us of their history. This statement is not meant to belittle Michael Ventris's decipherment of the "Linear B" writing. It is to say that such writing was used, it seems clear, for little more than country-estate accounting, that it was not a sufficiently flexible instrument for anything much more demanding, and that it seems to have been used, at least on the mainland of Crete, for no longer period than half a century or so. Its predecessor, Linear A, must have been an even more rudimentary instrument, and unless very unexpected discoveries are made the fact that it has not been deciphered can be accepted by the historian with no great regret.

All this may signify something more than that our knowledge of Minoan history cannot be great. It may mean that there is really not much history to know—happy are a people who have no history, and the Minoans were happy in the sea that surrounded and isolated them so long as they had command of it. It may mean also, from the very fact that they developed no efficient writing, that for all the sophistication and luxury of their later days they had not so very much in the way of thought and the immaterial inventions that was of lasting significance.

The greatest importance of the Minoan Empire is that it acted, rather as the Roman Empire was to act, as a carrier into Europe and so into the rest of the world of the benefits of civilizations that preceded it—duly stamped nevertheless with its own individuality in the process.

Let us not overdo the minimizing. For the stamp of Minoan individuality was certainly distinctive; and Minoan culture of the Second Millennium is a colourful, exciting and unique affair. It will be well to list its outstanding characteristics, shown by its relics, from tiny signet seals and delicate figurines to the whole sprawling but controlled mass of the palaces of Knossos and Phaistos. They are: a great architectural skill, particularly in the practical aspects of comfort, such as light wells and drainage; delicate artistic skill rivalling the Egyptian but much less bound by formality; a love of nature and of the decorativeness in particular of the creatures of the sea, as exemplified in the designs on their pottery and frescoes, and a love of brightness and colour, as exemplified in those same frescoes; a cheerful pleasure, not to say coquettishness, in dress and personal ornament, both male and female; a passion for athletics and spectacles of bodily skill.

The Minoans had their mythical great architect as had the Egyptians. But whereas Imhotep was also a great writer and healer, Daedalus was also a great artificer. After his indiscretion over Ariadne he successfully flew (or sailed?) away from the wrath of his king; but his own ingenuity betrayed him, for when he solved the riddle of how to place a thread from one end to the other of a spiral shell (by harnessing an ant and letting it do the job), the avenging King Minos knew that he had caught up with the man who had lost him his daughter. Daedalus is the cunning man, forerunner of Odysseus though rather undeservedly less lucky. Perhaps it was Daedalus, or a man of the school of Daedalus, who solved the problem of preventing the rainwater, that at Knossos ran down a series of flights of steps at right angles to each other, from pouring over the platforms at each junction. This he did by making the runnels at the side parabolic, giving the water its natural course in fall and thus so reducing its speed that it could be kept in bounds.

A spectacle for a pleasure-loving people: from a Minoan rhyton

Engineering and plumbing do not make a civilization, however, and it is a dull mind that is most impressed by the W.C.s of the palace of Knossos. Perhaps the greatest significance of the place is that it is a palace and not a temple and a palace for the living and not for the dead. Here is the difference from Babylonia and Egypt.

Which is not to say that the Minoans were irreligious, though it does illustrate a very different outlook.

There are the snake goddesses and the bulls. How do these connect; and did the Minoans merely play with the bull or worship it? To take the second question first, the answer can only be "both". The Minoans seem to be obsessed by bulls. But the wild aurochs is a most imposing animal, bigger than the modern bull and certainly more athletic than the walking steaks that lumber about our agricultural show-rings. And even now the bull is a symbol of lustiness. To tame it and then to match against its strength and grace the strength and grace of men and girls who also had superior wit and cunning, this was not an unnatural thing to do for a people who had the affluence and leisure sufficient to spend the time and energy required. The famous bull leap is at least something that, so far as we know, no one has ever had the temerity to try since the fifteenth century B.C. If Theseus succeeded in it before he carried off an admiring Ariadne, it would be interesting to know how many months' training he needed beforehand. The average life-span of the heroic bull-athlete—bejewelled, decorated, hair-curled, idolized— would also be an interesting figure to have.

All that is not religion, however, any more than plumbing is civilization, except in so far as a symbol of lustiness is also a symbol of a desired and worshipful Nature's fecundity. The Minoan god is a goddess. And her familiar and emblem is the snake, which, with his belly to the ground, is acceptedly a symbol of the earth. Here then can be nothing more than another emanation of the familiar Earth-Goddess of all antiquity, the comforting mother who like Egyptian Isis is the fount of all richness and life and beneficence. No primitive religion, however, has been merely cosy, at least not after the priests get hold of it. The snake element is a little sinister. Perhaps this was another Minoan example of man pitting himself *against* an animal. The female figures intertwined with snakes may all be priestesses rather than goddesses; and there is something heroic in conquering one's natural aversion of the reptile and sufficiently penetrating its dim mind to be able to control it—or at least something impressive and spectacular. Perhaps the Minoans were exhibitionists.

Another aspect of their earth religion—to give it its resounding scientific-Greek title, their chthonic religion—was even more sinister. This is where enters the probable connection with the bull; it is an interpretation made by Sir Arthur Evans and given in his own monumental *The Palace of Minos* and also expertly summarized in Leonard Cottrell's book that covers the exploits of both Henry Schliemann and Arthur Evans, *The Bull of Minos*. An unexpected aspect of the palace of Knossos discovered by Evans was the number of occasions, at least three, on which it was devastated and rebuilt. Evans knew of the propensity of Crete to suffer seismic shocks and had indeed personally experienced them. This led him to make inquiry into more recent historical times and to discover that the island experienced a major earthquake on average once a century. He believed, therefore, that the Knossos devastation was natural and not man-made: the Minoans must have had a very healthy fear, not to say horror, of earthquakes. But not only that. Evans found a connection between bulls and earthquakes. In unearthing a building that had obviously suffered ruin from earthquake he discovered the skulls of two bulls, placed near to tripod altars, obviously propitiatory sacrifices. There was also the line in the *Iliad*: "In Bulls does the Earth-shaker delight." Then he experienced a more serious earth-shock himself. From the safety of the ferro-concrete *Villa Ariadne* which he had had built for himself he watched and listened. The bells of Candia's cathedral were moved to chime, women shrieked, the roofs of two small houses crashed, a mist of dust arose, and "a dull sound arose from the ground like the muffled roar of an angry bull". There comes to mind obviously, as there came to Sir Arthur Evans's mind, the fable that King Minos kept in the depths of his labyrinth a terrible monster, the Minotaur, who was bull-headed. There was also the fact that the only obviously religious aspects of the palace, the lustral chambers containing sinks or stands for human anointing, the pillared crypt that provided for the catching of sacrificial blood, were all underground. Did on solemn feast days or at times of emergency King Minos, as high priest as well as monarch, don the ritual mask of a bull and make propitiatory sacrifice?

A religion, then, compounded perhaps of primitiveness, exhibitionism and fear, yet not observed with any great depths of passion, except for that fear which will drive any man to sincerity when it arrives. Such is not a very complimentary analysis. Put it rather that the Minoans seem less overwhelmed by superstition and the rule of the priest than any other of the early civilizations, a trait that we at least like to feel is European rather than Oriental.

And finally, two other aspects of Minoan civilization that help to give a picture that we can admire rather than deride. The first is that King Minos—title of a dynasty rather than the name of an individual— came down to the Greeks by reputation not only as a great ruler of an empire of the seas, a thalassocracy, but as a great law-giver. Like Hammurabi before him and Moses after him, Minos received the tablets of the law straight from the god himself, in this instance from Zeus in his awe-inspiring cave in the Cretan mountains. One cannot imagine the Minoans regimented; but they may in fact have enjoyed the protection of good laws and sound justice. The other significant aspect is that they are men of peace, with less evidence of weapons of war and certainly of fortifications to their cities than even the Egyptians. They depended upon their command of the sea.

That they finally lost that command becomes all too obvious, for their civilization is snuffed out almost as suddenly and completely as a candle flame between wetted finger and thumb. A description of their end, however, we will leave to an ensuing chapter. Here we will look at their history up to some fifty years before that catastrophe which came "on some spring day around the year 1400, when the wind was in the south".

There is in truth not much to tell. There are falls and rebuildings of the palaces and ensuing changes, not drastic, in styles of architecture and ceramics that enable the archaeologists, following Evans's lead, to make their divisions and subdivisions of Early, Middle and Late Minoan cultures. There are hints of an influence of outside events upon this isolated and self-sufficient people.

Early Minoan ended roughly at the turn of the millennium, 2000 B.C., or some would say as late as 1800. Middle and Late Minoan extend to about 1200 B.C., but the last two centuries are a time of enormously diminished greatness, the full flowering of the Minoan civilization being, therefore, a matter of only four or at most six hundred years. At its beginning Crete is for the first time united, culturally if not politically; Phaistos during the ensuing centuries may have been a rival of or a subsidiary to Knossos, towards the end almost certainly the latter.

The trading connections are already established and the Minoan ships have for long been commanding the surrounding seas. Trading stations may have led to colonies, in Cyprus as well as the Cyclades, for instance. Evidence of trade with the Hittites has even been found.

But soon after 1800 Egypt is suffering her second relapse into anarchy and then the comparative barbarism of the Hyksos rule. The effect is apparent. The Minoans turn their eyes northwards. They set up their trading stations and then their colonies on the mainland of Greece, on the Peloponnese. Up through Sparta and the fertile plain of Argos they come and then through the mountain pass to the Gulf of Corinth. The new sites of cities and citadels appear: Vaphio, Sparta, Asine, Tiryns, Mycenae, Argos, Corinth. Where now lies the slit of the

Corinth Canal porterage would have carried the trade goods from one arm of the sea to the other; and where there is porterage there are dues to be paid and the controlling prince grows rich. This sea route itself for that matter may now have been Cretan, taken over from the first important town of Troy, "Troy II" which fairly recently had succumbed very completely to some enemy unknown.

1580 or thereabouts sees a collapse of Knossos and a rebuilding, and conveniently dates for the archaeologist the end of *Middle Minoan* culture and the beginning of *Late*. Crete is now at the top of her curve of greatness, enjoying her Classical era, soon beginning to show signs of effeteness and decline. This is the time, too, of Egypt's return to greatness, and we now see depicted on her commemorative walls the "Keftiu", who by their hair-styles and their dress are wellnigh unmistakably Minoans. They appear not as captives nor as suppliants, but as equals, proudly bearing gifts.

1450 is the last date before the tragedy of 1400. It has a double significance. Phaistos but not Knossos appears to suffer about now some sort of catastrophe. The Linear A writing, which had displaced the earlier crude pictographic hieroglyphs a hundred years or so earlier, now in turn gives way to the Linear B. And the Linear B which the scribes and storekeepers are scratching on to tablets and shards is being scratched too on the Greek mainland, and the language it scratches, in all instances, *is an early Greek*.

We are led, obviously and inevitably, to the Mycenaeans.

Were the Mycenaeans Greeks or Cretans; were they Aryan-speakers, part of the tide from the north that had started to move at the turn of the millennium, or part of the original neolithic, "dark-white" Mediterranean population? It is important to answer this clearly. To say that they were probably a mixture does not help at all: all races soon become mixtures but they retain their original spirit and culture. To say that it is not easy to be clear is not helpful either: something can be done. One thing must be understood at the start: the Mycenaeans, once called more vaguely the Aegeans, are called so because Mycenae, lying where the plain of Argos lifts itself up northwards to mountains, was their principal citadel. Now it is true that here and about here the finds—seals and scraps of fresco—have shown a remarkable affinity to the Minoan—it was the *foreignness* of them that first set Arthur Evans on his search for an outside origin. But these finds are not wholly Minoan in character. The subjects depicted are hunting and fighting: the manner, in fact, is Minoan but the matter not so. On the one hand there are signs that, as has been said, Minoan traders were turning away from Egypt to Greece from about 1750 onwards; on the other there are signs that by this time or even earlier Aryan-speakers have penetrated into the Peloponnese and are ousting or subjugating in their masterful way the aboriginal "Pelasgians", as they called them. One of two things then: the first lords of Mycenae and its satellites were either Minoans who rapidly took on the way of life of the local Aryan-speaking aristocracy, or they were Aryan-speaking aristocrats who had allowed Minoans to teach them how to

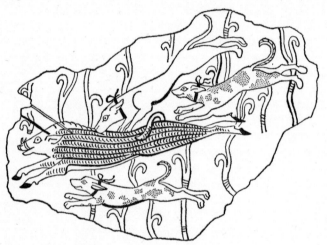

The manner Minoan, the matter Mycenaean: fresco (restored)
from Tiryns

become rich. From that uncertainty, however, we can go to a certainty. By the fifteenth century at latest the Mycenaeans have become entirely distinctive and entirely different from the Minoans. This has happened either by brute force—there is a fabled dynastic tussle at Mycenae—or by moral force. The Mycenaeans are "themselves", very distinctly so; and all their deeper affinities lie with those always masterful and aristocratic invaders from the north. The Mycenaeans *are* the first Greeks.

We are back in times as feudal, though on a smaller scale, as Egypt's Middle Kingdom. We are forward as it were in times as aristocratic and heroic as those of the Saxons and the Vikings, into times almost, it might be said, of the eighteenth-century English country gentleman, duly substituting for "hunting, shooting and fishing" hunting, shooting and fighting.

The sources for assessing the Mycenaeans are more plentiful than the corresponding Minoan. There are the archaeological finds, almost as spectacular; there is the Linear B script, deciphered by Michael Ventris with the help of John Chadwick and others and found on tablets at more than one Mycenaean site as well as at Knossos; there is the *Iliad* and the *Odyssey*. The three sources have to be treated with respect and

Mycenaean "treasure": a gold cup showing a bull ensnared by
a decoy

caution and the last with some measure of disbelief when it fails to tally with either of the other two. Homer, it must be remembered, is in time a very long way ahead. He wrote probably *in* the eighth century B.C. and *of* the early years of the twelfth century, when the Mycenaean civilization was rapidly approaching its end. However, if we can look at the Egyptian ways of life a thousand years apart and find them only superficially distinguishable, there is no reason to suppose that we cannot do the same with Mycenaean life in, say, 1650 (the probable dating of Henry Schliemann's great finds) and at 1190 which is generally thought to date very closely the fall of Troy.

Homer, too, was telling of what had come down to him; and when men have no writing to make them slack and lazy in the matter their memories are always quite phenomenally good. In point of fact Homer is a mixture, at times imputing to the heroes of Troy the customs of his own age—the burning of the dead, for instance—and at times remarkably accurate, even to the extent of contradicting himself. Usually, for instance, he speaks of round shields; but once he graphically describes a different sort: Hector returning to rally his townsmen and with his tall shield slung behind him and "tapping his heels as he walked". The tall type of shield is corroborated by finds both at Mycenae and—showing the Minoan influence—at Knossos. Perhaps Homer's most spectacular piece of detailed accuracy is his description of a cup decorated with doves which on one occasion Odysseus uses: its exact replica, except that it has two handles instead of the described four, was found by Schliemann in the shaft graves at Mycenae and dating, it is now believed, about 1650. Treasures in those days were kept and remembered.

"Treasure" is, in fact, one of the key words in describing the Mycenaean aristocracy. Though the primary point to realize is how very definitely it was an aristocracy. In Homer nobody matters except the heroes (and, of course, the gods, who help or hinder the heroes) and it is easy to see that nobody matters to the heroes except themselves —on the only occasions in which Odysseus has to deal with the lower orders he treats them harshly and as if to appeal to their better nature or sense of honour was, by contrast, a complete waste of time. On the big country estate, in the household or *oikos*, there is the noble family, of three generations (or even four if war has by good fortune failed to shorten life); there are the retainers, from chamberlains such as Menelaus's "my lord Eteoneus", or the young Achilles' squire and friend, Patroclus, down to the farm hand and old retainer such as Odysseus' Emmaeus, the swineherd; there are the specialists and experts, headed in importance by the metal workers; there are the slaves, predominantly female; and, hovering disconsolately on the periphery, the *thes*, the masterless man who owes allegiance to and can seek protection from no man. And the noble family itself lives in splendour. Homer describes it, no doubt with some loving exaggeration. Here is the youthful Telemachus, son of Odysseus, talking to his friend, the son of Nestor, after being dined in the great pillared *megaron* of King Menelaus:

"Look around this echoing hall, my dear Peisistratus. The whole place gleams with copper and gold, amber and silver and ivory."

And then Helen, a reformed and matronly but still beautiful Helen:

... Helen with her ladies came down from her lofty perfumed room, looking like Artemis with her golden distaff. Adreste drew up for her a comfortable chair; Alcippa brought a rug of the softest wool; while Phylo carried her silver work-basket, a gift from Alcandre, wife of Polybus, who lived in Egyptian Thebes, where the houses are furnished in the most sumptuous fashion.*

Now here is wealth and ostentation. Where did the wealth come from? Partly, of course, from the land that was farmed—there are references in the Linear B tablets to flocks of sheep of surprising magnitude, and these will be accounting figures and not literary ones and so much more likely to be accurate. But that source was not sufficient by a long way.

The first extraneous source is not exactly trade. It is its gentlemanly equivalent. It would not be quite right to call the Mycenaean seigneurs merchant princes. At times "robber baron" might be nearer the mark: the Prince of Mycenae, as did the Prince of Troy, sat himself at a strategic point and exacted his due from the trading caravans that had to pass that way. A better title would be Dispenser and Receiver of "Gifts". The Mycenaeans were not alone in this practice. There are the Keftiu on the Egyptian walls; we shall be hearing of bitter complaints by lesser breeds of Eastern royalty of the inadequacy and infrequency of the current Pharaoh's munificence; and there is even a strong resemblance in the modern African system of "dashing". It is really trade at one remove, and smelling sweeter to the proud and sensitive aristocrat by being given another name. Odysseus is affronted when one of Penelope's suitors, failing to pierce his disguise, suggests that he may be a trader—no, he is a player of games, and the dangerous game of shooting arrows in particular. All the Homeric heroes exchange gifts; and it would have been unthinkable for them not to have honoured their own side of the tacit bargain, and perhaps unthinkable too not to have had to suit the greatness of the recipient by the greatness of the gift.

*This and ensuing quotations are from E. V. Rieu's translation of the *Odyssey* (Penguin Books, 1945). Remains of Egyptian works of art, gifts from Amenophis II and III, have been found at Mycenae.

Each *oikos*, therefore, had its storeroom, as important a place as the megaron; and therein, meticulously accounted for, was kept the Treasure. It would have contained the more down-to-earth emblems of riches, the great jars of corn and wine and oil. But it would also have contained the gifts, the great works of art, in particular the works of metal made by those most important of the specialists, the resident smiths and tinkers, men who would be treated with special consideration—there is possible evidence of this on one of the Linear B tablets—lest he should take up his tools of trade and go elsewhere. The point of this system is that it is an aristocratic system, one that hid the sordid calculation even when it was present and that demonstrated magnificently the openness of hand and heart. It did not create wealth—the slave and the specialist did that—but it kept it in circulation and perhaps tended to give more to him who already had. . . .

The other method open to the Mycenaean princes of obtaining wealth, if not of creating it, was to go to war.

This they did with zest. Here was the advantage of obtaining wealth not from your friends but your enemies. It also obtained for you wealth-producing wealth, the slave. A proud title of the Homeric heroes is "sacker of cities". And when a city was sacked the usual fate of the men was death and of the women and children slavery, even the highest not being exempt, witness the sad forebodings in the *Iliad* of Hector's Andromache and the fact that one of Helen's women was, by repute, Aethra, who was none other than the mother of Theseus and had been taken captive on the Argive's revenge for Theseus' rash attempt to forestall Paris in the abduction of the most beautiful of women.

Now, these two methods of obtaining wealth and prestige have a deeper significance, in that they both illustrate a point of view, a tradition. The Mycenaeans may not have been alone in this, it may be a growing phenomenon in the world of the Second Millennium. But they possess the tradition paramountly. It is a tradition of pride, and of glory. Of heroism and of heroics. There is one task and one task only for a prince, and that is to gain glory. Says Hector hopefully of his baby son as he holds him in his arms for the last time:

"Zeus, and you other gods, grant that this boy of mine may be, like me, pre-eminent in Troy; as strong and brave as I; a mighty king of Ilium. May people say, when he comes back from battle, 'Here is a better man than his father.' Let him bring home the

"A prince of Mycenae". The gold death-mask discovered
by Schliemann

bloodstained armour of the enemy he has killed, and make his
mother happy."

Achilles is made a little to see the sadness of the tradition, the flaw
in it, which is the probability of an early death. But that is Homer
speaking, not Achilles. Whatever doubts or deeper thoughts they may
have had on occasion, the typical Mycenaean nursed unquestioningly
a tradition and code that had little regard for gentleness or mercy but
great regard for heroism and honour and glory in war. . . .

And like the Vikings after them, the Mycenaeans went out to seek
it. They did not, we may say on second thoughts, possess an empire,
but rather an area in which they raided. They went on doing it to the
end, in fact until they were made to swallow their own bitter medicine.
In the following chapters we shall see them doing it, sometimes no
more than apparently minor characters in events of greater import.
They had their own significance none the less.

CHAPTER XII

First Megiddo

*That vile enemy, of Kadesh, has come and entered into Megiddo,
and he is there at this moment. He has gathered to himself the princes
of all lands who were loyal to Egypt . . . their horses, their soldiers, and
their people. And he says—so they say—"I will stand to fight against
His Majesty here in Megiddo." Tell me what is in your hearts.*

So, by his records at Karnak, the great Pharaoh, Tuthmosis III, spoke
to his generals at a council of war. The year is 1468 or thereabouts and
it is only a couple of years since the once-young monarch had at last
freed himself from his outwardly peaceful but dynastically repressive
stepmother and aunt, Hashepsowe, and had come to be sole ruler.
He has wasted little time before setting out north and east across the
desert to show the world his prowess and to "extend the boundaries of
Egypt in accordance with the command of his father Amun-Rē".

His less heroic generals, so the record goes, objected that the road to
Megiddo was through a dangerously narrow defile (the entrance, in
fact, of the plain of Jordan into the mountains of Lebanon):

Will not horse have to go behind horse, and soldiers and people
likewise? Shall our own vanguard be fighting, while the rear stands
here in Aruna and does not fight? Now there are two roads here.

Tuthmosis, however, was resolute and bold, as befitted a New
Kingdom Pharaoh and an empire builder:

As I live, as Rē loves me, as my father Amun favours me, and
as I am rejuvenated with life and power, My Majesty will proceed
along this Aruna road.

Here is the curtain-raiser to those two centuries of vast turmoil and
change, the fourteenth and thirteenth centuries B.C.

By 1468 Egypt had reached half-way in her two-century span of
uninterrupted greatness and prosperity after the final expulsion of the

Hyksos foreigners and the inception of his New Kingdom. Amenophis I had changed the policy of his father Amosis, a second liberator, to one of extending the boundaries. This he had done mostly in the south, colonizing Nubia and leaving behind viceroys. His son, "raging like a panther", had first continued this process, returning triumphantly down the Nile with the body of a recalcitrant chieftain hung upside down at the prow of his vessel. Then he had, with the new-found war weapon that the Hyksos had bequeathed to him, the horse and chariot, made spectacular progress across Palestine and Syria to meet and subdue the people called the Mitanni, crossing the upper reaches of the Euphrates to do so. On his way back, in heroic and sporting vein, he had indulged in an elephant hunt. His son, Tuthmosis II, though seemingly a lesser man, also raged like a panther, and by punitive raids managed to keep the outposts of his empire relatively quiet, both south and north. There followed the reign of Hashepsowe, first alone and then ostensibly as no more than co-regent with this Tuthmosis III of the battle of Megiddo. She built, as we have said, magnificently, boasting of the wealth of gold that she used, and did much to restore Egypt's Hyksos-defiled religious sanctuaries and no doubt to a parallel extent her country's pride and self-respect. But the subjugated peoples on the outskirts of Egypt's empire would always revolt if left too long unimpressed by a sight of military power. Hence the rising of the Prince of Kadesh and his friends, and the first recorded battle of Megiddo or Armageddon.

Tuthmosis III

After three days' rest at Aruna the Pharaoh Tuthmosis III set out at the head of his troops, carrying before him the image of Amun. His boldness was justified and his army emerged from the pass unharmed. Now, however, he did accept the cautious advice of his generals, restrained his impetuosity and waited for the full strength of his army to form up in his rear. It was too late to join battle that day and his army bivouacked for the night. In fact they did not even attack the

9

next day, Sir Alan Gardiner in the book already mentioned suggesting that the pause was in order to observe the festival of the new moon. That is reminiscent of a much later battle, Alfred's first victory on the Berkshire Downs, where the young prince took the initiative from his elder brother who delayed battle in order to attend Mass; no doubt there have been many ancient battles lost—or sometimes won—by a strict religious observance. Tuthmosis at any rate did not suffer from the delay. He entered the battle "on a chariot of gold equipped with his panoply of arms like Horus, Brandisher of Arm, Lord of Action; and like Mont the Theban". And he routed his enemies, who, leaving behind their own disabled chariots of gold and of silver, were soon being ignominiously hooked up by their clothing over the ramparts of the town of Megiddo, the gates of which had been closed by its frightened citizens.

There follows a likeness to a much later battle, the German advance of 1918, and indeed again no doubt to many battles. The victorious troops slowed down their advance in order to loot, and the chance to storm an unprepared fortress manned by the demoralized remnants of an army was lost. Tuthmosis had to exhort his troops to patience and renewed effort: "All the princes of all the northern countries are cooped up within. . . . The capture of Megiddo is the capture of a thousand towns." The siege was certainly not so long as the reputed siege of Troy, but to the Egyptian troops, great home-lovers, it must have seemed long enough. In the seventh month Megiddo capitulated and the first victorious campaign of Tuthmosis III was over. There were very many to follow, but this was the one that the heroic Pharaoh seems always to have remembered most proudly.

The recurring campaigns proved necessary because Palestine and Syria were not like Nubia which could apparently be kept pacified by the leaving behind of viceroys and an occasional show of a corpse hung upside-down on a Pharaoh's barge. These lands were occupied by small townships or principalities, whose princes and chiefs—the Egyptian description of the Megiddo campaign lists no less than 350 of them—not only quarrelled amongst themselves and entered into an ever-shifting kaleidoscope of alliances but also sought protection from the greater and more menacing powers that existed to the north and east. In all, Tuthmosis III boasted of fourteen campaigns in this part of the world. The stele that tells of his exploits shows also that some diplomacy was used as well as pure force. Fresh princes of Egypt's choosing were installed, their brothers and children taken away as hostages, while Egyptian skilled cultivators were sometimes left behind; where necessary, on the other hand, a policy of ruthless harrying of the land was adopted. Coastal ports were equipped with rations and stores, so that at least some of Egypt's army could be moved by sea to a point of danger.

The greater kings behind this Palestinian frontier must have watched and listened and been impressed. But a mere show of force and efficiency was by no means enough to keep them quiet. Or at least so Egypt feared and believed, and probably with good reason. If Palestine and Syria were a simmer of unrest, the lands of Asia Minor and of the rest of the Fertile Crescent were intermittently boiling. Babylon, after that spectacular early raid of the Hittites that seemed to have overtaxed their strength, had been taken over by the Kassites, probably yet another, easterly, branch of the overwhelming Aryan-speaking tide and the eventual colonizers of Persia. These were being relatively quiet, though later we shall witness their kings writing importunate or impertinent letters to the reigning Pharaoh. North of them the Assyrians, at their capital of Assur, are as it were biding their time before bursting into the pages of history. But westward of them and extending to the Euphrates (which here flows only some hundred miles from the tip of the Mediterranean's eastern coastline) existed a people already much more militant. Here was the land of the Mitanni, an already powerful kingdom which, judging by what is known of its language, had already come to be Aryan-led, the bulk of its population (and so of its rank-and-file soldiers) being probably Semites known as the Hurrians. Farther west, into Asia Minor, are the redoubtable Hittites, suffering at this time trouble on their western frontier from princelings of coastal towns, as numerous and restless perhaps as those of Syria and Palestine, and on their eastern borders from these same Mitanni.

Gradually in the light of recent excavations the Mitanni are assuming a greater importance, and it may be that we should earlier have accorded them the status of Empire, along with Egyptians, Babylonians, Hittites, Minoans and Mycenaeans. The site of their capital city has not yet, however, been discovered, and our knowledge of them comes mostly from the records of their enemies (or on occasion suspicious allies) the Egyptians and the Hittites.

If Megiddo, in fact, was the most memorable to Tuthmosis III of his campaigns, his eighth, against the Mitanni, must have been the most difficult and spectacular, taking him as it did as far afield as his grandfather, Tuthmosis I, and so far as any Pharaoh for 800 years had penetrated. As illustrating the might of fifteenth-century Egypt, this campaign merits some description—or rather quotation from Tuthmosis's contemporary description. (The river referred to is, of course, the Euphrates, "Nahrin" is the Egyptian name for the country of the Mitanni, and "the-mistress-of-Byblos", that is to say its goddess, signifies the town itself. "Chariots" equal wagons).

My Majesty crossed to the farthest limits of Asia(!). I caused to be built many boats of cedar on the hills of the God's Land in the neighbourhood of the mistress-of-Byblos. They were placed on chariots, oxen dragging them, and they journeyed in front of My Majesty in order to cross that great river which flows between this country and Nahrin. Nay, but he is a king to be boasted of in proportion to the performance of his two arms in battle—one (person, not arm) who crossed the Euphrates in pursuit of him who attacked him; first of his army in seeking that vile enemy over the mountains of Mitanni, while he fled through fear before His Majesty to another far distant land.

The pronouns in the second part are a little confusing; but the feat described in the first part is clear enough and need not be doubted. It represents a porterage of 250 miles, greater one would imagine than ever any desire for trade could have instigated. The Pharaoh's campaign was successful, though not successful enough to down the Mitannis for long. On the way home Tuthmosis imitated his grandfather in hunting elephants in the swamps of the Orontes, and then found that he had to subdue the Prince of Kadesh once more. This prince, learning perhaps from the Mitanni, who were by repute great breeders of horses, nearly won his battle by a ruse to cause havoc and confusion amongst the Egyptian stallion-drawn chariots by means of a mare let loose. A general named Amenemhab, however, slew the innocent mare and presented her tail to his majesty, as earlier he had jumped into the water, hewn off an elephant's trunk and presented that also to the Pharaoh. At least, so Amenemhab had it stated on his tomb. There are many other informative Egyptian tombs of this period, including the famous one of the Vizier Rekhmirē. They shadow forth an elaborate magnificence, with officials carefully accumulating treasure from the tribute and gifts that come from Nubia and the land of Cush in the south to the land of Khatti in the north.

Amenophis II, son and successor of Tuthmosis III, had obviously been brought up to become an heroic prince. He emulated his father in prowess with the bow and was in other ways a great athlete, a skilful horseman too, able to drive for long distances without causing his steeds to sweat. He emulated his father's ferocity, and exceeded it. At Nye on the Orontes he did not hunt elephant but contented himself with passing by, so that "the Asiatics of this town, men and women, were on their walls adoring His Majesty and showing wonderment at the goodly god". He then gave a display of target-shooting—so, when it seemed politic, could an Eighteenth Dynasty Pharaoh unbend. There is another interesting item in the rather sickeningly boastful description of the Pharaoh's first campaign. Riding south in the Plain of Sharon, famed in the Bible for pleasanter things, this man of war came across a messenger of the Mitanni, complete with his clay-tablet message slung round his neck. There being no diplomatic immunity in those days, the man was taken prisoner and made to trot along by the side of the Pharaoh's chariot. He duly arrived in Egypt; and with him were, it is boasted: 550 prisoners of the Maryannu, with 240 of their wives; 640 Canaanites; "children of princes, 232; female children of princes, 323", together with very much else including musicians with their instruments and horses with their chariots. The instruments are stated to be of silver and gold, which may well have increased their attractiveness. This was a successful expedition that seems to have penetrated up into Asia Minor to the outskirts of the Hittite country. Perhaps we may pause for a moment from surveying the course of history to reflect what multiplicity of misery this ruthless habit of the carrying away of hostages must have caused. Even if we halve or quarter the numbers, as probably we must, the truth is grim enough. "Maryannu", incidentally, is an Indo-Iranian word indicating the highest rank of fighting-men, the heroes who rode and fought in horse-chariots. The description of this campaign ends with the boast that the Princes of Nahrin, of Khatti and of Sangar—Mitannis, Hittites, Babylonians (the same word as the Biblical Shinar)—vied with each other in sending tribute to this "ruler of rulers, raging lion". Amenophis II had not penetrated into their lands; but he had paraded his strength and the three northern enemies had no unity with which to oppose him.

This Pharaoh executed one more Syrian campaign. And then, for the rest of his reign and for that of his successor, Tuthmosis IV, a period of twenty-five years or more, there is mention only of good deeds done at home.

With the accession of the next Pharaoh, Amenophis III, the magnificent, who has been called the Roi Soleil of Egypt, we come to the year 1405 and very close to the opening of the fourteenth century. Bar a probable early expedition south to Nubia, this king did not go a-soldiering. He left that to his generals, but in any case ruled more by diplomacy. We come now to the period when the rival rulers not only exchange gifts but exchange sisters and daughters for each other's harems. And in this it is certainly the most powerful who appears to get the best of the bargain. Amenophis III received the sister of King Tushratta of Mitanni (together, it is stated, with a retinue of 317 other women), the sister of the King of Babylon, and finally the daughter of Tushratta. This last the Mitanni king insisted should become not merely a member of the harem but the principal or "great" wife, thus enabling him to talk patronizingly of the magnificent Pharaoh as his son-in-

Amenophis III

law. Amenophis was old by then, however, and soon died; Tadukhipa, the Mitanni princess, was duly passed on to the successor, Amenophis IV, later to call himself Akhneten. What happened to her then is not known, for it is not at all likely that she was one and the same person as Akhneten's famous and beautiful wife, Nefertiti.

Amenophis III continued in magnificence to the end of his reign of thirty-seven or thirty-eight years. As Louis XIV built himself Versailles so the Pharaoh built himself a festival hall in which to hold his thirty-year jubilee, and a palace and pleasure lake for his queen, Tiye. The walls of her palace were painted with frescoes of birds and water plants and the like, executed possibly by Minoan artists whose fathers had learnt from the Egyptians, as had their rulers exchanged gifts of fine vases with the Pharaohs over the last few reigns.

But meanwhile the palace of King Minos had been burnt to the ground. And the letters that Amenophis III received so negligently from these monarchs who sunned themselves or wished to sun themselves in the glory of being tied to him by marriage tended to grow more openly demanding.

CHAPTER XIII

Minos Falls, Suppiluliumas Rises

THE two vital centuries, the fourteenth and thirteenth, can be looked upon in several ways. They are centuries that lead to the rise of Assyria, and see the decline of the Mitanni. They are the centuries of the Hittites' real greatness. They witness the enormous wealth, energy and vitality of the Egyptian Empire, and its first decline. Finally, they begin and they end with resounding events that reflect the even greater vitality of the Mycenaean Greeks.

These two events seem to us, who can only read such records as exist, somewhat isolated and disconnected with the rest of the events in that Middle East which is still the heart of civilization. This is not true, however, and both the Fall of Knossos and the Fall of Troy are of the greatest importance in that they show the pressure of the Aryan-speaking peoples, which is there all the time in these centuries and is the most fundamental phenomenon of all.

We begin, then, with the collapse of the Minoan civilization, but then shift back to the Fertile Crescent where the main protagonists are Egyptian and Hittite and where the disturbing Aryan influence is much less *obviously* present.

All the Cretan palaces fell, burnt and devastated, at about the same time, and comparative dating gives the year—it is generally but by no means universally accepted—as approximately 1400 B.C. Here, it must be remembered, is a date unlike its Egyptian counterparts, where dispute can only range over half a dozen years or so; here, as yet, have been found no records of names of kings and their years of reigning. We can only go to the ruined sites, and see the signs as Sir Arthur Evans saw them at Knossos.

Those signs are dramatic enough and to an extent revealing.

The stones still show the blackening of fire, always towards their northern end. There are signs of work suddenly stopped: a stone jar half finished, a block of basalt half sawn through. And in the king's inner throne room, where is the lustral sink for anointing, there was discovered confusion, with a ritual vessel on the floor and an overturned oil jar in one corner. "It looks," says John Pendlebury in his *Archaeology of Crete*, "as if the King had been hurried there to undergo, too late, some last ceremony in the hopes of saving the people."

The mind turns, romantically but naturally, to the legend of Theseus: surely it was the Mycenaeans who were at the gates, the heroic Achaeans impatiently throwing off a tutelage that had become a tyranny. But now there is a difficulty in such an interpretation. For, as we have already noted, by the evidence of the Linear B tablets the Greeks had been there and in command for half a century. One can, of course, assert that the script is not in the Greek language, which some still do. But that is to credit Michael Ventris and his helpers with a self-deception that is monstrous. One can believe that dates have some-how got stood on their heads. But it would be difficult to collect evidence for this. The most likely explanations are either that Knossos and the other places were destroyed once more by earthquake and not by invasion at all, or that there now occurred a second and fiercer invasion of Greeks that overwhelmed everything including an aristocracy that had already become Greek-speaking or at the very least employed Greek scribes.

The difficulty, however, does not go very deep. Whichever way it went at the very end, the Minoan civilization, with all its signs of over-sophistication and decadence, had run its course and the Mycenaeans had arrived. To quote another expert:

Everything testifies to the arrival of a new population in Crete. The Egyptian documents mention the Keftiu no more. Suddenly short-headed men prevail over the long-headed men who had hitherto been preponderant. From beneath the Dorian speech which was implanted in Crete two centuries later, a few elements emerge of the speech which was that of the Peloponnese also before the Dorian invasion. . . . Every characteristic of the mainlanders is now found in Crete. The men are no longer clean shaven. . . . For the first time there appears in Crete the northern house with a megaron. Funerary architecture is transformed, and the beehive tomb and the rock chamber are adopted: even the beliefs to which Crete had converted the Mycenaeans come back to her in a primitive, childish form.*

The Keftiu do indeed disappear. But there appear instead in the

*p. 49 of *The Aegean Civilization* by Gustave Glotz .

Date	Greece / Europe	Palestine / Asia Minor	Egypt	Assyria / Babylon	India	China	Date
1400	Fall of Knossos	First Megiddo / Tushratta / Suppiluliumas		Rise of Assyria / Babylon in correspondence with Egypt		Chinese writing	1400
1300	Mycenaeans at height	"Troy VIIA" / Muwatallis	Amenophis III / Akhneten / Tutankhamen		Aryans spread in India		1300
1200	Spread of Battle Axe People / Agamemnon	Battle of Kadesh / First use of iron / Moses	Rameses II / Exodus of Jews / Merenptah	End of Kassites			1200
1100	Dorian Invasion	Fall of Troy / Decline of Hittites / Judges / Peoples of the Sea	Rameses III / Decline of Egypt	Tiglath Pileser I		Chou Dynasty	1100
1000	Dark Ages	The Philistines / David / Solomon / The Phoenicians	Libyans in Egypt	Temporary decline of Assyria		China united	1000
900	The Celts	Phrygians		Ashur-nasir-pal	The Rig Veda		900
800	Homer lives (?)	Ahab / Elijah	Carthage founded				800
700	Rome founded / The Greeks colonize	Phoenicians spread / Lydians / Greek colonies / Midas / Jewish prophets	Ethiopians in Egypt / Assyrians conquer Egypt	Tiglath Pileser III / Sennacherib		China records an eclipse	700
600	Iron Age in W. Europe / Homer written down(?) / Solon and Thales	Jewish exile		Fall of Nineveh / Birth of Nebuchadnezzar		China disunited	600
			(Hanno's voyage soon)	(Chaldean Empire)	(Buddha and Confucius soon)		

records of the Fertile Crescent the Akawasha (Egyptian) or Ahhiyawa (Hittite), and, later, "The Peoples of the Sea". If the Minoans are ended, Homer's *Achaeans*, to wit the Mycenaeans, are at the height of their power and have another couple of centuries to run.

Rather as nowadays in a motor-car and wishing to avoid a large town one finds all the roads leading inwards and oneself inevitably dragged into it, so in these two ancient centuries the pull is always to Egypt, which even in her careless self-absorption, or her aberration, or her desperation, seems to dominate. Nevertheless, the fourteenth century at least we must allow as the Hittite's century, if not the thirteenth as well. If we knew more, or even if what we do know we had known sooner, the names—outlandish but resoundingly beautiful—of Suppiluliumas and Muwatallis would be as familiar to us as Tuthmosis and Rameses, as Pericles even or bold Horatius.

Let us renew our acquaintance with the Hittites, whom we left in their mountain fastness evolving their laws and endeavouring to cure their political weaknesses after the surprising and premature effort at empire-building wherein they captured not only Aleppo but distant Babylon. We saw them, having suffered from the Mitanni, begin to return to fighting greatness by a second conquest of Aleppo, possibly in alliance with Tuthmosis III.

But, as we know and in spite of his boasting, the Pharaoh was far from destroying the Mitanni; and these people, themselves having trouble from the Assyrians to their east, turned to give trouble once more to the Hittites. Thus the new empire started with hard times. "In earlier days," wrote a later king, "the Hatti-lands were sacked from beyond their borders. The enemy from Kaska came and sacked the Hatti-lands. . . . From beyond the Lower Lands came the enemy from Arzawa, and he too sacked the Hatti Lands." The lugubrious recital goes on until all the points of the compass are covered, including the east. There must be some exaggeration here; but we do know that the Arzawa, living where later the Lydians and Phrygians lived, were of sufficient power and importance for their king to correspond on something approaching equal terms with the Pharaoh, and no doubt the Mitanni king was playing off the smaller states against his Hittite rival.

Then came the truly great man of the Hittites, Suppiluliumas,* who reigned from about 1375 to 1335, a period that covers the latter part of

*Sometimes spelt with "b's" instead of "p's".

the reign of Amenophis III, and all the reigns of Akhneten and Tutankhamen.

Suppiluliumas fortified his capital city of Hattusas with a great wall. He built roads. He united his own country into a feudal and a not wholly undemocratic kingdom and ringed himself with allied princelings who also owed him feudal service. He was then able to devote himself to his main task, which was to settle accounts for all time with the Mitanni.

His first campaign was a failure and a defeat: the Mitanni monarch was able to add to his prestige by handing over some of his booty to the Pharaoh in the eternal game of present-swopping. Suppiluliumas, apparently undismayed, decided upon a more strategic plan. He subdued the tribes around the upper reaches of the Euphrates, crossed that river, and took the Mitannis in the rear. The capital was apparently invested and sacked with hardly any opposition. Suppiluliumas marched south into Syria to receive the homage of the small states there. The King of Kadesh, however, of whom we have already heard, and a vassal now to Egypt, came out to battle. Amenophis III was in his dotage and not interested; and the King of Kadesh and his men, failing support from Egypt, went down before the Hittite chariots. Leaving his son to rule the south, Suppiluliumas returned home.

But Mitanni was discredited, not defeated. Tushratta, its king, was busy allying himself by marriage with the Pharaohs. In effect he backed the wrong horse, a horse not at the moment interested in the race. And he suffered for this weakness from his own people, a rival faction who allied themselves—a portentous sign—with the Assyrians. Tushratta was murdered; and the Assyrians from being nominally the Mitanni's vassals became by treaty independent. The power of the Mitanni was by now virtually ended, Suppiluliumas having had his job completed for him. He was thereby enabled to consolidate and extend his power in Syria, so that by the time of his death a Hittite Empire had been formed that extended from the Euphrates to the Aegean, and that was earning at the moment the awed respect and later the jealous fear of powerful Egypt.

The sources for our information about the Hittites of this time and of their friends and enemies are fairly extensive. There are firstly the famous El-Amarna letters, a cache of cuneiform tablets, written mostly in ancient Akkadian, which was the then diplomatic language of the whole Fertile Crescent. They were discovered on the site of Akhneten's new capital—of which more later—and covered the diplomatic exchanges of his reign and of the latter part of his predecessor's. The second great source for the knowledge of the Hittites is the finds over the last fifty-odd years at the site of their capital, Hattusas, which site is known as Boghazköy, after the nearby Turkish village. These comprise not only tablets which corroborate and at times actually duplicate the Egyptian but a great deal in the way of statuettes and the like and particularly of stela and rock carvings that are highly revealing.

There is the series of four tablets that comprise a manual for the training and acclimatization of horses. It is by one Kikkuli, a Mitannian, which shows whence the Hittites obtained their skill in chariotry and that they must have been apt learners. The manual is elaborate and technical and a little portentous. And perhaps that is the sort of thing the Hittites liked. There is another manual, a book of instructions which concerns the ritual of the great yearly royal religious festival. Here is a part of it:

> Two palace-servants bring the king and queen water for the hands from a jar of gold. . . . The king and queen wash their hands. The chief of the palace servants gives them a cloth and they wipe their hands.
>
> Two palace servants place a knee-cloth for the king and queen. The verger walking in front, the "table men" step forward.
>
> The verger walks in front and shows the king's sons to their seats.
>
> The verger goes outside and walks in front of the chief cooks, and the chief cooks step forward.
>
> The verger again goes outside, and walks in front of the "pure priest, the lord of Hatti, and the god's mother of Halki", and shows them to their seats.
>
> The Master of Ceremonies goes inside and announces to the king. They bring forth the "Ishtar" instruments—the king says, "Let them bring them forth!"

A formal, serious people apparently, believing in having things done properly; a religious as well as a military people. Does this mean that the Hittites were as superstition-ridden, magic-ridden, priest-ridden, as their Egyptian and Semitic neighbours of the Fertile Crescent? Up to a point it probably does, though it, of course, also means, to look on the brighter side of the same picture, that they equally needed the binding powers of a state religion and the outlet and safety valve of common ritual and observances. The religion of this warrior nation does seem to have a tougher, opener, less dark and moody aspect than some of its contemporaries. The generalization is sometimes made that the Earth-Goddess religions tend to be dark and moody and the Sky-God religions the opposite. It is an obvious over-simplification: after all, the Egyptian great god was by now in his major manifestation a sun god. It might be said in defence of the idea, however, that Egypt's sun, like for that matter Mexico's sun, is a different sun from that of higher, less brazen-skied latitudes, a cruel sun by appearance rather than a kindly one. The Hittite religion, remarkably like the later Greek, shows actually a combination of an earth and a sky religion, with the sky element, however, greatly predominant. The god of these people of the mountains, again as of the early Greeks, was the Storm God and the Weather God, a counterpart of Zeus, whose emblem is the lightning shaft and the thunderbolt. He is worshipped most fittingly, and with most naturally evoked feelings of awe, amongst the craggy hills.

The protective god. Rock carving at Boghazköy

Outside the site of Boghazköy have been found wonderful rock carvings that show a long procession of priests and priestesses and gods. Here is little similarity with the carving of the rugged soldier who guarded the king's gates of Hattusas; here are long robes and high ceremonial hats. But in two ways the carvings are distinguished from others of their kind. There are very few of those theramorphic figures, nightmare combinations of man and beast or beast and beast, that disturb us in contemplation of Egyptian and later Assyrian and Babylonian carvings. There is, on the contrary, the outstanding and often-reproduced figure of the king and the god. The god, a tall,

powerful but benign figure, has his arm round the shoulder of the
king and firmly and protectively holds his wrist. No doubt too much
could be made of this. But it does convey an idea of true and sincere
religious feeling, and give a profound impression of godly protection
and, surprisingly perhaps, even of love. Suppiluliumas and the best of
his successors allowed themselves to be good diplomatists as well as
good soldiers and do not seem to have been cruel conquerors. No doubt
they were fierce. But at least they do not boast of their ferocity.

We need not, however, accord fourteenth-century diplomacy a very
high morality. Nor indeed is it always very diplomatic. The letters of
El Amarna which the potentates of the Fertile Crescent sent to the
Pharaohs are amazing in their frankness, their naïve wiliness, and their
cupidity.

There is only one from Suppiluliumas, addressed to Akhneten and it
is, as we might expect, relatively dignified.* It starts with the usual
fulsome greetings:

Thus hath Suppiluliumas, the great king,
king of Hatti-land, to Huria (Akhneten)
king of Egypt, my brother, spoken:
I am well. With thee may it be well.
With thy wives, thy sons, thy house, thy warriors, thy chariots,
and in thy land, may it be very well.

This is the almost universal greeting, sometimes put a little more
flowerily, and usually coupling horses as well as chariots with the
recipient's wives and warriors. Suppiluliumas proceeds:

My messengers, whom I have sent to thy father
in respect to the wish which my father expressed for mutual
relationship, let us establish it. And, O king,
I have not refused anything of that for which thy father has asked.
O king, verily I have done all; and all that
for which I asked thy father, thy father has in no wise
refused. He has, verily, given all.
When thy father was living, the messages which
he sent, why, my brother, hast thou refused them?

*The Tell El-Amarna Tablets, edited by S. A. B. Mercer (Macmillan, Toronto, 1939).
The lines are not as might first appear some form of blank verse but correspond to the
cuneiform lines.

Now, thou, my brother, hast ascended the throne of thy father,
and, just as thy father and I
mutually requested presents,
so will also thou and I be mutually
good friends. And after I
have expressed a wish to thy father, so to my
brother let it be not trifling. We will mutually fulfil it.
Whatever was requested of thy father,
thou, my brother, withhold it not.

The rest of the tablet, which from now on is a little mutilated, refers
to the actual exchange of presents. The sender's, of silver, are listed and
their weight carefully given. It is suggested that the Pharaoh might like
to send in return the two statues of gold that his father had apparently
promised.

This letter, of which it is hardly necessary to say there is no trace of
an answer, is in very many ways an extremely mild edition of all the
others. The kings and princes of the Mitanni, of Babylon, of Assyria,
of the Arzawa, of "Alasia" (probably Cyprus), and of Syria and
Palestine write to their "brother" seeking friendship, reflected glory
and gifts. So far as the last goes they seek in particular gold, for Egypt
by repute was fabulously rich in gold: as one king simply puts it,
voicing the scrounger's typical reaction, there is so much that the
Pharaoh if he sends some cannot possibly miss it. The importuner
usually explains that he needs it for some great religious building that
he is having erected, and, having no qualms about looking a gift horse
in the mouth, he complains bitterly if he does not receive what he
expects or is promised:

In respect to thy messenger, whom thou didst send,
the twenty minas of gold, which he brought, were not complete;
for when it was put in the furnace, it did not come forth five minas.

It is the King of Babylon complaining.

References to the Pharaoh's father, and to how much friendlier and
more munificent he was, are frequent. One writer puts it the other
way: his relationship is ten times closer with the reigning Pharaoh than
was their respective fathers'; he would therefore please like ten times
as much gold.

This theme of gold becomes a little sickening. The theme of the exchange of brides is more humanly interesting, and more important. Amenophis III is the chief collector of foreign wives, but he had not been the first. Occasionally the traffic went the other way; but one cannot help receiving the impression that the Pharaohs were a little superior and even a little careless about the matter. There is an extraordinary answer from Amenophis III to the King of Babylon who has complained that he can get no news about the sister whom he has sent to the Pharaoh's harem and that he does not even know whether she is alive or dead. Amenophis in reply denies the charge and accuses the Babylonian messengers of telling lies—they are such unreliable and unpleasant messengers that he has ceased giving them presents. It is not true, he continues, that he complained that the girl was not beautiful. It is not a sign of her disappearance that her father has received no gifts from her lately, for she has received no gifts from her father. And finally, if the king wants his daughter anointed with oil let him recollect that he has only sent one present of oil for the purpose. This seems to us more the language of back-street pawnbrokers than of Kings of Kings. This same Babylonian on another occasion suggests that if the Pharaoh is unwilling to send one of his daughters he might at least send any beautiful woman: after all, if he says she is a Pharaoh's daughter who is to know the difference? The search for prestige is thus unashamedly stated.

The letters from Tushratta the Mitanni king, besides reflecting on the whole a less sordid and more genuinely friendly relationship, furnish information of greater historical importance. They appear to refute, for instance, the suggestion from other sources that Akhneten acted for a while as co-regent before his father's death, and they show the importance of Akhneten's mother-in-law, Tiye. Even so, the bargaining over royal brides and their dowries are protracted and close, and Tushratta is not above harping on the current theme: "gold in Egypt is as abundant as dust". There is one interesting letter to the ageing Amenophis. Tushratta sends an effigy of the goddess Ishtar—"Thus saith Ishtar of Nineveh, mistress of all the lands: 'To Egypt to the land which I love, I will go.' " This idol was sent apparently not only as a token of friendship but as a prophylactic.

Two years later, however, Amenophis III was dead. And at much the same time Tushratta was assassinated. There is no more correspondence in the Amarna letter between Mitanni and Egypt. The one is declining. And the other is concerning itself with an internal revolution.

CHAPTER XIV

The Preoccupied Emperor

AKHNETEN was the son of Amenophis III and Queen Tiye, a luxury-loving monarch and a forceful woman, both pure Egyptian and, one would imagine, normal people. Akhneten was not normal.

Much has been written about this highly interesting Pharaoh and, upon somewhat slender foundations, much praise has been bestowed upon him as the "First Great Rebel" and the first founder of a mono-theistic and universal religion. However, it is also true to say that his reforms were utterly ephemeral and that he caused great misery by not facing up to the obligations of monarchy and of empire. He was the Edward the Confessor of his time, concerned with religion (though hardly in so orthodox a manner) at the expense of State, and doing proportionately more harm since his State was the greatest of the then world. The over-praise afforded to him engenders in one a desire to debunk him; but that is really too easy. We must struggle hard to be fair. It must not be forgotten, for instance, that the neglect of the Egyptian Empire had not begun with him but with his father; it is also possible that this empire was really such a ramshackle affair, or at least so amorphous and from the start so beset by enemies, that no one could have kept it intact for long.

Akhneten's god was a sun god. There was certainly nothing new in that. Firstly, however, his sun god was not a fierce and cruel or a provincially jealous god, but a god of righteousness and truth and beneficence—it is indeed possible, since his first wife before he married the Egyptian Nefertiti was a Mitanni princess, that he did imbibe something of the Indo-Iranian openness of religion that was to lead to the Persian God of Light. Secondly, Akhneten's god was truly a sole god. That was a revolutionary idea to advocate, and a brave act to try to spread the idea.

The conservative Egyptians never discarded anything, whether in their hieroglyphics or their religion. Their gods, therefore, were by now an inconsistent muddle of ancient fertility deities and local deities,

headed by the hyphenated Amun-Rē, Lord of Thebes and Lord of the
Sky, who had as many attributes and tortuous symbols as any of his
subsidiaries. What was more significant was that this pantheon with
Amun-Rē at its head had a tremendously powerful and tremendously
rich priesthood. We have seen how in the Old Kingdom the Pharaoh
had tried to curb that power and curtail those riches. But in spite of any
reform the accumulating process had gone on. The pride of any
Pharaoh who brought back prosperity after unsettled times was that he
rebuilt the temples. The desire of the Pharaoh, and of his nobles and
officials too, was to assure a happy after-life for themselves by providing
the Egyptian equivalent of our chantry chapel and endowed establish-
ment. The power of the priesthood had grown so great apparently that
they sought to influence the royal succession, having in the case of
Akhneten's grandfather, Tuthmosis III, succeeded.

Akhneten, helped a little it seems by a trend of feeling that his father
had started, nevertheless did not dare to make his great gesture until
he had been five years upon the throne. He had begun by shifting the
accent of sun god worship to the *Aten*, the actual, physical disc of the
sun, not in itself at all a spiritual idea but chosen rather as an attribute of
the god that was neither anthropomorphic nor heavily burdened with
associations with the old religion. He instructed his artists to replace
the old symbol of a winged sun with a golden sun that shone benefi-
cently over himself and his new queen Nefertiti, its rays ending in
caressing hands that spread the symbols of life and power upon them.
He changed his name from "Amen is Content", Amenophis IV, to
Akhneten, "Serviceable to the Aten". Then he took his prodigious step.
No doubt feeling stifled in priest-dominated Thebes, he set out to found
a new royal city.

He chose his site with practical good sense, at a spot some two
hundred miles down the river where the eastern mountains receded to
leave a crescent-shaped plain some eight miles long by three miles
broad. On the western side there was a broader expanse giving scope
for the agriculture that his city would need to support it. He was well
situated to intercept the wealth from empire and allies that still flowed
down from the river's mouth. However, on the great boundary stelae
that he set up he gave a less material, more mystical reason for his
choice: after sacrificing to the god he had fared forth in his golden
chariot, and the sun himself by shining upon him had shown where the
spot should be. Gratefully he swore an oath on the spot: by his father,
the Aten, and as he hoped that his queen and his daughters would

attain old age, he swore that he would never pass again the boundaries that he was setting up.

So far as is known he kept his vow. It meant more than that he would never lead his soldiers out to preserve his empire as his immediate forefathers had done; it meant that he would never even travel

Akhneten and Nefertiti, in the beneficent rays of the sun

through his own country on the tours of inspection and the showing of personal interest in his people that all his forefathers had made. From henceforth, for the eleven years of his life that remained, he was not a Pharaoh but the architect of a new city and a new religion, the genie who from the bare plains beside the river brought to life Akheteten, *The Horizon of Aten.*

He possessed the power and he possessed the wealth. He, and those who came with him and whom he promoted to high position, must have had a thrilling time. They were free of the priests, free of the ancient, elaborate, oppressive ritual, free of the old men who always said, "this is the tradition, this is the way it has always been done". The only older men known to have come away with the Pharaoh were his brother and the rather sinister Ay, who became Superintendent of the King's Horses, a more important post than it sounds; the mayor of the new city bore the significant title, "Akhneten created me". The New Men watched a new city grow up, temples and palaces and, as of old, a pleasure garden for the queen, though this time caged animals as well as flowers seem to have been set there to beguile her. They watched too their own mausoleums being erected in their lifetime, which was a practice not in the least new.

Nor was there anything new in the sycophancy that seemed still to surround the king: "How prosperous," wrote one courtier on the wall of his intended tomb, "is he who hears the Doctrine of Life, and is sated with beholding thee." Akhneten himself seemed to encourage this subservience in that the sculptures and wall reliefs, besides showing the aggressive, at times exaggerated, naturalism that he insisted upon, did not fail to make him the centre of the picture.

If the times were thrilling they cannot have been without their difficulties. One difficulty Akhneten was spared. He was not molested in his self-erected prison, and there was no hint of civil war: were the priests of Amun so self-confident as to let this aberration of a Pharaoh play out his little game of revolt undisturbed? Akhneten seems, nevertheless, to grow more bitter and more fanatical. There increases that unhappy habit of the Pharaohs, of deleting from the monuments the names and the images of those of whom they disapprove. Akhneten deletes the name of Amun and anything to do with the old god, even any word that by its sound fortuitously suggested the old god. Then, more unhappily, the name and image of his wife Nefertiti begins to be displaced. She has borne him six daughters. But she leaves the royal palace to live separately; and on the mural carvings her place is taken by one of her daughters. Has she ceased to be the obedient disciple, or is it possible that she was the more fanatical of the two? A glance at their effigies makes the latter unlikely, as does that part of Akhneten's boundary oath which referred to the possibility of his wife trying to make him change his mind. . . .

Our knowledge of Akhneten's religious teaching comes, apart from the evidence of his actions, almost wholly from his famous *Hymn to the Sun*. Too long to be set down here in full, it assuredly deserves to have its theme set down and its significant phrases quoted. It begins:

> Thou arisest beauteous in the horizon of heaven, O living Aten, beginner of life when thou didst shine forth in the eastern horizon, and didst fill every land with beauty.
>
> Thou art comely, great, sparkling, and high above every land, and thy rays enfold the lands to the limit of all that thou hast made. . . .

There follows a description of the terrors and the negation of night, when the sun has departed. But then:

> The earth grows bright, when thou hast arisen in the horizon, shining as Aten in the daytime. Thou banishest darkness and bestowest thy rays. The Two Lands are in festival, awakened they stand on their feet, thou hast lifted them up. Their limbs are cleansed, clothes put on, and their hands are upraised in praise at thy glorious appearing. The entire land does its work. All cattle are at peace upon their pastures. Trees and pasture grow green. Birds taking flight from their nest, their wings give praise to thy spirit. All animals frisk upon their feet. . . . Who causest the male fluid to grow in women and who makest the water in mankind; bringing to life the son in the body of his mother; soothing him by the cessation of his tears; nurse (already) in the body, who givest air to cause to live all whom thou makest. . . .

Even the chick speaks and testifies in his shell and "walketh upon his two feet when he comes forth from it".

> How manifold are thy works. They are mysterious in men's sight. Thou sole god, like to whom there is none other.

The Aten is the creator of all things and of all countries, of all men of every speech and complexion. He has blessed Egypt with the Nile-flood and other countries with a "Nile-flood in the sky", which is to say rain. He makes the seasons. He has made the sky, in order to shine in it and, being both near and distant, to see from it all that he has made.

There comes finally the theme of "there is only one god and I am his only prophet": "There is none other that knoweth thee except" Akhneten, "thy son who came forth from thy body, the King of Upper and Lower Egypt, living in Truth. . . ."

Here is certainly a monotheistic religion, and one informed with a poetic and a perhaps rather cold spirituality. It is not grossly anthropomorphic, depending for its appeal upon "graven images"—though Akhneten cannot avoid the inconsistency of claiming that he is the god's son, issuing from his body. It cannot, however, put forward any great claim to be a universal religion, merely on the grounds that other countries are accorded the same divine authorship and even have been afforded a second-best substitute for the Nile-floods. Of ethical teaching it has none, wherein it is inferior to the common people's Osiris worship, which equally with the rest Akhneten sought to displace and which did at least contemplate the triumph of good over evil and a reward to men in after-life for their righteousness in this.

As for Akhneten's neglect of his empire, it was tragic.

There is a kind of El-Amarna letter quite different from the bargaining of "brother" with "brother" and which as time goes on takes the place of the other. Such letters come from the Pharaoh's regents and governors in the cities of Palestine and Syria; and they ask not for gold but for help.

> To the king, the sun, my lord.
> Thus saith Abi-Asratu,
> thy servant, the dust of thy feet:
> At the feet of the king, my lord,
> seven times and seven times I fall down.
> Behold, I am a servant of the king and
> a dog of his house, and
> the whole land of Ammuri
> I guard for the king, my lord.

But it was not even at all clear that Abi-Asratu did guard the whole land of the Amorites for the Egyptian king. There are many letters from one, Rib-Addi, Governor of Gubla, which is none other than the already long-famous trading town known to classical times as Byblos. Rib-Addi tells how Abi-Asratu changes sides and how his son Aziru, "this dog!" is even a worse traitor. The appeals for help from Rib-Addi are long and impassioned. He asks for archers, or chariots and charioteers—only a few, a mere show of Egyptian strength and the whole situation will be changed overnight. He does apparently get one reply from Akhneten, which is a dusty one—as is shown by Rib-Addi's bitter answer:

> The king, my lord, says: "Protect thyself, and protect the city of the king that is in thy care." I say: From whom should I protect myself and the city (of the king)? Formerly a royal garrison was with me, and the king gave grain from Iarimuta for their provisions. But, behold, now Aziru has again oppressed me.

One other irritation gets under the skin of Rib-Addi, that such a man as Aziru should dare to set himself up against the might of a Pharaoh:

> What are the dogs, the sons of Abdi-Asirta, that they act according to their hearts' wish and cause the cities of the king to go up in smoke?

But this is a different Pharaoh. Though Rib-Addi sends his son personally to Akhneten, though he writes letters to his friends at court, pleading, "Say this to the King!", though he reports, "And behold now they bring soldiers from the Hatti-lands to conquer Gubla"—yet no help comes. The letters grow more urgent and more despairing, until at last: "If the king, my lord, does not change his mind I die." Then silence. Perhaps the king had not any mind on the subject to change.

One more despairing cry from a Governor may be quoted, of another coastal town, Tunip:

> But now Tunip,
> the city, weeps,
> and her tears are running,
> and there is no help for us.
> We have been sending to the king, the lord, the king of the
>   land of Egypt,
> for twenty years;
> but not one word
> has come to us from our lord.

That involves Amenophis III as well as Akhneten. Or else both Akhneten and his successor.

The two immediate successors to Akhneten are the boys who married his first and third daughters respectively, the first to reign three years and the second, Tutankhamen,* to reign eight or nine.

It was Tutankhamen who set the reversing process in full motion. Now it was *Aten* that had to be expunged as the hated name and *Amun* to be reinstated. Everything was to be as it had been—except that a spectacular but rather shoddily built city lay on the banks of the Nile to moulder and twenty-odd years of misery through neglect had passed.

This Pharaoh is famous purely by reason of the exceptional chance that his tomb remained almost wholly unrobbed until discovered in our own century. He is believed to have died at the age of eighteen, and little more can be said of him than that he was likely to have been the ideal occupant of the throne for those patient but powerful priests of Amun who took their opportunity to stage a triumphant return. Perhaps the superb wealth of his funeral was a reward for complaisance. It certainly shows how rich was the land of Egypt even yet. One find which is in complete contrast to these funerary riches is worth recording, since it brings back—by all the canons of sentimentality and probability—the widow of Tutankhamen and so the main stream of history. At the entrance to the fabulously stocked, gold-crammed tomb were found the withered but unmistakable remains of a bunch of flowers—a widow's farewell gesture?

Queen Ankhesnamun (called during her parents' lifetime Princess Ankhesenpaten) was yet another Egyptian lady of character. Widowed at an early age—she cannot have been more than in her early twenties— she was sensibly aware that the Egyptian line of succession ran ostensibly through the female side, that in other words some ambitious man would wish to marry her as a very considerable step towards the Pharaoh's throne. She must also have been aware that the aged renegade, Ay, first among the supporters of her father Akhneten and now first among the blackeners of his memory, would be the man most likely to claim her. She therefore wrote a most extraordinary letter.

Its recipient was King Suppiluliumas of the Hittites who, reaching the end of his reign and life but still actively campaigning to enlarge his empire, was laying siege to Carchemish. The letter—found on the site of the Hittite capital—ran as follows:

*The spelling of Tutankhamen (rather than-amun) is so familiar that it is retained. He began his life as Tutankhaten.

My husband has died and I have no son, but of you it is said that
you have many sons. If you would send me one of your sons, he
could become my husband. I will on no account take one of my
subjects and make him my husband. I am very much afraid.

That is surely one of the most dramatic and amazing documents of
any time. To ask for a daughter in marriage was one thing. But for
the Pharaoh's widow to ask for a man's son so that that son might
become the next Pharaoh was another. King Suppiluliumas was no
doubt a proud man and certainly a successful one. But by Egyptian

Akhneten's daughters

standards he was an upstart and his empire a despicably new thing.
He too, therefore, was amazed, and indeed suspicious. He sent an
envoy to the Egyptian Court to find out the truth.

The messenger came back with a stinging reply, but a reply no less
urgent:

Why do you say, "They are deceiving me"? If I had a son [who
would have by right become the next Pharaoh], would I write to a
foreigner to publish my distress and that of my country? You have
insulted me in speaking thus. He who was my husband is dead and
I have no son. I will never take one of my subjects and marry him.
I have written to no one but you. Everyone says you have many
sons; give me one of them that he may become my husband!

King Suppiluliumas did not hesitate a second time. A son was sent. Unhappily the little drama ends in disaster: the intended husband never reached his destination.

What happened to the courageous Ankhesnamun is not known; whether she was forced to marry the traitorous Ay is not known. What is known, however, is that for four years Ay sat upon the throne of the Pharaohs. If a man with the blood of Suppiluliumas had sat on it, ensuing history would surely have been different.

CHAPTER XV

Kadesh Exhausts

WE have reached the thirteen-thirties B.C., a third of the way only through the double century of great events. We are also still in the Bronze Age, though nearing the end of it. That fact seems now barely relevant—unless perhaps there is used with it the phrase "bronze age heroes".

It is a long time since we looked at events in the way more natural to their earlier course: what are man's achievements, inventions, increases of power over his environment? And if we do so now the answer seems at first sight to be a blank. But there is a better answer; and it is "the horse and chariot". Here is the invention which has altered the scene, that has caused roads to be built and has sent the kings' messengers along them, that has made empires possible, that has revolutionized warfare to make it more mobile, more romantic and more deadly. And if to control one's fellow-men—or rather one's unfellow-men, the stranger, the rival—is to control one's environment, then the introduction of the horse and chariot is a great and significant achievement. The taming of the horse certainly affected the course of history.

Much can be legitimately made of this. It is not fantastic to look upon the horse and its taming and use as a great changer and developer of human character. The horsey man is the same throughout time and place, a worshipper and practiser of the manly and aristocratic virtues, courageous rather than intellectual, extrovert and—we come back to the word—heroic. And it is undoubtedly from the steppe lands of Euro-Asia that the use of the horse arrives. It is parallel to the use of the Aryan language; and even further than the language, it spreads. We have seen the Hittites borrowing Mitanni horse trainers; we have seen how throughout the Middle East it has become customary for potentates to ask after the health of horses as well as wives. It is not only the Mycenaeans, now growing more wealthy and more adventurous, who possess the heroic outlook; it has even affected profoundly the once-peaceful Egyptians.

Indeed, after the Akhneten aberration it was as if the Egyptian rulers felt shame at falling from the high standard into the pit of intellectualism. At any rate, to put it more practically, they did their best to regain control of their crumbling empire. It is significant, and in line with our theory, that the man who followed Ay upon the throne was an army general. This man, Haremhab, paved the way for Egypt's second most famous dynasty, the last of her native dynasties of any repute, the Nineteenth. This is the first dynasty of the Ramessids. It was to resume and bring to a head the struggle with the Hittites and finally to make a peace with that country for fear of a common enemy. The real enemies, however—to all the combatants, and not only to their bodies but even and more so to their significance and fame—lay quite unsuspected, either miserably in their midst or out of sight beyond the northern borders.

We have now to tell of the battle of Kadesh, the events that led up to it, and its sequel.

Haremhab, the efficient military dictator, took his New Men from his friends in the army. He brought back law and justice to the land, stern justice such as no doubt seemed necessary, with savage punishments for crimes of violence. He built and restored religious sites, as did all Pharaohs of these times. Egypt was becoming her old self again.

But that she should have changed was inevitable, and the changes are apparent. Sir Alan Gardiner writes of these times: "It is impossible not to notice the marked deterioration of the art, the literature, and indeed the general culture of the people. The language which they wrote approximates more closely to the vernacular and incorporates many foreign words; the copies of ancient texts are incredibly careless, as if the scribes utterly failed to understand their meaning. At Thebes the tombs no longer display the bright and happy scenes of everyday life which characterized Dynasty XVIII, but concentrate rather upon the perils to be faced in the hereafter." A sadder and a spiritually impoverished country, but by no means yet an exhausted one.

Haremhab was apparently childless; at any rate he did not seek to establish his own dynasty. He chose for the succession a man of relatively humble origin, who first appears as a mere "captain of troops" and later—that familiar stepping-stone—as Superintendent of the King's Horses. This man, taking the name of Rameses I and coming to the throne late, reigned for less than two years.

His son, the next Pharaoh, was Sety I (alternatively called Seti,

Sethos, Setekhy). Under him the drive to regain greatness and an empire up to the Euphrates got fully under way. Sety I did his best to make himself popular at home—as a member of a recently established dynasty with no lineal claim to the throne, this may have been particularly necessary. He devised an elaborate code protecting priestly privileges. He built a temple at Abydos, which place was particularly holy to the popular trinity Osiris Isis-Horus. He even remembered the most lowly and miserable and had a well built on the road traversed by the gold miners, being careful to see that his thoughtfulness was duly recorded in stone. Then he mounted into his golden chariot and followed the way across the Sinai desert that the last great conqueror, Tuthmosis III, had traversed. But the political scene had changed in the interval. . . .

Prisoners captured by Sety I

One of the last acts of Suppiluliumas had been to re-enter the Mitanni capital and put his own nominee on the throne, in fact Tushratta's son in place of Tushratta's murderer. Nevertheless, this placing by the Hittites of a friendly buffer state between themselves and the Assyrians was not destined to last for long, and soon the land of the Mitanni was swallowed up by the Assyrians, who thus faced their enemy the Hittites across the Euphrates. Nor were the successors to the great Suppiluliumas free from trouble in other directions; indeed they were pressed from all directions, particularly from the northern and western coastlines of Asia Minor, coastlines that were suffering pressure from other restless peoples.

Troubles other than from human causes were also suffered by the Hittites. Apparently both Suppiluliumas and his heir were carried off by pestilence. Another son of the great king came to the throne, Mursilis II, and he has left behind prayers to the Gods in Time of Plague that show him to have been a pious, reflective and expressive man as well as an active soldier:

The matter of the plague I have laid in prayer before all the gods, making vows to them and saying: "Hearken to me, ye gods, my lords! Drive ye forth the plague from the Hatti land—either let it be established by an omen or let me see it in a dream, or let a prophet declare it!"

The gods being unresponsive, Mursilis sought to discover for himself the reason for the divine visitation: what wrong things had been done or right things left undone? Of the second, offerings to a certain river had been omitted. Of the first a campaign of his father's against Egyptian territory now seemed to the king to have been made treacherously, the Hattians though under oath to the Storm God having "ignored their obligations". Here, incidentally, historical information is given as well as the ways of thought of a fourteenth-century king. According to this king's prayer it was Egyptian fear at his father's hostile act that had caused to be sent the famous widow's request for a king's son in marriage which we have already noticed, and it is here that we learn that a son was actually sent and was murdered on the way. So, the prayer explains, was the tale of misfortune continued:

My father let his anger run away with him; he went to war against Egypt and attacked Egypt. He smote the foot soldiers and the charioteers of the country of Egypt. The Hattian Storm God, my lord, by his decision even then let my father prevail; he vanquished and smote the foot soldiers and the charioteers of the country of Egypt. But when they brought back to the Hatti land the prisoners which they had taken a plague broke out among the prisoners and they began to die.

So the plague was introduced and spread. And Mursilis, in short, offered expiation for his father's sin and threw himself upon the mercy of the great Storm God:

From my heart drive out the pain, O Lord, and from my soul lift fear.

Mursilis does seem to have risen refreshed and strengthened from his prayers. He now had to meet on his Syrian border the Egyptian Sety I, who had progressed victoriously through Palestine and like his warlike forefathers had reached the River Orontes. Sety, however, got no farther. He must have been met with a great show of strength, and he retired. The Hittite Empire was, in fact, at the turn of the centuries from the fourteenth to the thirteenth, as strong as ever it had been, tried by the fires of adversity and kept fit by the threatening ebullience of her dependencies and neighbours.

Very soon two new monarchs were facing each other, the Hittite Muwatallis and the Egyptian Rameses II. Which was the greater king it would be impossible to say; but as to which left behind for posterity the larger claim to greatness there can be no doubt whatever. Rameses II is Shelley's Ozymandias, King of Kings—"Look on my works, ye Mighty, and despair!" As may be imagined, his rumoured greatness was not long in reaching Muwatallis—who, realizing that a trial of strength was imminent, cast about to see what help he could get from his vassals and allies.

There need be no qualms about debunking Rameses II; the style of his boasting demands it, and the trouble has been that until the Hittite evidence came to light the process had never gone far enough. We can at least accord him the virtue of personal valour—which is by no means nothing—and also the *nous* to employ an expressive and imaginative writer, as well as a sycophantic one, to record his deeds.

Rameses II

Rameses marched north with four army corps behind him, which was one more than his father had had: not only the First Army of Amun, "Powerful of Bows", the First Army of Rē, "Manifold of Bows" and the First Army of Seth, "Victorious of Bows", but also an Army of Ptah. Reaching the mountains above the town of Kadesh, he held the usual army conference and made the usual bold Pharaonic decision. But this time the decision was not a good one.

Early in the morning and with one corps only, the Army of Amun, Rameses II descended to the ford over the river Orontes south of the

town. Here were captured two Bedouin deserters. Brought before
the Pharaoh they repeated their story, that the Hittites were still away
to the north in the land of Aleppo. They may have been spies. But in
any case they were believed. Without waiting for his other three
corps—the Army of Seth never reached the battle at all—Rameses
pushed on. Striking camp in order to rest his tired troops and seating
himself on his portable golden throne, he then received a great shock.
Two more prisoners were brought in; and they told the truth. The
Hittites were in strength and in hiding to the east of the town. Rameses
reproached his officers: the Egyptian intelligence service had not been
good. Then the Hittites, passing round to the south of the town and
also fording the river, were upon him.

Rameses gave direction that his children—Pharaohs travelled in
domestic comfort as well as with panoply—should seek shelter behind
the palisade of the as yet unfinished camp, and sent his vizier back for
reinforcements. Then he turned to face the enemy.

The Egyptian account at this point becomes so intent upon extolling
the personal prowess of the monarch that it reflects unconsciously, and
one would hope exaggeratedly, on not only his foolhardiness but also
on the inefficiency and cowardice of his army. The braggadocio of
the account soon grows tiring to the modern reader; but now there
comes something more, the true feelings of the Pharaoh or at least
what the writer felt ought to have been the Pharaoh's true feelings.
Having complained naïvely that "the wretched chief of Hatti" is too
frightened to make a head-on advance but comes upon the Egyptian
army "as it marched unheeding and unready for battle", the narrative
continues:

> His majesty issued forth like his father Month [or Mont, a war
> god], after he had seized his panoply of war, and had put on his
> corselet; he was like Baal in his hour. The great span [horse-chariot]
> which bore his majesty was called Victory-in-Thebes and was from
> the great stable of Rameses. His majesty rode at a gallop, and charged
> the hostile army of Hatti, being all alone and having none with him.

Soon two thousand five hundred chariots encircled him, filled with
the warriors of wretched Hatti and of all their allies (duly enumerated)
and holding not two to a chariot as in Egypt but three. Rameses
prayed to his god and reasoned with him:

"What is it then, my father Amun? Hath a father indeed forgotten his son? Have I done aught without thee? . . . How great is the Lord of Thebes, too great to suffer the foreign peoples to come nigh him! What are these Asiatics to thee, Amun? Wretches that know not God! Have I not fashioned for thee many monuments, and filled thy temple with my captives?"

The list of benefits to the god continues. Then:

"I call to thee, my father Amun. I am in the midst of foes whom I know not. All lands have joined together against me, and I am all alone and none other is with me. My soldiers have forsaken me, and not one among my chariotry hath looked round for me. If I cry to them, not one of them hearkeneth. But I call, and I find that Amun is worth more to me than millions of foot-soldiers, and hundreds of thousands of chariots. . . .

"Amun hearkeneth unto me and hearkeneth when I cry to him. He stretched out his hand to me, and I rejoice; he calleth out from behind me: 'Forward, forward! I am with thee, I thy father. . . .'

"I have found my courage again, mine heart swelleth for joy, all that I was fain to do cometh to pass. I am like Month. . . ."

The prowess of the Pharaoh then becomes unbelievable. The enemy princes are there before him. "I caused them to taste my hand. . . . One cried to the other, saying: 'This is no man that is among us; he is Seth, great of strength, Baal is in his limbs.' . . . I slew among them and none escaped me. I shouted out to my army: 'Steady, steady your hearts, my soldiers!'" Rameses then proceeds to reason with his soldiers rather as he had with Amun: "There is not one among you to whom I have not done good in my land. Stood I not as lord there, while ye were in poverty? Yet I caused you to become notables, and daily ye took of my sustenance." Reluctantly the soldiers creep back to his help. But there is left no doubt in the mind of the reader that the Egyptian victory which ensues is due primarily, if not entirely, to the phenomenal prowess of one man, the Pharaoh.

We may leave this boasting, mixed as it is with some evidence of human frailty—there is one revealing phrase in the Pharaoh's prayers, "Would that I were in Egypt like my fathers, who saw not the Syrians!"—and return to the probable truth, as can be extracted from the multiple Egyptian records, duly tempered by the Hittite.

There can be little doubt that Rameses II very nearly suffered utter defeat and was only saved by two things: the enemy's indiscipline and love of loot, such as was the Egyptian undoing at Megiddo, and the appearance of reinforcements in the nick of time. These seem to have been no part of the four armies but apparently some garrison troops already in the country; they attacked the Hittites in the rear, those who were not busy causing havoc in the Egyptian camp.

The description by the imaginative Egyptian writer ends with the Pharaoh reading out to his generals a Hittite letter grovelling for peace and his generals magnanimously recommending mercy. But this is fantastic nonsense. In fact, Rameses "held out his hand in peace on the march to the south" not from magnanimity but because he had to, because he was retreating. At best the Battle of Kadesh was for the Egyptians an ignominious draw. The Hittite records dismiss the battle in a sentence: "At the time that Muwatallis took the field against the king of the land of Egypt and the country of Amurru (the Amorites), and when he then had defeated the king of the land of Egypt and the country of Amurru, he (the Pharaoh) returned to the country Aba." This is around present-day Damascus. And even from here Rameses retired and the area became a Hittite dependency. Another Hittite tablet tells how the Amorites after the battle changed their allegiance away from the Egyptians. Finally, if we wish to believe the Hittite records no more than the Egyptian—though they are never so boastful —the ensuing event makes it clear that the resounding victory that the uncontradicted boasting of Rameses II made the world believe in for over three thousand years never came to pass.

This event was a treaty of alliance between the Egyptians and the Hittites, the terms of which we possess from both country's records. It is not only an offensive treaty but, what is significant, a defensive one: not only do the parties agree to refrain from invading each other's territory but also to help each other in case of attack from another quarter. It ends with this resounding curse:

And as for these words which are written upon these silver tablets for the Land of Hatti and the Land of Egypt, whosoever does not obey them, may the thousand gods of the Land of Hatti and the thousand gods of the Land of Egypt destroy his house, his land and his servants!

The treaty *was* observed, at least on the defensive side. It was in the interests of each to do so, for each was to be increasingly beset by other enemies. The treaty, made about the year 1270, was sealed by the marriage of the long-lived Rameses to a Hittite princess. The occasion was made one of great mutual display and pomp, and the princess even arose to the position of the Pharaoh's Great Wife. It is typical of Rameses, however, and perhaps of his subjects' mental attitude, that the

Hittite king presenting his daughter to Rameses II

very unmagnanimous Egyptian account of the affair makes it not a bond between equals but an effort at propitiation by a miserable and terrified Hittite king who brings "gifts of homage to the good god (the Pharaoh), so that he may give us peace and we may live".

The reigning Hittite king, Hattusilis III, brother of the now dead contender at the Battle of Kadesh, was not in the least a miserable or terrified monarch but a great one. He had, in fact, usurped the throne from his ineffectual and short-reigning nephew, and he shows a political conscience rare in those days in writing a sort of *Apologia* for his deeds. He gave to his people a generation of peace, or at any rate near-peace, and of prosperity.

He was succeeded by one Tudhalyas IV, who is the king to be seen in the rock carving enveloped in the loving arm of the god. The Hittites, in the latter part of the thirteenth century, had a pious man rather than a soldier for their king. And, as in the preceding century in Egypt, a country in those very troubled times could not afford a pious king. From the east and from the west, from Assyria and from coasts facing the Aegean Sea, troubles began to multiply upon the Hittites.

The Egyptians too were facing trouble, from the Mediterranean coast to the west of the Nile Delta and soon from raiders whom they called "The Peoples of the Sea".

The Battle of Kadesh was an important and decisive battle for the two giants who fought it and for the lesser figures of the nations who helped or watched. But it was, in fact, a battle between giants already beginning to be exhausted and who would have done better to have saved their strength. They did have the sense to compose their differences after the event. But even a pair of Goliaths are not going to trouble over-much those peoples who have the youth and self-confidence of a David.

CHAPTER XVI

Assyrians, Exodus, and Troy

IT is not only the ancient giants who are concerned in this story of the two centuries. There come into the picture now, or re-enter the picture, three utterly different peoples. One makes itself known to later generations by the sort of monumental boasting—monumental in both its meanings—that Rameses II delighted in; the other two leave behind literary monuments that are the greatest of the Western world, the *Bible* and the *Iliad*. The peoples in question are the Assyrians, the Jews, and the Homeric Greeks (which is no more than a later name for the Aegeans or Mycenaeans). All three will survive the holocaust that ends the twin centuries, most certainly to appear in history again, though changed in varying degrees and ways. What we have to tell now is briefly of their activities before the holocaust came.

The Assyrians are the people of the Land of Assur, or Ashur, their capital city on the upper reaches of the Tigris before they founded, still farther north, their famous or infamous Nineveh. They have so far entered the story only as rivals of the Mitanni and, earlier and with deceptive mildness, as merchants who left behind for us tablets giving some description of the Sumerians amongst whom they had elected to live. For very many centuries they remained an unimportant, agricultural people, benefiting from and imbibing Sumerian and early Babylonian culture, and suffering from both the raids of tribesmen from the north and the interference and brief dominance of a Sargon and a Hammurabi from the south. They are a Semitic people. They are neither men of the mountains as were the Hittites nor men of the plains such as the Sumerians and Egyptians, but something in between. Their land, though never producing the phenomenal crops of a carefully controlled Nile or Euphrates, was fertile, growing fruit as well as grain, flock-supporting. The control of Syria and the coast that the Hyksos exerted probably kept their kings and merchants poor, and their land quiet.

With the revival and expansion of New-Kingdom Egypt, Assyria finds herself dragged into the imperialistic struggle, her country part of the Middle East cockpit. She must become military or perish—and she certainly does not perish. Throughout the fifteenth and fourteenth centuries she was playing her hand carefully and gradually asserting her independence and enlarging her recognized frontiers. She appears in the El Amarna correspondence: her first king of historical importance Assur-uballit, following the practice of his imperial colleagues, asks the Pharaoh for gold, whereupon the King of Babylon complains that his "subjects" the Assyrians have no right to enter as equals into this correspondence between royal brothers. The Assyrian king, however, has no need to take notice of this slight. Before his reign is over he has helped the Hittites to interfere in the dynastic troubles of the Mitanni and finally to invade that country and, as we have seen, to divide its spoils and so face the Hittites across a common frontier. But as events were to turn out the Assyrians never experienced the need to engage in a full-scale war with the Hittites.

That they engaged in other full-scale wars, that they were indeed outstandingly a military nation, is well known. They bestraddled the Middle East with their chariots and their bearded bowmen from the fourteenth to the seventh century, though with a break in the middle of something like 250 years. It is the second period that is marked with the familiar names, largely because it is in that that they entered biblical history, but their characteristic behaviour had marked the world before then.

Colossal winged and human-headed bulls of stone; lion hunts; and the everlasting heavy, square, curled beard: that is the impression we receive of Assyria. It is not a wrong impression, though it would be nearer the mark if, even more than in Egypt, the face and figure of the king himself were present. The Assyrian monarchs are religious. They have a pantheon of gods as in Egypt and are as fond of composing strange beast-men to symbolize them; they are the god's earthly representative as were their Sumerian mentors and predecessors. But there is a difference: ostensibly the servant, the monarch gives the impression of nothing so much as in truth the master of the god, as he is master of everything else. If Babylonian Hammurabi was the essential Eastern potentate, the Assyrian kings are the essential Eastern despot. With them we enter fully into the world that the Bible has made familiar, of a Royal Court of portentous elaboration, with the chief cup-bearer and the head baker, the scribe of the harem and the chief eunuch, the king's physician and sword-bearer and mace-bearer, the captain of the guard, the keeper of the gate. The king's sorcerer, too, and interpreter of dreams and omens are there: the Assyrians, for all their military efficiency, are slaves to the whim of the gods and their attendant demons and must seek out and obey their wishes and propitiate their wrath. The Assyrians are, of course, not alone in their times in having that outlook; but they do seem to have carried it to excess. There is little sign of a religious conscience such as the Egyptians and the Hittites show in their different ways. But there is great effort to drag in the god on the right, that is to say on one's own, side.

The Assyrians were adepts at interpreting the significant be-haviour of birds, and the signifi-cant changes in the aspect of the quivering entrails of the animals they sacrificed, that curious and rather revolting habit that yet was to continue into Roman times.

Sooner or later the omens must always have been interpreted as favourable so far as the king's entry into battle was concerned. For with his army, which rapidly changed from a militia to a pro-fessional army, the Assyrian kings invariably and inevitably set out to war. By 1200 B.C., the end of our twin centuries of great events, the Assyrians have become the most powerful nation in the Middle East, and we must describe briefly how the change was made.

An Assyrian king (Sargon II, of the eighth century)

It was about the year 1270 that Rameses II and the Hittite king signed their famous offensive and defensive alliance. They must obviously have had Assyria in mind, for the first king of that country to be called Shalmaneser had at that time been successfully campaigning in the old Mitanni land. But it was to Babylonia that the next Assyrian king turned. He invested the city of Babylon, brought back its king in chains, and put himself on the southern throne, assuming the ancient and forgotten title of King of Sumer and Akkad. About 1240 he was assassinated by his son, and the records for a hundred years or so become sparse and confused.

Meanwhile on her western borders Assyria was being, quite simply, lucky. After the Battle of Kadesh the Egyptians retired from Syria for three centuries. And as for the Hittites under their pious Tudhalyas IV and his two successors, they were suffering tremendous pressure from still farther west and were with amazing rapidity sliding down to complete loss of empire and the eclipse of all their greatness—what is known of their collapse, which is indeed little, will be related in the next chapter.

What is even more significant, however, than Assyria's climb to power is the means by which she climbed. It was the habit of her kings to report their campaigns to their gods; and here is a selection from their reports:

> Lands, mountains, cities and princes, enemies of Ashur, have I conquered and their territories have I subjugated. . . . Peer in combat, rival in battle have I none. . . .
>
> I inflicted a defeat upon them. I slew their warriors with the sword, descending upon them like Adad when he makes a rainstorm pour down. In the moat I piled them up, I covered the wide plain with the corpses of their fighting men, I dyed the mountains with their blood like red wool. . . .
>
> I slew in battle 10,000 of their experienced soldiers. . . .
>
> The terror-inspiring glamour of Ashur, my lord, overwhelmed him and he seized my feet. . . .
>
> Sidquia, however, king of Askelon, who did not bow to my yoke, I deported and sent to Assyria, his family-gods, himself, his wife, his children, his brothers, all the male descendants of his family. . . .
>
> I deported their survivors and settled them in Samaria. . . .
>
> Himself I flayed; the rebels I killed in their cities and established again peace and harmony.
>
> I tore out the tongues of those whose slanderous mouths had uttered blasphemies against my god Ashur. . . . I fed their corpses, cut in small pieces, to dogs, pigs, zibu-birds and vultures. . . . After I had performed this and thus made quiet again the hearts of the great gods, my lords, I removed the corpses of those whom the pestilence had felled, whose left-overs after the dogs had fed on them were obstructing the street. . . .

I . . . killed the officials and patricians who had committed the crime and hung their bodies on poles surrounding the city.

I beat the warriors to death before the gate like lambs. . . .

From some I cut off hands and fingers, from others noses and ears; I deprived many of sight. I made one pile of the living and another pile of the heads. . . . Their young men and maidens have I cast into the fire; I have destroyed the city, devastated it, and delivered it to the flames. . . .

The harvest, subsistence for its people, and the hay, subsistence for their cattle, I set alight. . . .

Into their sacred groves whither no stranger had penetrated nor crossed the boundaries thereof, my shock-troops penetrated; they beheld the mysteries and delivered them over to the flames. . . .

Over the ruins my shadow rested; in gratification of my wrath I find contentment. . . .

The voice of man, the steps of flocks and herds, the happy shouts of mirth, I put an end to them. . . .

At home a slave-and-aristocracy society, a man-dominated society, obeyed and suffered the king's laws:

If her (a thief's) husband does not wish to ransom her, the owner of the stolen property shall take her and cut off her nose.

If a woman has crushed a seigneur's testicle in a brawl, they shall cut off one finger of hers, and if . . . she has crushed the other testicle they shall tear out both her eyes.

If a seigneur . . . has kissed [the wife of another seigneur] they shall draw his lower lip along the edge of the blade of an axe and cut it off. They shall flog her (a harlot discovered going about unveiled) fifty times with staves and pour pitch on her head.

If a woman has had a miscarriage by her own act, when they have prosecuted her and convicted her, they shall impale her on stakes without burying her.

It is the duty of the historian to be fair, and in an effort to be so most writers about the Assyrians have been at pains to point out that they were efficient administrators and often bequeathed order and peace; by their boasting, they suggest they paint an unfair picture of themselves. But this is a leaning over backwards to be fair. It may be true that there were in these centuries others nearly as bad, that even the

Egyptians had descended to cruelty and ferocity; it is no doubt true that the Assyrians did not spend all their time in destroying men, body and soul. But in the name of a merciful god how much is there left with which to damn them! Even if the Assyrian conquerors did not quite achieve all that they boasted of, the very fact of boasting shows what was their ideal; even if they were merely the worst of a bad lot, yet they were the worst. It is right that the Assyrians should go down to history as the very epitome of bloody-minded cruelty. From a land of agriculturists they turned their country into a war machine that from its size and duration, let alone its ferocity, puts Sparta into the shade. It is a symptom of the times that were coming that, with intervals, Assyria should have flourished for so long. The two other peoples of this chapter are alike only in their unsuspected power to change the world.

The Israelites are essentially the sufferers from the terrors and harshness of these times, a people who extracted good out of evil and spiritual unity and faith out of their tribulations. They were one of very many peoples in the disputed area of Palestine and Syria, who, however, rose for a time to prosperity and for all time to distinction. The Egyptians apparently had a word for them and other bedouin of their like; this was Habiru or Hapiru, which, whether or not it is the word from which is derived "Hebrew", meant for them no more

Servant of a war machine: the Assyrian soldier

than bandit. And, to give a balanced picture, let it be remembered that the Israelites were capable, in the process of welding themselves into a nation, of being at times nearly as ruthless as the Assyrians.

The Egyptians had a habit, after all a very understandable habit, of not writing about people and events that they did not like and wished to forget. That, we may imagine, is why they have left behind for us precisely nothing that corroborates the story of the entry into Egypt of Joseph and his brethren or of the Exodus under Moses. Neither event may have been of great importance to the Egyptians. But they were of obvious importance to the Israelites and, since generally speaking archaeology has done so much to substantiate the fundamental truth of legends, we may at the very least accept both as facts and not fiction. The entry of the Israelites into Egypt was probably during the time of the Hyksos, one of the peaceful parts of the invasion. The Exodus, which was once thought to have been earlier, can now with something approaching certainty be placed in the reign (1290 to 1224) of Rameses II. It is perhaps to be expected that if the event was in the very least as the Bible depicts it this horribly boastful Pharaoh would not have had anything to say about it. Or perhaps he was so engrossed with what he considered more important matters that he genuinely was not much affected: pestilences of one sort or another were no doubt a fairly common ill, and Rameses was not the sort of person to have the tender conscience of his contemporary, the Hittite Hattusilis III, who, as we have seen, made public expiation and prayer in time of plague.

The biblical story of the Exodus and subsequent conquest of the land of Canaan is a long-drawn and occasionally repetitive affair, interspersed with much detail of Mosaic laws and rules and priestly rituals; it is written by a person or persons long after the event and intent upon illustrating the thesis that the Israelites were the chosen people of God and succeeded precisely for that reason. But, as with Homer, remarkable accuracy of detail has often been proved by archaeology; and, making due allowance for exaggeration and tendentiousness—and ignoring the cries of the Fundamentalists whose piety only helps to mask the truth—we can accept the story and seek to put it in its historical setting. There is something fascinating in watching this event unfold, so completely ignored by the "Great Powers" of the time, so minor compared with the two centuries' rise and fall of empires, and yet of so great an importance in the history of thought.

The Israelites, in the land of Goshen, which lies between the Nile Delta and the Gulf of Suez, had fallen into a state of servitude, having with all other lowly Egyptians to do their stint of *corvée*, or "King's Work", but hating it. In the reign of Rameses II matters came to a head: "Therefore they did set over them task-masters to afflict them with their burdens. And they built for Pharaoh treasure cities, Pithom and Raamses." They were, in fact, caught up in the passion for building indulged in by this megalomaniac Pharaoh. Pithom is probably Pi-Tum, a granary town, the remains of which now lie half-way down the Suez Canal; Raamses is Pi-Ramessi, the House of Rameses, which was none other than the new northern capital that this Pharaoh built for himself on the east shore of the Delta, where indeed the Hyksos kings had once built their own capital, Avaris. Moses, the Sargon-like myth of whose romantic upbringing need not make him any less real for us, had his rebellious career begun for him when, fearing discovery of his murder of an Egyptian found "smiting an Hebrew, one of his brethren", he was forced to flee the country. Soon he was to receive from his god in the burning bush the call to return and champion his fellow-countrymen; and he showed himself both humble and by no means wholly willing to take up the task. Like Joan of Arc Moses had begun to hear his voices. There is something similar here, too, with the long communings with their gods that the Homeric characters indulge in. But, significantly and typically, whereas the Greek heroes are as it were doing no more than listen to the dictates of their conscience or better nature, screwing their courage or having it screwed to the sticking point, for instance, Moses is receiving genuine inspiration. The ensuing instructions to Moses on his return to Egypt we may, however, discount a little: the biblical author is so intent upon showing the greatness of the Hebrew god that in the matter of the plagues and the continual hardening of the Pharaoh's heart he succeeds only in portraying a deity who is willing to give his chosen people a most unhappy time so that his own might may be apparent. It is perhaps a likely truth, however, that the Israelites managed conveniently to borrow jewellery from their neighbours and to "spoil the Egyptians" before they went. They cannot have been very unpopular, nor for that matter can they have been altogether miserable, since afterwards in the desert they were continually indulging in nostalgic

Semitic types as seen by the Egyptians

memories of the fleshpots, "the fish . . . the cucumbers, and the melons, and the leeks", of the land that they had left behind and which was after all the only home they knew.

One of the major impressions to be got from reading the story is, in fact, of the recalcitrance of the people whom Moses led out of Egypt.

They are highly individualized but not highly disciplined; they are not heroic. They complain of the monotony of manna (a real food incidentally and not a magic one, an exudation from sap of the tamarisk when pierced by its plant lice); they slip back into observing a less austere religion when they get the chance; they are more anxious when they reach the borders of the Promised Land to fraternize with the natives than to make the necessary effort to oust them.

Such is the main point of the Exodus story, that the Israelites have to be *shaped* into an efficient instrument. Though they have been afraid to take the direct route from Egypt into Palestine and go first south and so right round the edge of the Sinai peninsula, yet this part of their wanderings takes less than two years. When, however, they are faced with the task of breaking their way into the Promised Land—which as well as flowing with milk and honey has experienced a tough history for the last couple of centuries and is clothed with well-manned and high-fortressed cities—they are quite unable to encompass it. The solution is a retirement into the desert that lies immediately south of Palestine—the steppe country might be a juster description—so that they may continue for a while as a nomad people and may, as it were, be hardened off. Whether the whole process did indeed take forty years—"forty" being a favourite term throughout the then Middle East, "a couple of score" as we might say—is perhaps doubtful; but there is the insistence that it had to be long enough for all the original immigrants to have died.

At last, a tried and tough instrument in a very warlike age, they are ready for the test. Moses has died, after no more than a sight of the Promised Land, and the Israelites are now under Joshua who is a strategist and a military leader. We may credit him with all the strength and assurance that belief in the backing of a stern but righteous and extremely partisan god can give him, but not with the improbable miracles that make his strategy and his trained troops unnecessary. The Jordan is crossed and the great and ancient bastion city of Jericho is stormed and invested. Archaeology can only say that probably between Hyksos times and about 1400 B.C. the site had been deserted but after that date had grown great again; subsequent demolition has unfortunately prevented much knowledge of the city during the latter half of the thirteenth century, which would be the time of its fall to Joshua. However, the key had been turned, and a spreading over the land, half warlike, half peaceful, became possible, though with some of the fortress towns with discretion left intact. More troubles were yet to be faced by the Israelites and fresh enemies. But they had entered into the land which a masterful leader had promised them and in which a shaky but yet never-dying faith had made them believe.

In the wider view of history, they had been lucky. They entered the vacuum—if it can be called a vacuum—that an Egypt which was in process of retiring from the ownership of empire had created. They were not disturbed over-much by the decaying Hittites, and the Assyrians were not ready to take notice of them. As for the Mycenaeans, they must, at about this time, have been contemplating or preparing for what we can imagine was the biggest and we know was the last of their heroic-cum-practical expeditions of piracy and conquest.

To switch thus suddenly from the Bible to the *Iliad* may be disconcerting. We have to adjust our outlook. Since, however, the later Greeks were to regard Homer as highly and as much a symbol of nationhood as were the Jews to regard the Old Testament, and since each story, it is now fully realized, tells of historical and not merely mythological events, it is as sensible to pay regard to the one as to the other. We may believe with the late Sir Gilbert Murray that the story of the siege of Troy, as it were, telescopes into one drama the memory of a great number of different expeditions. We must remember that the Linear B tablets show the Mycenaean civilization to have been richer and more elaborate and more sophisticated than ever Homer dreamt of showing it. But when all is said the poet was collating what had been handed down to him, and hidden in the flesh of his fancy and of the fancy of the line of bards before him there is likely to be a strong skeleton of truth.

We have already considered the character of the Mycenaeans; we come now to see these heroes, rather unexpectedly, in the final role of tragedy.

Agamemnon of Mycenae, and his blood relations round about the Peloponnese and allies from farther afield, must have entertained, like most extroverts, highly mixed motives. Their favourite activity was fighting; their need, their next most persistent obsession perhaps, was the acquiring and retaining of wealth—they were, in fact, not unlike most aristocrats. We may accept, then, something of both the story-teller's reason for the Trojan expedition, which was to avenge the rape and abduction of Helen, and the later historians', who point to the strategic position of the site of Troy at the trade gate to the Black Sea and the fertile lands that lay around it. We may take due notice of the

fact, attested by more than one geographer, that Troy commands a
strip of land where sea traders would have to resort to porterage, there
being currents along the shore-line that would make it almost impossible for ships depending on oars and sails that did not tack to enter the
Dardanelles. We may allow, on the other hand, that "Avenge Helen,
wife of our Leader!" would have made the necessary good battle-cry:

Two things are outstandingly significant in the story of the siege of
Troy, both of them tragic. The first is that the protagonists of both
sides are caught up in an inexorable code of behaviour, the aristocratic
warrior's code, that leads all too many of them to their doom. Prowess
and honour alone matter to them; and there is fierce competition to
establish the one—even to win in funeral games is important—and
nothing must stand in the way of retaining the other. Achilles, insulted
in the matter of the sharing of the spoil and the taking away from him
by Agamemnon of his slave girl, has no way open to him but to
withdraw from the fight though it brings the Greeks to the brink of
defeat. Hector can only accept the challenge of Achilles though he
knows and all his side knows that he stands little chance and that his
defeat is more than likely to lead to the final defeat of the Trojans:
"What if I were to offer surrender and promise to return Helen and all
her possessions and to pay in amends half the wealth of Troy? Achilles
would kill me, unarmed as if but a woman." They are cruel and bloody-
minded, these Greek and Trojan aristocrats, these "Sackers of Cities".
But theirs is not the refined, pathological cruelty and lust of the
Assyrians. It is an accepted form of competition. It is a way of life and a
way of expressing themselves, and they know no other. Perhaps the
Hittite aristocracy, also of Aryan-speaking origin, felt somewhat
the same.

The second tragic point of the story is the doom that awaited those
of the victors who survived. They come back to chaos and oblivion.
In two instances the chaos is described, both King Agamemnon on his
return to Mycenae and Odysseus on his final return to Ithaca meet
revolt and treachery: the morale and stability of their *oikos* have disappeared. As for the rest of them, the very lack of story is significant.
Menelaus and Helen are in the *Odyssey* allowed a rather improbably
gracious retirement. But for the rest: it is silence. The multitudinous
legends of the later Greeks cover Agamemnon and his contemporaries,
and their fathers and sometimes their grandfathers. But only a few
of their sons and daughters appear, and none of the next generation
at all.

Troy fell in the first few years of the twelfth century, a date held for a long time and still accepted. It ends these two centuries of great happenings that began with the destruction of Knossos and continued with the rise and fall of the Hittites, the emergence of the Assyrians, the last hysterical flaring up of Egyptian greatness before its decline, and the Exodus of the Israelites. It ends an epoch and in deterioration. Even if such individuals as Hector and Achilles and Odysseus never existed, the spade of the archaeologist shows the extraordinary fact that not only was Troy razed and gutted but that the fortress towns of the victors were very shortly afterwards to suffer the same fate.

CHAPTER XVII

Dark Ages, Iron, and the Peoples of the Sea

THERE arrives now a time of chaos; and there is not much known about it for the very simple reason that the chaos destroys the records or prevents them being made. Nor would the details of this chaos, were they known, be of any great significance.

There will be threads to follow through, nevertheless. They are those that lead to the revival of civilization and a new and different world. Violence has no significance except as it hinders or, paradoxically and certainly without intention, helps that revival: the soldier who killed Archimedes is not known because he was a soldier; and Daniel is more important than the king who put him in the lions' den. Not that either of those characters will appear in our story—which ends when the new world that leads to our modern world and creates the heritage of Western civilization is no more than surely on its way.

When the twelfth century had not as yet grown very old, fresh waves of Greek-speaking, probably iron-using invaders, the Dorians, began to come down into the Balkan peninsula from the great reservoir of the Steppes, while similar tribes of Phrygians flowed into Asia Minor. This sort of thing had been happening, of course, for the best part of eight hundred years, constantly an infiltration, occasionally swelling to invasion. Here, now, was the last of these, perhaps the greatest and almost certainly the most desperate. The pushers may have themselves been pushed from behind, or rather from the East where lay the Mongols; changing climate may have been the even more fundamental cause. Certainly the latest arrivals effected great damage. We may picture a kind of snowball of movement and depredation, one band of harsh and hungry people creating by its onslaught, whether from sea or land, another band made equally homeless and even more harsh and hungry. With the Minoan power long disappeared, the Aegean Sea had become, and would remain for centuries, a piratical sea; no avenging fleet of a thousand ships controlled by a powerful Mycenaean "King of Men" thrusts through the wine-dark sea, but the lone marauder even more lost and desperate than the ship of Odysseus.

All the great fortress cities of the Mycenaeans come to an end at this time; some such as Thebes and Corinth may revive in classical times, but others such as Menelaus's Sparta, the site of which is as yet undiscovered, and even Mycenae itself, will sink for ever into mere villages. At Pylos, the reputed home of Homer's garrulous elder statesman, King Nestor, a batch of the Linear B tablets tells us, in an elliptical, tantalizingly incomplete way what may have happened as the new wave of Greek-speaking barbarians arrived.

Most of these tablets, as has been said, and whether discovered on the Greek mainland or in Crete, are no more than the storekeeping records of the king's treasure or the equivalent of his Domesday Book:"Wheelless chariots, 2"; "One pair of wheels, bound with bronze, unfit for service"; "One footstool inlaid with ivory lions' heads and grooves"; "at Pylos, twenty-two sons of the bath-attendants, eleven boys"; "the priestess holds (this land) and claims that the deity holds the freehold"(?). But we know from archaeological evidence that Pylos was attacked and defended and burnt to the ground at about this time; and, *on the assumption* that an attack was expected, some of the tablets seem to show forth a dramatic story. One tablet states that a contingent of thirty rowers, drawn from the coastal villages, is to go to Pleuron; and if this is the Pleuron mentioned by Homer then the contingent would be travelling to the most northerly point of the kingdom. Other tablets list rowers to a total of over 400, including some who are "absent"—with or without leave is not stated. Then there is a group of tablets dealing with the *o-ka*, believed to be a military unit of command. The significant introductory phrase is translated by Michael Ventris and Professor John Chadwick—these details are taken from Chadwick's book, already mentioned—"Thus the watchers are guarding the coastal areas". Ten commands are listed, with the name of the commander and sometimes the location, the largest unit being of 110 men and all units being in multiples of ten. There comes the phrase, "and with them is the Follower". Now these Followers appear to be a kind of high-ranking king's bodyguard or king's messenger, chariot-owners. If the previous deductions are correct, then we may legitimately imagine a dramatic scene: slavering horses, helmeted hero dashing up to the aged King Nestor with the news of invasion. But, as we have seen and as John Chadwick puts it tersely, "in the event, the preparations proved vain". Pylos was not a walled fortress, and it fell. Mycenae must surely have put up a longer resistance. Unless, that is, the Dorian invasion was only the final cause of the collapse of the once great Mycenaean civilization and already, like the Minoan, it was exhausted and had within it the seeds of decay. It does seem obvious that something so specialized, artificial almost, as this treasure-hoarding, bronze-weaponed fighting aristocracy, was not going to last indefinitely.

Gordon Childe has made a point here, in his book, *What Happened in History*.* It has to do with the introduction of iron. The arrival of the use of iron we have so far mentioned only casually, and since so much has been made of Bronze Age and Stone Age this may seem odd. But when civilization has reached so far in so many other ways the significance in the change is not so very great; it has more import on the outskirts and we shall consider this in the next chapter. The fact, nevertheless, that this last tide of Aryan-speaking peoples usually wielded iron weapons may have constituted a very real practical reason for their success. The first really successful smelting of iron—a technically difficult operation needing a much higher temperature than copper—seems to have come first in the land of the Mitanni. The Hittites developed it to some extent; but they, like the Philistines after them, were careful to do their best not to let the knowledge of the process or the product itself spread—a request from the Pharaoh to his Hittite brother was politely turned down. The Hittites, however, were trying to do the impossible and by the twelfth century the use of iron was spreading.

Iron, though it corrodes so easily, does make a better weapon. Gordon Childe's point, however, is something more than that. He calls its introduction the "democratization" of warfare—of agriculture and industry, too, for that matter. Iron, by comparison with copper and tin, is not a scarce metal; once the processes are really mastered, tools, and weapons, are no longer fabulously expensive. "With iron weapons a commoner could meet on more equal terms the Bronze Age knight. With them, too, poor and backward barbarians could challenge the armies of civilized States whose monopoly of bronze armaments had made them seem invulnerable."

Iron had not reached beyond the scarce and precious stage with the thirteenth-century Hittites, and their collapse before the new hordes from the north was as sudden if not quite so complete as the Mycenaean.

To what extent the Hittite collapse was due to Phrygian invasion—as Homer has it—or to the treachery of a once-friendly neighbour on the Anatolian coast, or to displaced Mycenaeans, is perhaps not really

*Pelican Books, 1942.

very important: the truth may well be a great mix-up, both politically and genetically, that would make nonsense of our careful efforts at sifting and categorizing. Whatever the truth, it is interesting to see the already mentioned Ahhiyawa coming into the picture again; and when it is explained that Homer's name for his Greek heroes, the "Achaeans", was then spelt with the archaic Greek *digamma* or W, *Achaiwoi*, the suggestion that the Hittites' Ahhiyawa and the Homeric Achaeans were at least originally one and the same people does not seem far-fetched.

The story of the Ahhiyawa's defection from the Hittites goes back a hundred years or more to the reign of Mursilis II, the strong successor to the famous Suppiluliumas. All is sweetness and light then, for in the way of those days the Ahhiyawans sent an image of their god to help cure the Hittite king of a sickness. Later there is friendly correspondence in which the Hittites ask their ally to extradite a certain troublesome pirate or freebooter, and into which there enters a personal note. His messenger, says the Hittite king, "is a man of some importance; he is the groom who has ridden with me in my chariot from my youth up, and not only with me but also with your brother and with Tawa-galawas". This euphoniously-named individual has been identified by one modern philological expert as the Homeric Greek Prince Eteocles (or Etewoclewes), but the connection is a little slender. The tie between the two countries, however, is obviously the reverse of slender. This correspondence must have been either with Mursilis II, duly recovered no doubt, or his son and successor Muwatallis, the king who fought the boastful Rameses. We jump now three-quarters of a century to the pious Tudhalyas IV. He includes among a list of kings "who are of equal rank to me" the Ahhiyawan monarch, though an effort to erase this particularly entry on the tablet seems to suggest that this was something that he was not sure of or did not wish to recognize. Then the trouble begins. In the reign of Tudhalyas' successor and the last but one of the dynasty, a certain Attarissiyas of Ahhiyawa (some see under the disguise none other than the Greek Atreus, father of Menelaus and Agamemnon) attacks a western and minor ally of the Hittites. The Hittites help in the fight against the one-time ally and the outcome is inconclusive. But then the minor ally transfers its allegiance wholly to the Ahhiyawa and joins in on a sea raid upon a western Hittite dependency. Worse follows when the minor ally swallows up the nearby and once-powerful state of Arzawa. At the same time the Hittite kingdom is threatened from the north-east by an adventurer by the name of Mitas. The rot is beginning to set in; and the name Mitas, if it is the same as Midas, signifies the dynastic name of the royal line of the Phrygians. The last king to be enthroned in the Hittite highland capital, the second Suppiluliumas, reigns for a few years as the twelfth century begins, and then all is silence. Archaeology tells us that the Hittite capital is gutted; the reigning Pharaoh, Rameses III, tells us how "the isles" (of the Aegean) were disturbed and the Hittites fled into Syria in a great multitude which, with other fugitives and with "the Peoples of the Sea", was soon to menace Egypt. The rest of the Hittite story, of a minor revival in a new land, connects with the story of the Israelites and is more proper to the following chapter.

The Peoples of the Sea begin to trouble Egypt before the fall of Troy; that is, if our relative dates are correct. They comprise, by the Egyptian account, a mixed collection of races, almost certainly Hellenic, but when they begin to include men of the last, Dorian, invasion is not clear.* What matters historically is that Egypt is now not only in contact with the peoples of the coasts and islands of the troubled Eastern Mediterranean but is in danger from them. The most famous of the successors to Rameses II, Merenptah and Rameses III, are still Pharaohs of a fighting Egypt. But the fighting is on home ground; Egypt is on the defensive.

It is a tribute to Egypt's past greatness, and a witness to its long-lasting influence upon the minds and hearts of its peoples, who certainly had no way of knowing that historically they were on the way out, that her self-defence was for many years highly successful. Perhaps she surprised, as well as pleased, herself; she certainly surprised her enemies, who after Kadesh and the long-drawn-out and increasingly priest-ridden end to the reign of Rameses II had obviously no great opinion of Egypt's strength.

The first attack on Egypt by the Peoples of the Sea was made in conjunction with a chief of Libya. He brought his wife and family and possessions in the expectation of being able to settle down. He and his friends met with a resounding defeat—and the Egyptians, no doubt

---

*A list of names would only be confusing. Suffice it to say that experts see in them the Danaans, another Homeric title for the Greeks; the Achaeans again; the peoples who were to become the Sicilians and Etruscans; the Sardinians, and the Philistines, who it is believed came from Crete. Cretan population has by now become well mixed with Mycenaean Greek and is soon to receive its quota of what Odysseus (speaking of Crete) calls the "long-haired" Dorians. As Sir Alan Gardiner cautiously puts it, "some at least of the proposed identifications are likely to be correct".

conscious of being saved from a terrible danger,
raised a shout of exultant joy:

> The families of Libya are scattered as mice
> on the dykes.
> . . . The vile chief of the Libu, who fled
> under cover of night alone without a feather
> on his head, his feet unshod, his wives seized
> before his very eyes, the meal for his food taken
> away, and without water in the water-skin to
> keep him alive! The faces of his brothers are
> savage to kill him, his captains fighting one
> against the other. . . .
> Great joy has come about in Egypt, rejoicing
> is gone forth in the villages. . . . They talk of
> the victories which Merenptah has gained. . . .
> Pleasant indeed it is when one sits and chats.
> One can walk freely upon the road without
> any fear in the hearts of men. . . . Men go and

A "person of the sea"

come singing and there is no cry of people that mourn. . . .

The Egyptians, lovers of peace, never seem to have expected
retribution for having inflicted the opposite upon others!

This Pharaoh, Merenptah, did even copy his predecessors and issue
forth some way onto the old battlefields:

> . . . Canaan plundered with every ill; Ashkelon is taken and Gezer
> seized. . . . Israel is desolated and has no seed. . . .

This is the sole Egyptian reference to the Israelites, and a typically
boastful and optimistic one at that.

There followed a time not so happy nor so good, wherein the
Nineteenth Dynasty ended with four short reigns, one a woman's—
that a woman can climb to the throne is seldom a good sign in Egypt—
and then a short kingless period. Then came Rameses III (about 1182
to 1151), the second Pharaoh of the Twentieth Dynasty, who might be
called the Napoleon III of Egypt, modelling his names and his conduct
on an illustrious predecessor, and seeking to re-create a glory that had
departed. On the whole he made a better job of it, however.

In the eighth year of this Pharaoh's reign Egypt's enemies thought

they saw another chance to invade and settle. They attacked not only
the Nile Delta but Palestine, and by both land and sea. The sea attack
on the Delta at least was successfully met and though probably not
such an overwhelming naval victory for the Egyptians as depicted,
with the Sea Peoples in their feathered headdresses tumbling over-
board and being triumphantly rowed home as bound captives, yet a
victory it was and Egypt is saved from complete foreign domination
for another four hundred years. Rameses III, by copying some of the
temple scenes of Rameses II, tried to give the impression that he too
reached the River Orontes and attacked the Hittites. But this is nonsense, and his greatest authenticated achievement, apart from the great
one of fending off invasion, was to defeat some bedouin tribes south
of Palestine—"It looks," says Sir Alan Gardiner, "as though the defeat
of these relatively unimportant tent-dwellers was the utmost which
Rameses III could achieve after his struggle with the Mediterranean
hordes."

Egypt, in fact, was exhausted. This particular Pharaoh was to end his
reign meting out punishment for a sordid but nearly successful harem
intrigue against his life and throne. As for the Twentieth Dynasty as a
whole, it was to last until the beginning of the eleventh century, a
couple of generations or so before Israel was to find herself a line of
strong kings, and it was to peter out in a long line of undistinguished
Rameses', whose main concern would be to keep the Twin Land of
Egypt united and the power away from the priesthood, and who would
fail finally in both endeavours.

The glory had departed. It had departed from the land of the
Pharaohs, as it had from the land of the Hittites, as it had from the
land of those gilded warrior-potentates who had taken over something
of the culture of the already half-forgotten Minoans.

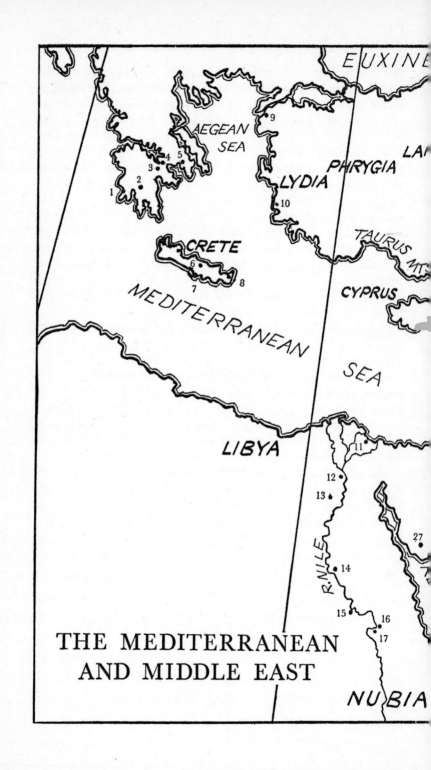

THE MEDITERRANEAN
AND MIDDLE EAST

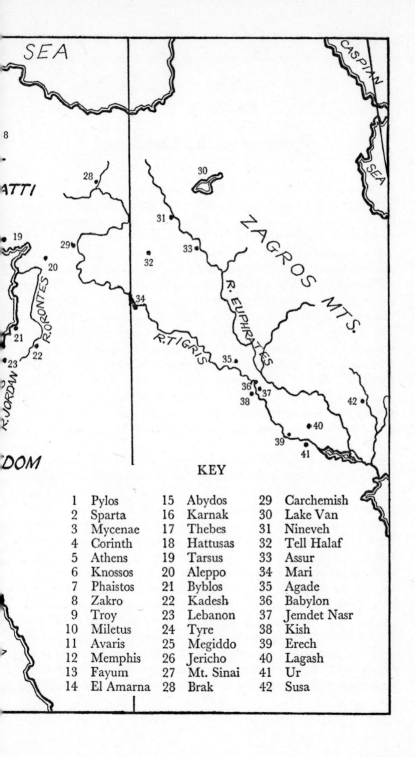

SEA

CASPIAN

SEA

8

ATTI

28

30

ZAGROS MTS.

19

29

31

20

32

33

R. EUPHRATES

R. ORONTES

34

R. TIGRIS

21

35

22

36

23

37

R. JORDAN

38

42

40

39

DOM

41

KEY

1	Pylos	15	Abydos	29	Carchemish
2	Sparta	16	Karnak	30	Lake Van
3	Mycenae	17	Thebes	31	Nineveh
4	Corinth	18	Hattusas	32	Tell Halaf
5	Athens	19	Tarsus	33	Assur
6	Knossos	20	Aleppo	34	Mari
7	Phaistos	21	Byblos	35	Agade
8	Zakro	22	Kadesh	36	Babylon
9	Troy	23	Lebanon	37	Jemdet Nasr
10	Miletus	24	Tyre	38	Kish
11	Avaris	25	Megiddo	39	Erech
12	Memphis	26	Jericho	40	Lagash
13	Fayum	27	Mt. Sinai	41	Ur
14	El Amarna	28	Brak	42	Susa

CHAPTER XVIII

Progress in the Outskirts

HAVING reached the entrance by the centre of civilization into the Iron Age, not a very happy entrance, and having left the outskirts either within or only entering the Bronze Age, we must return again to the outskirts. The aim of this book is to tell of the events that led men to the state of affairs wherein they could found the great traditions of Western civilization; it stops when it is apparent that the disciplined thinking of the Greeks and the religion of righteousness of the Christian are going to be a possibility. That being so, it is the centre, the centre that yet remains about the Eastern Mediterranean, that matters most. The outskirts have significance for us only to the extent that they are influenced by or influence the centre—though naturally our interest is keener because we know that in the subsequent course of history the centre will shift to various parts of the outskirts. If, therefore, this chapter is no more than a series of snapshots or very sketchy outlines, the reader, who will undoubtedly have his own peculiar interest, must please not complain when that interest appears to be slighted.

Africa, those parts of it that were habitable, did little to contribute to or hinder the progress of civilization up to the eighth and seventh centuries B.C. when our story begins to fade out. The regions of the Sudan and Ethiopia are, if anywhere, the exception: Nubia is bound up with Egypt and will yet be seen interfering actively in Egyptian affairs. But mostly she is Egypt's pupil and dependency; only in the seventh century B.C. does her capital city of Meroe become of some importance, in the next few centuries producing even her own hieroglyphic script. In truth the Egyptians were no more enamoured of the outside world of barbarians than were the later Greeks, and considerably more afraid of them. To her neighbours, therefore, and so in decreasing effect to the rest of Africa, she acts in a double and a contradictory role. Through trade and military expedition—we have seen that the two can hardly be separated—Egypt's influence and knowledge, such as of methods of agriculture and stock-rearing and pottery-making, spread inevitably abroad. But her policy nevertheless was fundamentally one of "hands off Egypt", and her influence was nowhere near what it might have been. In absence of that influence Africa did not much change or progress. Her rock paintings and engravings from the already mentioned Capsian times and right out beyond our period, are Africa's chief claim to fame. They start in the Sahara and spread eastwards and southwards. They are another example of man's skill in drawing animals and his refuge in queer symbolism and tortuous obliqueness when depicting himself.

Northern and western Europe, by and large, enjoys a Bronze Age at the best part of a thousand-year shift from the Middle Eastern source. In Chapter IX there was described the spread of the "Neolithic Revolution" of farming and stockbreeding, and then the spread of the use of copper and bronze and gold; and it was suggested that the reason for the first was largely an ecological one—it started when Nature made it easiest to start and spread when Nature's exhaustion made it necessary to spread—whilst the reason for the second was little more than that the metals were scarce and had to be found. There was nothing, except lack of thought and initiative, to prevent the outer Europeans from developing their own trade and industry in metals: it is almost as if the men of the outskirts had formed a habit of depending upon the men of the centre. They were to prove apt learners nevertheless.

There were others who sailed and trekked into northern and western Europe besides the Beaker People, the prospectors, and the Megalith Builders: the picture is by no means a simple one of movement outwards. We have already witnessed the vast and recurring movement inwards of the Aryan-speakers from the steppe lands of Europe and Asia. Now we must look at a movement from one part of the periphery to another. This is the movement of the Battle Axe People. These once again are Aryan-speakers; and by the evidence of their weapons and rich burials they spread from the area of the Eastern Ukraine. They may indeed, for all we know, have been close relations of those who were to be called Mycenaeans or Hittites or Phrygians or Medes, failing only by the accident of their migration to a non-literate part of the world to achieve a less generalized and archaeological-sounding name. They sweep across Europe, these Battle Axe People, about the time that the Hyksos were sweeping into Egypt, to end up in meeting the Beaker People around the Rhine and in Scandinavia. They are essentially stock-breeders and not agriculturists, and, as we might expect from their origin, their way of life is an aristocratic one and they bury their great chiefs with pomp. Here is a description of such a burial in their land of origin, by Geoffrey Bibby in his book, *The Testimony of the Spade*:

> In stone- or log-lined pits the dead princes lie on their sides facing south with weapons of gold-mounted bronze, gold drinking cups, bronze statuettes inlaid with gold, circular or kidney-shaped "sun-discs" (for they appear to have been sun-worshippers), and above all else, battle-axes of silver or copper.

The axe, says Geoffrey Bibby, is the old antler-axe of the original forest hunters, translated by the bronzesmiths into copper; and as the migration goes westwards, where metal is scarce or even as yet unknown, the copper axe is translated back again into polished stone imitated even down to reproduction of the casting seam. The western burials are not so grand, or rather with the grandeur of the poorer but proud. There they lie, these barbarians but not wholly uncivilized chieftains, mute, inglorious Akhnetens perhaps or, a closer parallel and to parody Gray further, Agamemnons guiltless of any Trojans' blood.

And "guiltless" may not be altogether the wrong word. Hardly so to start with, for these Battle Axe people came in large numbers and are not likely to have won a hold for themselves and their cattle without opposition. But, unlike the Middle East, here there was land enough and no existing empires to be met and overcome. It does seem as if the newcomers settled down with the old inhabitants—the new in a superior position to the old, no doubt—and that in Europe a long Bronze Age period of peace ensued. There appears little sudden change of culture anywhere, such changes being a sure sign of war and destruction. Though bronze is scarce it is used with increasingly great art and skill. And then there are the rock carvings of this age, as far apart as Scandinavia and northern Italy, but chiefly around the southern coast of Norway. These, utterly different from anything else in the world, show signs of an elaborate religious ritual of sun-worship; and elaborate rituals do not develop unless there are peaceful times in which they can do so.

Yet the accent, nevertheless, is still on weapons, particularly in the burials of the chief. It is reasonable to suppose that the weapons were as much as anything a badge of rank, that these aristocrats lived in a heroic tradition of personal combat and prowess and treasure-exchanging and the rest exactly as did the Mycenaeans' noblemen, but that fortunately for them and even more fortunately for their peoples there was little real and serious fighting to be done.

The typical rock engraving shows the Sun God being rowed across the heavens in a well-manned ship; and perhaps it would be fairer to say that the accent, in the European Bronze Age art that has survived for us, is not only on weapons but on ships. The ritual ships depicted are not drawn from imagination, in a void. That the handles of bronze razors were very often modelled as ships is also significant. In Europe, as well as in the Mediterranean, the Bronze Age must, in fact, have been very much an age of ships and sea-borne trade and adventurous voyaging. We spoke of the Minoan civilization growing rich on the trade in objects of bronze and amber and jet and other such unbulky luxuries—beads of faience, and bright blue fused glass, were now to become popular. The fall of Knossos did not stop the trade, for the Mycenaeans must largely have taken it over. People moved about in those days; and it is now well known that the later, Bronze Age, Stonehenge shows traces on its trilithons of carvings of Mycenae-type daggers and one of the double axe. There are sure signs that the island of Madeira was reached. It has even been suggested that Plato's description of "Atlantis" does not show forth memories of the glories of ancient Crete, or not wholly so, but embalmed a legend of the first and unknown Bronze Age discoverers of America.

That is as it may be. Western and northern Europe, which does not suffer the disturbance of the Iron Age until after our era is closing, does during the Second Millennium show a picture, if not of a sophisticated civilization or certainly of a literate one, at least of a largely peaceful yet adventurous and prosperous age.

Of India there is even less to tell. We left the Indus valley civilization waiting in decline for invasion from the north-west, from the plateau of Iran. It came about 1700 and within a couple of hundred years Mohenjo-Daro and Harappa are no more. There are signs of fighting and massacre. It is, yet once again, the same story: hordes of people on the move, partly Aryan-speaking and probably Aryan-led.

Our sources of evidence are the collection of hymns and prayers and epic chants called the Rig Veda, and archaeology; and neither are extensive enough to give a very clear picture.* It seems certain,

---

*The newcomers seem to have been builders in wood—an Aryan characteristic— which practice does not give archaeology much chance.

however, that the Aryan conquests were much less disruptive of continuity than the composers of the epics would have us believe. Hindu religion has retained Indra, the Aryan's Storm and War God, but it has also retained Siva and much of fertility worship, ritual cleansing and regard for animals from the Indus valley civilization. Whatever may be the final results, nowhere in the world do the invasions and infiltrations of the Aryan-speakers produce in the short run startling or deep changes in thought or peaceful skills. The rest of India before the invasions had been in some state or another of Stone Age culture, with the possible exception of the Ganges Valley, where some use of copper had been or was about to be achieved. After the invasion there is a slow progress, least apparent in the south, and benefiting in the north no doubt from the skills and knowledge of the displaced Harappans. These Harappans had used a rather primitive pictographic script (so far undeciphered); but this disappears, as it did in the Aegean, and literacy does not come back to India until the Mauryan Empire, which is after Alexander's time. An earlier stirring-up occurs with the introduction of the use of iron in the second half of the First Millennium B.C. With this there also comes to India, so late, the building of megalithic tombs. The connection back to passage graves of Europe and the beehive tombs of Mycenae must be there but is difficult to trace. When Darius I invaded at the end of the sixth century and Alexander at the end of the fourth, they found what seemed to them no more than a collection of petty and warring counts and kingdoms. But in the earlier of these two times Gautama Buddha flourished, and an India that could produce him was obviously the reverse of barbaric.

China remains isolated. We have said that this country's civilization is not the oldest. What China can truthfully claim is that she has possessed a civilization that for by far the longest time remained virtually unchanged. Rather like the city of Babylon with its culture and trade and prosperity, China rode over wars and revolutions and dynastic changes and remained serenely herself. She had her palaeolithic and early neolithic period and then her gradual development of a fertile river valley, the Hwang-ho or Yellow River, which significantly is in the northern part and the part where contact with the West—along the later Silk Route, south of the Gobi desert, north of Tibet and into Turkestan—was at least possible. Even the use of bronze may have been, as the archaeologists say, "intrusive" and not original. But then, with the Shang Dynasty and the middle of the Second Millennium, China asserts her individuality and retains it—no doubt it was there before but archaeology has yet to make much leeway in that part of the world before it can substantiate and illustrate the country's legends, even the discoveries at Anyang, the Shang capital, being very recent and not yet completely reported.

There is a legend of a Chinese city besieged and in a desperate plight. The commander carefully observed in the hearing of one whom he knew to be an enemy spy that he did hope the enemy would not think of opening the tombs of the city's ancestors, for that would indeed force a surrender. The enemy duly proceeded to desecrate the tombs, which were just outside the city gate, and the people were seized with such fury that they made a victorious sortie and annihilated the enemy.* Here was the distinctive religious outlook of the Chinese—not unique as such but unique in its intensity—that was now, during the four hundred or so years of the Shang Dynasty, forming itself out of a more generalized and primitive fertility cult. "The temple of our ancestors," says the *Book of Odes*, the oldest collection of poetry preserved in China:

> The temple of our ancestors grew
>   mightily.
> Armies of men brought earth in
>   baskets
> And, shouting joyfully, poured
>   it into the frames
> They rammed it in with ringing
>   blows . . .

Chou dynasty bronze chalice

And this somewhat primitive building method did produce walls to last. Much less primitive were the ritual vessels of bronze that this culture and the next, the Chou, produced. These imposing and beautifully executed "chalices" were of varying type, each type being strictly used at some stage of the ritual of ancestor worship. By the end of the Shang Dynasty the distinctive and elaborate pictographic writing also has developed, the number of

*As quoted by Ernst Diez in his book *The Ancient Worlds of Asia* (Macdonald, 1961).

separate characters then having reached the comparatively modest figure of about two thousand.

There were also signs of primitiveness and of less amiable or peaceful qualities. Not only were servants and wives buried with the great ones but a fairly extensive sacrifice of war prisoners took place. The inquiry of omens and oracles was very prevalent and had been before the period of the Shang. This again, of course, is not unique but the particular method of creating changing and unpredictable signs is so. The Second Millennium Chinese scratched questions upon bone or tortoiseshell, cast them in the fire—and acted on the interpretation that the experts gave to the ensuing heat-produced cracks. Of warlike evidence there are the horse chariots, not unlike the Mycenaean, that towards the end of the period were buried in the tombs of the great. Something of a feudal empire was being formed. And at the very end of the millennium one of the feudatories, the Chou, revolted, and took over control.

The new régime was not likely to have been achieved without bloodshed, and the *Annals* of the time speak of the penalty of death meted out not only to a culprit for the sin of disobedience but also to his wife and family. The dynasty, however, possessed with later generations a reputation for peaceableness, as it had indeed of every virtue, the first acts of the founder being thus described:

> On the way home, travelling westwards, when he had crossed the Yellow River he set the war horses free . . . he had the chariots and armour daubed with ox-blood and stored away in arsenals to show that they would never be used again.

In fact, if not a golden age, the next four or five centuries, times of darkness and only slow recovery for the lands of the Mediterranean, were for China times of phenomenal progress. It was a literary and well-mannered age, an age in which all China's traditional virtues were founded, an age that ended with the appearance of Confucius.

The youth of the noblemen were taught literary composition, and music, and to shoot straight with the bow, and to drive the horse chariot. Even shooting with the bow was made a polite sport, since it was set to music and the shot that was out of time was not counted even though it should hit the bull's-eye. Men wore tablets, as Hamlet did, at their belts, in case they should wish to commit anything to writing; and indeed everything was committed to writing, by a meticulous and conservative bureaucracy. The old were highly respected, so that it was a great aim to survive to old age. Drunkenness was frowned upon but, as shown by the annals and the poems, was not unknown. Cookery was a well-practised art. Poetry was a greater:

> . . . Then with their sharp ploughshares
> They go off to work in the fields which lie to the south.
> They sow all manner of cereals
> Each seed contains a germ of life.
> The tender shoots spring up in long rows
> And the tender feathery stalks climb higher. . . .

But there are poems of much more personal tenderness, that no Egyptian would have thought of, even in Akhneten's time:

> I climbed the crumbling wall
> To watch for you coming round the hill;
> And when I did not see you
> My tears flowed unchecked.
> But when I did see you coming
> I laughed and I joked.
> You said that you had asked the tortoise-shells
> And the reed-sticks
> And that their answer was not unfavourable.
> "Come then," said I, "with your cart,
> And I will follow you with all I possess."

and

> The cricket sings in the grass
> And the grasshopper leaps o'er the green blade,
> Yet I cannot see my beloved.
> My heart is filled with sadness.
> Ah! Could I but see him
> And hold him close to me.
> Then would my grief be cured.

Only the Israelites at the time of David and Solomon, and the Greeks in a time yet to come, have been such an expressive people as these Chinese of the early First Millennium. The previous Shang period has been likened to the early Sumerian, but the Chou has been likened to a rather gayer and more enlightened medieval Europe—it could in some aspects be likened to Elizabethan England. Then followed, after an "Age of Confusion", the Han Dynasty, which spanned a period of two hundred years on each side of the life of Christ.

There is nowhere else in the world during these times a comparable advance to China's. No doubt we do scant justice to many unknown heroic pioneers in stating briefly that the many scattered groups of islands in the Pacific continued to fill sparsely with men. Australia achieved and remained in a culture which it is fair to call not more advanced than mesolithic. There remains the continent of America.

To start backwards but to make clear from the beginning what is sometimes forgotten, the civilizations of Central and South America, Pueblo, Maya, Aztec, Inca, flowered wholly in our Christian Era. Having said that, we may take a short look at the progress of the original hunters and fishers who came across in waves from Asia and who slowly but successfully spread over a double continent, not even failing to populate its cold and inhospitable southern tip.

There are two great points about American Stone and Bronze Age history, one to be expected, the other hardly so. The first is that this new, strange, clever mammal, spreading over the virgin continent, reacted specifically to his environment and so produced for himself varying ways of life. The second is that, with at any rate no proven help from outside, he paralleled remarkably the progress of the fellow-humans that he had left behind. That is, he made parallel progress up to a point; the failures are as significant as the successes.

By and large, the early Americans—Amer-indians to give them their usual archaeological name—developed three ways of living. Those who stayed north—and for that matter those who finally reached farthest south—developed a fishing-hunting culture, more fishing than hunting one would guess. Those who streamed down to the east of the continent's long mountain divide met the great grazing beasts, bison in particular, and became the expert and adventurous hunters that their European forefathers had been, and contentedly remained so to become the Red Indians of a later day. Those who kept to the west of the Rocky Mountains, meeting more desert conditions (though less desert than now) were stimulated, quite simply, to find themselves a living in any way possible, learning to net and snare the little animals and gathering the seeds and roots. They must have been a sparse population and often a nomadic. The higher and colder climate made them seek cave and rock shelter, and they were the forerunners of the Pueblo

Indians. They were also probably the first to take the great step to food cultivation instead of food gathering; it seems likely that history was repeating itself here and that it was not the affluent hunter but the poor scraper and picker-up of Nature's unconsidered trifles who made the advance. Gourds, squashes, potatoes were grown, and in particular maize.

We may break off here to look at the tools and inventions of the Amer-indians. Their flints were from the beginning good and varied and they produced one distinctive weapon, now called the Folsom Point, from its place of discovery in the State of New Mexico. This is a two-inch-long flint, brought to a rather obtuse point and then flaked longitudinally on both sides, presumably to fit into a split spear-shaft. These and other tools were often beautifully made, more beautifully than utility demanded, though this is about the only sign of conscious art that the early Stone Age people show. They did not do much with bone and ivory—though the Easterners hunted the mammoth—but the Westerners became great basket-makers.

Then, with those who were following the neolithic way of life, came, just as in the Eastern world left behind, the inventions of weaving and pottery, and chances taken to exercise artistic skill. Where maize would grow easily and where men wished to grow it—which would not be on the prairies where the big beasts could be hunted—villages turned to the first towns and men learnt to build. At the same time they learnt to exercise their imaginations and to foster an expert, the priest, to show the way in which the exercise should be conducted.

We reach now, in Western dating, the middle of the Second Millennium, not long before Knossos fell. There are reached, too, the first tentative beginnings of civilization that are paralleled in pre-dynastic Egypt and Sumer, what is known as the "formative" era of the cultures that were finally to become—after the best part of some two thousand years had passed—the four classic civilizations that we have already mentioned. Before the middle of the First Millennium B.C. pyramid or Babel-like temples are being built—do all men naturally lift up their eyes to see God?—and the use of copper has begun.

After their very late start the Americas had made great leeway. When, two thousand years later, the Western world on the other side of the Atlantic discovered America it discovered civilizations in some ways already decadent and with some curious gaps in their knowledge and techniques. The knowledge of astronomy and mathematics and writing was serving mostly an incomprehensible preoccupation with time; skill was great with copper and silver and gold, but there was no use of iron. None of the civilizations knew of the plough, or the wheel, or money. Two of them had, as is well known, an obsessive regard for death and sacrificial killing. Even the freer, opener Indians of the plains seemed to brood in a harsh and gloomy outlook, setting much store by physical endurance and the ability to rise above self-inflicted pain.

Why the great and wide continent should have bred such sadism and masochism it is hard to say. But for that matter the world to which we shall now return was not free from these vices.

CHAPTER XIX

The Chosen People

THE rest of our story is of the development of two peoples of rugged, poor but stimulating hill-countries, the Greeks and the Hebrews.* They are not stories that would have often, as it were, supplied the international news headlines of the times. But to follow these two lines of development is the best if not the only way to make sense of these very turbulent and troubled centuries. Indeed, it is really something more than that: for posterity these two stories constitute the only true focus of the times.

It will be well first to give a quick resumé of the centuries that are left to us, from the point of view, that is to say, of what might have been the headlines.

Rameses III, the second of the Pharaohs successful against the Peoples of the Sea, died in the middle of the twelfth century. After him Egypt was to be weak, often with two rulers, north and south, sometimes with rulers of Libyan or Nubian blood, but still capable of bursting forth on occasion to make her mark abroad. Assyria at this time pushed her boundaries north to Lake Van and then stayed quiet. The Peoples of the Sea, the creators of the Aegean Dark Age, gradually settled down. The Hittites, shifted eastwards, were experiencing around Carchemish a period of secondary glory before becoming absorbed into the Semitic Phoenicians and Arameans.

At 1000 B.C. King David had been anointed or was about to be so and the greatness of King Solomon was to follow. By 900 Assyria had become resurgent. After three-quarters of a century of terror for her neighbours she mercifully quietened for a while to attend to dynastic troubles and civil war. Then she burst forth again. She invaded Egypt, and swamped Palestine, the Israelites suffering from the new Assyrian policy of shifting conquered populations. The end of the eighth century had now been reached, and at this time the kingdoms of Asia Minor suffered from a fresh invasion of northern barbarians, the Cimmerians.

*Israelites is no longer the best name to use, since Israel and Judah are at the end of the tenth century to split apart.

The Phoenicians' power and wealth had begun to wane but Greek commercial and colonial expansion had begun to take its place.

Assyrian power, however, was beginning also to wane. Rent by internal dissension, failing to help Asia Minor against the Cimmerians, she had no friends. As she sank a new empire appeared, the Chaldean, which was to bring Babylon to her most fabulous greatness, a greatness, however, that lasted less than a hundred years. At the beginning of the sixth century the Hebrews had suffered their second deportation; by 539 B.C. Babylon once more had fallen. Then arose the might of the Medes and Persians. In another couple of hundred years, never having swamped the Greeks, the Persian Empire will have fallen to a Greek Macedonian, Alexander.

So much for an outline of these confused centuries; now to see how the Hebrews steered a difficult and harassed course through the confusion.

> And the children of Israel did evil in the sight of the Lord, and served Baalim:
> And they forsook the Lord God of their fathers, which brought them out of the land of Egypt, and followed other gods, of the gods of the people that were round about them, and bowed themselves unto them, and provoked the Lord to anger.
> And they forsook the Lord, and served Baal and Ashtoreth.
> And the anger of the Lord was hot against Israel, and he delivered them into the hands of spoilers that spoiled them, and he sold them into the hands of their enemies round about, so that they could not any longer stand before their enemies. . . .
> Nevertheless the Lord raised up judges, which delivered them out of the hands of those that spoiled them.

Here is the constant theme of the biblical narrative so soon as the Hebrews had established themselves in the Promised Land. For Baal we may read Sky God and for Ashtoreth, Earth Goddess: that is near enough and all that matters, the deities that the Hebrews hankered after were the familiar deities who under a hundred names had sufficed millions of their fellow-people for thousands of years.* Having been welded into a fighting force and having been reasonably successful,

*Baal means "Lord" or "Possessor", so the previously quoted Baalim means "lords of the land" or all the local gods.

the Hebrews now wanted only to relax. Left to themselves they would almost certainly have been absorbed into their Canaanite neighbours and have lost their sense of mission and their very identity. Two things saved them, one from inside, one from without. The first was the "Judges", for which we may read inspirers, heroes, leaders: the poetess Deborah, the Herculean Samson, the king-maker Samuel, men and women in whom the heroic spirit burned fiercely. The second was those "Peoples of the Sea" who had settled down along the strip of the Palestinian coast, the Philistines. Perhaps the grandfathers of these people had known an un-splendid Knossos or had looked up at the Cyclopean stones of the deserted fortress of Mycenae—their pottery had Mycenaean affinities. Whatever their origin, they possessed now and for a while the advantage of a monopoly of iron-smelting and iron weapons. The Hebrews, who in any case were being "spoiled" by some other of their neighbours, had by the time of the last of their Judges, Samuel, become desperate. Even their holy shrine and talisman, the Ark of the Covenant, being

A Canaanite goddess—Ashtoreth?

brought into battle and at first striking terror into the Philistines by its presence, had been captured; even its return did not mend matters. Their thoughts went, therefore, to a king who would lead them in battle, and Samuel's warning of the tyrannous habits of the breed would not deter them: "Nay, but we will have a king over us, that we also may be like all the nations." It was another backsliding, for they should have had faith in the spiritual power of their god, passed on through the mouths and will of his prophets. But they had their way.

There follow the superlative stories of Saul and of David. Histories is a better word, for no one can doubt the authenticity of this passionate pair who in the Bible come so vividly alive; and as William Albright shows in his book, *The Archaeology of Palestine*,* the results of modern digging corroborate the ancient written word. Werner Keller, in his book, *The Bible as History*,† quotes an interesting example of even the detailed accuracy of the biblical narrative. In Allenby's Palestine campaign of 1916 a certain British officer, finding himself near Michmash, consulted his Bible, where (in Samuel 13 and 14) he read of Jonathan's daring raid upon the Philistines in that place, which led to a Jewish victory. With his armour-bearer, Jonathan had made his way through a defile upon either side of which was "a sharp rock". The British officer sent out a patrol, the defile and the sentinel rocks were found—and the Turks were subsequently surprised and history repeated itself.‡

That escapade of Jonathan had indeed led to a victory for Saul. But the sequel was disastrous. The Philistines advancing beyond the hills in which Saul's guerrilla tactics had been successful, met the Hebrews on the plains and utterly defeated them. Jonathan was killed, Saul committed suicide, and the bodies of both were displayed by the Philistines on the walls of Beth-shan. David, who by his own tactics against Saul had hardly helped to prevent the defeat—though perhaps his actions were forced upon him—was left to mourn Jonathan, to retrieve the bodies, and to take up the burden of kingship, entering into his task at a moment as unpropitious as did our own King Alfred at Athelney.

David's is a fascinating personality, amazing compound of good and evil, always passionate and wilful, ruthless at one moment, sensitive the next. His life ended in disgrace and tragedy. But he was a great king; he broke for good the terrible threat of the Philistines, he extended his kingdom southwards to use the iron and copper of the Negeb—the latter one of Solomon's great sources of wealth—and so he paved the way for the Hebrews' sudden and surprising flash of material greatness under his son by Bathsheba, Solomon.

Solomon's wealth and status, though as nothing compared with the past grandeur of Egypt, were very real. His alliances, with the Phoenicians to his north and west and Egypt to the south, were no doubt political triumphs, though it is doubtful whether the latter ever did him or his successors any good. But the face of the Hebrew nation was changed. It was rather like the change that Rome suffered when the rugged integrity of her Fathers gave place to empire. There was now a

---

*Penguin Books, 1949.
†Hodder and Stoughton, 1956.
‡This story appears originally in *The Romance of the Last Crusade* by Major Vivian.

bureaucracy; there were the very rich and the very poor; there was forced labour, to escape which the Israelites had faced the wilderness; there was a Court, cosmopolitan and suffering from foreign influence and customs and religions, boasting of a harem, which is ever the home of intrigue. The faith and integrity and sense of unity of the people was now attacked not by hardship and disaster, which tended on the whole to increase the virtues attacked, but by prosperity; and the attack was more insidious and successful.

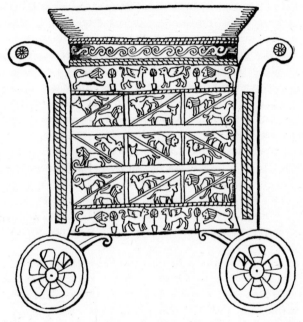

The art and magnificence of Solomon's time: a brass laver
from the temple

The Hebrews now played the game of power politics, and in the process not only found themselves split into two often warring parts but each part finally dispersed and led into captivity. As with David, perhaps their conduct was forced upon them, living as they did in the everlasting cockpit of the Middle East; but, if so, the fact that it was a necessity did not save them.

The politics and military campaigns of this long period of over three hundred years are too complicated to be described in any detail. For the sake of clarity the first things to say are: that the period begins with the split, north and south, into the two kingdoms of Israel and of Judah; that the first near-two-hundred years end with the downfall of the north before Assyria and the second period with the downfall of the south before Chaldean Babylon.

"And Ahab"—and this king and that king—"did evil in the sight of the Lord"; that is now the recurring theme of the Bible story, mercifully lightened by the few kings who did do good. The prophets of the Lord, the exhorters and the brave tellers of unpleasant truths, are there to warn the kings, later even to advise them as to their conduct, and to remind the people all the time of the basic teaching of their leader Moses, that righteousness and morality were attributes that their god, unlike the vast majority of the gods that had ever before existed in men's minds, demanded. Ahab, though no doubt a cunning king in diplomacy, was a bad king for his people by almost any standard. The Hebrews since the death of Solomon in 933 had suffered division and civil war. And meanwhile, Assyria, in her first period of resurgence and under her king Ashur-bani-pal II, had swept across the Euphrates and the Orontes and extracted submission from the rich Phoenician harbour towns of the coast. The Syrian Damascus had been in the line of advance, but having shown little or no resistance was left intact. Farther south the Assyrians had not penetrated. The Jews, therefore, were like a house or village in modern times that the bombing aeroplanes had missed: they would have done well not to make their presence apparent.

However, Ahab of Israel, Ben-hadad of Damascus, and the King of Hamath in the valley of the Orontes formed a triple alliance against the Assyrians. There was an indecisive battle on the river that had seen so many battles, and the Assyrians retired. Ben-hadad, however, had suffered heavy losses. Ahab saw the opportunity of settling an old score against his temporary ally, and with Jehosaphat, King of Judah, attacked the King of Damascus. In the ensuing battle he lost his life.

His death was the signal for further bloody strife in Israel. Ahab's wife was the Syrian Baalizabel or Jezebel, and in religious observances he had pleased his wife and not his people, and certainly not the prophets. Elisha now stirred up rebellion against Ahab's dynasty, by assuming the role of king-maker as Samuel had done before him and anointing a ruthless young man, Jehu, son of Nimshi. Jezebel was thrown down to the dogs at the contemptuous command of Jehu, and the reigning kings of both Israel and Judah were murdered. Soon the Assyrians were striking into Syria again. Jehu could only buy them off with rich presents: on a great stone obelisk of Shalmaneser II one small panel shows the Jewish king paying tribute. Jehu is not an admirable character; but he was preferable to the line of Ahab, who had legitimized the worship of Baal.

There now followed civil war in Assyria and, on a familiar pattern, assassination and a new line of kings. The Hebrews were left in peace for about eighty years. But they did not make good use of the respite.

There appeared, in the persons of Amos and Hosea, a new kind of prophet, not miracle-makers nor even king-makers but expressive men and of a deep and a new conviction. They had no illusions that Assyria as a power was finished; and they saw the Court of their kings as luxurious, sensual and corrupt. The denunciations took on a deeper note. Jehovah is no longer the god only of the Jews. He is the Lord of Hosts, god "not of national armies, but of the hosts of heaven and earth".* And if his chosen people would not mend their ways then the Lord of Hosts, using the terrible Assyrian enemy as his weapon, would make an example of her before all the world. "The virgin of Israel is fallen; she shall no more rise; she is cast down upon her land; there is none to raise her up."

So far as Israel, the northern kingdom, is concerned the prophecy is completely fulfilled. In the middle of the eighth century an Assyrian army general by the name of Pul pushed his way to the throne, took on the ancient name of Tiglath Pileser, brought Babylon to his heels and turned his attention to Syria and Palestine. The kings of Israel and Damascus had with great foolhardiness attacked King Ahaz of Judah, and Ahaz, with even greater folly, and against the advice of the prophet Isaiah, had sought help from Egypt. Tiglath Pileser defeated Israel and a number of other Canaanite kinglets in his stride, reached the confines of Egypt, and then set about the new Assyrian policy of pacification by the transfer of populations. Israel suffered her first deportation.

Assyria had reached her offensive peak. After the usurper there followed another Shalmaneser and then kings with names that have remained in the memory of man ever since: Sargon II—another who assumed an ancient name—Sennacherib, Esarhaddon, Ashur-bani-pal (or Sardanapallos), these five reigns covering one hundred and one years. Assyria's iron-equipped army was now at the height of its efficiency, with great siege weapons, battering rams and scaling towers,

*See Chapter III of W. G. de Burgh's great book, *The Legacy of the Ancient World* (a one-volume Pelican book in 1961).

with a combination of arms, chariotry, cavalry and unmounted bow-men, that was hardly to be improved upon until gunpowder in two thousand years' time changed the scene. The final weapon was propaganda, the advertisement of Assyria's terror—which almost, it seems, defeated its own object by creating at times the courage of despair.

Whether from despair or foolhardiness, Hoshea, who had succeeded to the throne of Judah and had continued to send "gifts", decided to depend on the support of Egypt and to defy Assyria. The result was disaster. Egyptian help was not forthcoming, and Samaria, the Jews' northern capital, after a long siege and a respite and renewed but false hope as the familiar tale of regicide and usurpation was once more enacted in Assyria, finally fell.

An Assyrian king (Shalmaneser II) receives tribute from a Jewish one (Jehu)

In the ninth year of Hoshea, the king of Assyria took Samaria, and carried Israel away into Assyria, and placed them in Halah and in Habor by the River of Gozan, and in the cities of the Medes.

For so it was, that the children of Israel had sinned against the Lord their God, which had brought them out of the land of Egypt, from under the hand of Pharaoh king of Egypt, and had feared other gods.*

A total of 27,290 men, women and children were said to have been deported and other peoples put in their stead: the Samaritans of the New Testament would so be formed and the Ten Tribes of the Jewish northern kingdom were dispersed, to lose their identity and their traditions for ever.

*II Kings, xvii, 6 and 7.

There remained only Judah. Judah was saved from Assyria by the strength imparted to her kings and people by Isaiah and by the increasing difficulties that the great enemy was creating for herself by her ferocious ambition. No Assyrian king could now stay at home for long to increase the beauty of his city and practise the arts of peace; for rebellion would break out somewhere, or a previous slight had to be repaid or a shameful failure rectified. Sargon had to sweep over Asia Minor and the states facing the Aegean; he ended triumphantly in Babylon. Sennacherib failed to conquer Egypt but took his revenge upon a revolting Babylon which he not only razed to the ground but drowned under the diverted waters of one of its own canals.

Now came the attempt to wipe Judah out of the way as Israel had been wiped. King Hezekiah reluctantly stripped even the temple of its gold so that he might placate Sennacherib. But the gift was useless. Sennacherib finally decided that Jerusalem was in his way but left the job of reducing it to one of his generals. The general failed, and to his own amazement. The shouted conversation between him and the courtiers of Hezekiah is recorded in the eighteenth chapter of the Second Book of Kings:

Speak ye now to Hezekiah, Thus saith the great king, the king of Assyria, What confidence is this wherein thou trustest?

Thou sayest, (but they are but vain words), I have counsel and strength for the war. Now on whom dost thou trust, that thou rebellest against me?

Now, behold, thou trustest upon the staff of this bruised reed, even upon Egypt, on which if a man lean, it will go into his hand, and pierce it: so is Pharaoh king of Egypt unto all that trust on him.

But if ye say unto me, We trust in the Lord our God: is not that he, whose high places and whose altars Hezekiah hath taken away, and hath said to Judah and Jerusalem, Ye shall worship before this altar in Jerusalem?

Now therefore, I pray thee, give pledges to my lord the king of Assyria, and I will deliver thee two thousand horses, if thou be able on thy part to set riders upon them.

The reply of the courtiers was to ask the general not to speak in Syrian, which the defenders could understand; and the general's reaction was to take the opportunity to appeal to the Hebrews direct:

Hath any of the gods of nations delivered at all his land out of the hand of the king of Assyria? . . .

Who are they among all the gods of the countries, that have delivered their country out of mine hand, that the Lord should deliver Jerusalem out of mine hand?

But the people held their peace. . . .

And soon the hosts of the Assyrians were smitten with a plague, and Sennacherib, foiled of his plan to conquer Egypt, and incidentally Judah, "departed, and went and returned, and dwelt at Nineveh"— where, according to the Bible, he was assassinated in his own temple by his own sons.

His successor, Esarhaddon, began with a pacific deed, perhaps a mistakenly pacific deed, the restoration of Babylon. But he had set his heart upon succeeding where his predecessors had failed, on the invasion and final humbling of Egypt. First capturing the Phoenician Sidon (and underlining his might by sending back to Nineveh a nobleman with the King of Sidon's head hung round his neck), but mercifully leaving Judah alone, he succeeded in capturing Memphis, the capital of Egypt's lower kingdom.

His success was shortlived, and from their upper capital, Thebes, the Egyptians managed to oust and destroy the Assyrian garrison. Death prevented Esarhaddon's revenge, but his son, the great Sardanapallos, took it, and invested Thebes as well as Memphis, destroying the latter as Sennacherib had destroyed Babylon, after stripping her of much booty. Here was the culminating destruction of most of Egypt's power and all her prestige. Here too was the beginning of the decline of Assyria. In simple terms, she had stretched herself too far and created too many bitter enemies.

Sardanapallos died in 626 B.C. Fourteen years later, to the exultant shouts of the world, Nineveh was meeting the sort of fate that its kings had meted out to so many other cities; it fell to the new Chaldean empire of Babylon. By the turn of the century the remainder of the Jews, at last defeated, were being sent by King Nebuchadnezzar into the Babylonian captivity. In the interim Judah had suffered from the Pharaoh Necho II, who killed their king at yet another Battle of Megiddo.

That at this second disaster the Jews did not lose either their spirit or their identity is a miracle and an everlasting testimony, if one is needed, to the strength of ideas and the truth that the pen is mightier than the sword. Judah—with some bad lapses—benefited from the extra hundred-odd years' respite granted to her after the fall of Israel. Under Hezekiah and Josiah she purged herself of all foreign forms of worship and strengthened and codified her rituals and her laws. She also produced the greatest of her prophets, Isaiah and Jeremiah, and listened to them.

Jeremiah's name has become synonymous with gloom, but this is unfair. Both these prophets inveighed against the sins of their people with unbridled rhetoric and prophesied woe if the sinful did not turn from their ways. But there did now enter a gleam of hope: the Chosen People were not merely there to suffer as a terrible example for the rest of the world. Some of the utterances of Isaiah were, of course, to become famous, familiar to the whole Western world through the New Testament, disputed everlastingly as to their authenticity and interpreted in varying ways: "And there shall come forth a rod out of the stem of Jesse, and a Branch shall grow out of his roots" . . . "For unto us a child is born, unto us a son is given." There remains enough undisputed to show that Isaiah genuinely established among his contemporaries a feeling of hope. "Therefore, said the Lord, the Lord of hosts, the Mighty one of Israel, Ah, I will ease me of mine adversaries and avenge me of mine enemies; and I will turn my hand upon thee, and purely purge away thy dross." The process would be painful, but the final outcome triumphant. As for Jeremiah, he did seem to despair of national virtue or repentance: "Can the Ethiopian change the skin; or the leopard his spots? then may ye also do good, that are accustomed to do evil." He saw in the invasions of the Scythians, "the evil from the north", who at this time were beginning to come down through the Cimmerians, not as a welcome menace to the Assyrians but only as an instrument of an avenging and disgusted god. But if he despaired of the Jews as a whole, he did not despair of the individual. Even in much of the reforms of Hezekiah he saw only formality and legalism—"the pen of the scribes is in vain". He turned, therefore, to the possibility of a personal covenant, between God and anyone who wished, and was fit, to make it. In that alone Jeremiah saw hope, and with optimism he preached it: "I will put my law in their inward parts, and write it in their hearts; and will be their God and they shall be my people . . . for I will forgive their iniquity and I will remember their sin no more."

So fortified, the men and women of Judah went into captivity.

They were not as a whole badly treated and many of them prospered materially. But their national and religious consciousness was strong enough; and their memories were poignant, and nursed: "By the waters of Babylon we sat down and wept." They were safely encased in their own habit of separateness. There are the stories of the steadfastness of Daniel and the later and less pleasant triumph of Esther. Then under the clemency of the Persian Artaxerxes they returned, not in the least to peace, but possessing their great body of law and custom and ethics, and with an incomparable literature intact.

CHAPTER XX

The Intelligent People

WE turn to consider finally that other vital people of a small and rugged country, the Greeks. Their rise to so great a position of influence is on the face of it equally miraculous, their background if anything even less propitious.

It took the lands round the Aegean something like three hundred years to recover from the spoiling of the Dorians. Between waves of invasion, however, and as the waves diminished and ceased, there cannot have been continued violence. Rather there was a return to bucolic simplicity: the Dorian, having taken for himself the best land, farmed it with contentment and kept clear for a few generations, as the Saxons did in Roman Britain, of the ancient towns and fortresses, which he regarded with either disinterest or distaste, or even awe.

At sea the position was something similar. The waters of the Aegean had still borne ships on their surface. But for some generations the ships themselves bore not so much merchandise as men bent on unpeaceful or unhappy pursuits: pirates, marauders, raiders, refugees. Gradually, however, that traffic changed again, and though merchandise came back the movement of men did not cease. It is hard for us in these days to realize to what extent, with few roads and no motors existing, the Aegean Sea was for the mountainous lands surrounding it the prime form of transport, the easy and obvious link. But it has to be realized. In simple terms, the stream of men in the ships continued but their intentions and emotions changed: no longer fierce and frenzied, driven out by the pressure of hunger or the ferocity of others like themselves, but eager and optimistic, driven by nothing harsher than the hope of gain and adventure or of a new and more spacious home. No doubt there would be fighting sometimes at the destination, later if not sooner; but, by and large, this peaceful picture is a fair one.

In other words, the first act of the Greeks when they had found their feet again was to spread, to colonize, to found an empire, a process contrary to the trend of recent centuries when countries have tended to found empires at the end of their time of greatness rather than at its beginning. From the second half of the eighth century B.C. and for the next two or three hundred years, Greece as it were duplicated, triplicated, herself abroad: westwards in Sicily and Italy and beyond; northwards both up the Adriatic and past Troy and around the shores of the Black Sea; eastwards and, in particular, the short distance to the in-shore islands and the mainland valley-heads of the Asia Minor coastline.

And by this time the Greek mainlanders had at length progressed beyond the rustic stage. Occasionally in the old places, much more often in new places, cities were again being built. Yet city, as we all know, is really the wrong word, as town is the wrong word, giving to us the wrong, the too large, picture. The word *polis* has to be used, however much the textbook's use of it has tired us of its sound: the *polis* with its *acro-polis*, the tight, small, self-contained city-state centring round its "peak", its topmost part, where gradually the fortress will change to the religious and administrative centre. It was the *polis* idea that was spread by the Greeks across the seas; and to use the word "empire" at all in conjunction with Greece is probably misleading. Italy would for a few centuries come to be called Magna Graecia. But she was not a colony, a dependency of Greece. More simply, she was Greek: wherever there was a *polis* there was Greece. The homelanders might despise the outlanders for their uncouth accent and manners, their "solecisms"; but that was purely by the way.

This act of colonizing helps greatly to make understandable the Greeks' rise to greatness.

First of all the very act gives us a clue to their character: they possessed an abundant vitality. Invasions do not always revivify a country, but most Aryan invasions did so, and this one did so outstandingly. No one could thrive in a country such as Greece without being hardy; and the hardihood and the thriving, with its attendant increase in population, made the effort of colonizing the only successful solution. The Greeks eagerly faced up to the necessity. Then it is true that from the Second Millennium onwards the people coming down into Greece had shown themselves an open-minded, open-handed lot, willing to learn from the people that they displaced and absorbed, and conquered so far as culture went rather than conquering. Once again with the Dorians, though their initial destruction was very great, this same thing must have happened. There is also the point that their conquest was not universal. Athens, for instance, the Athens of Aegeus and Theseus, escaped almost entirely, becoming a receiver of refugees rather than of invaders. And it was from Athens in particular, so Thucydides tells us, that the most successful and culturally important of the colonies, the Ionian, along the southern end of the eastward-facing Asia Minor coast, were formed.

Here arrives the second point in an explanation of Greece's miraculous rise to greatness. Always willing to learn, the Greeks by their very spread over the face of the near-eastern seas put themselves the much more into a position to learn. From Egypt, from Mesopotamia through the filter of Cyprus and the coastal states such as Lydia, from the trading Phoenicians, the new Greeks, sometimes innocently credulous but more often healthily, even disdainfully, sceptical, relearnt and learnt better the ways of civilization. Their open good sense made them extract and absorb the knowledge and practical skills rather than the faiths and beliefs, though perhaps unfortunately not wholly so.

The Greeks learnt particularly from the Phoenicians and the Lydians. We have done less than justice to the Phoenicians. They were, of course, the great traders; and, rather like the almost equally great traders of the city of Babylon, they went their ways and largely persisted in their prosperity, suffering sometimes from history but not often making it. Nor have they left behind any great account of themselves, in spite of their invention of the first genuine alphabet; or perhaps, more true to say, such an account has not yet been dug up by the archaeologist's spade. Byblos and Tyre and Sidon are their most ancient towns, the first going back to the Third Millennium; there follow, farther north and south on the Palestinian coast, Ugarit and Joppa. Then in the twelfth century the Sea Peoples descended upon them: the result, a concentration in Tyre and from there in due course a process of colonial expansion that very much paralleled the expansion of the Greeks. Both nations were great traders and great seafarers, and in the times to come beyond our period they will be not only rivals but at war. It is practical accounting rather than the need to set down poetry and story that creates an efficient medium of writing, and it is in the natural order of things that the Phoenicians who also invented the abacus should have handed down to us, through the Greeks, the alphabet we now use. The significant thing, the surprising thing, is that though the Phoenician owed much in this to what had gone before, the Greeks all around the Aegean had lost for three centuries the art of writing and by all the signs had become completely illiterate. At least, they were now to make amends.

From the Lydians outstandingly the Greeks—and, of course, not only the Greeks—inherited the use of money. Lydia, a later entity than Phoenicia, grew rich as an intermediary between the Greek coastal colonies and the East; and it was Croesus, a king both fabulous and real, who before destroying himself in his rash attack on the Persians, established in his country a standard gold and silver currency. This was, of course, a very different matter from possessing a standard of value by which exchange could be made—that, whether as cattle or a stamped metal bar, had existed for a very long time. Now, as we would say, loose change came into existence. Before, barter had been eased and regularized; now—in due course that is to say, when coins became more or less universal and plentiful—barter became unnecessary. In fact, if iron democratized weapons, then the simple sign-for-sound alphabet democratized writing and coinage democratized exchange. All three were inevitably pronouncing doom upon the illiterate, bronze-brandishing, trade-despising aristocrat who seems to have been the typical early Aryan and who, if he had had his day, had also had his uses in pushing along the processes of history. . . .

Just that necessary process largely constituted, in fact, the final effort of the pre-classical Greeks, both in the homeland and elsewhere. In the *polis* the prince became often a merchant prince, and, as often, what the Greeks called a tyrant. Such a ruler, though he may often have been benevolent, though he may have constituted a necessary phase in the development of Greek city government, earned inevitably the virulent dislike of a people who loved personal initiative and freedom; and with the entry of the wonderful sixth century, the end of our period, the tyrants are themselves on the way out—making way for oligarchy or democracy or, very often, a continual struggle between the two.

Tyranny, oligarchy, democracy: they are Greek words and Greek ideas; and we must try, before we leave them and however briefly, to assess the real, the non-material greatness of the Greeks.

The Greeks were not going to have an easy time, as the Jews were not going to have an easy time; even more than the Jews perhaps they would sadden all those who came after them by the tale of their gross imperfections and mistakes. Even so: they created, quite simply, a new world.

It is significant that one of the first uses they made of their regained literacy was to create a literature. At this time—at the end of the eighth century in all probability—Homer lived and created the epics of his countrymen's half-mythical, half-historical past; and then, or not long afterwards, they were put into writing.

What is yet more to the point is that they had been put into writing in a language that possessed all the potentialities of a most flexible and subtle instrument and that the Greeks rapidly made the potentiality actual. In fact, if the Jews showed a religious genius, the Greeks showed an intellectual one. *They showed an inquiring mind.* They showed a persistently inquiring mind, a persevering and sometimes a dis-

From a Greek vase

respectful mind, disrespectful that is to say of traditional taboos and hushed awe in the presence of the always accepted. Socrates asking pertinent, fundamental, and irritatingly searching questions in the market place is the essence of Greece—and unless we become too uncritically enthusiastic in this matter let it be remembered that even Socrates could be a little naïve in his reasoning, a little self-deceptive in his worship of the logical approach.* The great thing about the Greeks was that they were using their brains in new ways for the first

*Or is made to appear so by Plato, as in the earlier part of the *Phaedo* for instance.

time, and we must allow their methods to creak sometimes from newness.

It would not be right, however, to continue generalizations about the great Greek contribution to civilization without substantiating them with liberal quotation; and this is not the place for such a display, and the present author is not the one to make it. Let someone entitled to summarize do so—a quotation again from William de Burgh in his book *The Legacy of the Ancient World*. Having called them "great talkers", he continues:

What distinguishes the Greeks above other nations who have loved talking is that they talked also about what was most worth discussion: law and freedom, moral duty and the end of government, the nature and causes of things, art and poetry, virtue and the good for man. Above all, their talk was reasoned and logical, the expression of clear thinking and grasp of fact. No people have ever thought so deeply or talked so well on these high subjects as did the Greeks. No people have ever drawn with so firm a hand the line between illusion and reality, or set themselves so resolutely to understand and master the world of nature.

CHAPTER XXI

The Old World is Young Again

No people before the Greeks had ever tried at all hard or for long at a time to "understand and master the world of nature". Always before had returned, sooner rather than later, the old taboos, the old fears, the old and ever-present preference of men to stop thinking and fall back on a muddle-headed belief in the powers of magic and of gods who could be influenced but not understood.

No people before the Hebrews had worshipped a god of righteousness who also had regard for the individual man; for the religion of the older world was essentially a tribal religion that always sacrificed the desires of the individual to the believed good of the whole. The material progress of the old world had only been made possible through the medium of the "closed society" of a tribe grown large, which was the State that was run by a despot.

Tribalism writ large in this double way, religious and political, had grown monstrously to produce a world of ever-clashing empires. The Greeks and Jews did not introduce a perfect world or even a golden age. But they made possible a new beginning.

Nor were they alone. It is significant that in the sixth century B.C. lived both Confucius and Gautama Buddha.

That century, when the old world was somehow so generously new, is just two-and-a-half millennia away, a hundred generations or less. A span of the same length in the opposite direction brings us to the beginnings of the first civilizations, the pre-dynastic eras of Egypt and Sumer. Add on again all that period, 5,000 years, and we are back at the earliest beginnings of the Neolithic Revolution. Beyond that the Old Stone Age extends for a length of time that in comparison seems almost unending. Yet it includes, at a distance as far away from the first embryo farmer as that farmer is from ourselves, the artists of the caves of Lascaux and Altamira. *Homo sapiens* did not improve on his basic nature, physical or mental, during the time under our review, nor for that matter has he done so since. His potentialities were always the same. Cro-Magnon Man could have been as wise as Solon, as inspired as Jeremiah, as subtle as Plato. But he was not yet equipped. His brain was not yet trained nor his animal instincts curbed.

It took a great deal of effort and suffering to make the change. But made it was.

Index